AF803238

Crime and Justice in the Trump Era

Crime and Justice in the Trump Era documents the impact of Trump administration policies on (1) violence against women, (2) the treatment of persons of color, (3) corporate and environmental crime (both domestic and international), and (4) federal crime control policy.

First, the book examines how the policies of Donald Trump's administration have affected the rights and safety of female Americans—in particular, violence against women, including sexual assault. The book then goes on to explore President Trump's very public stances devaluing people of color—whether they reside within the nation's borders or are seeking entry into the United States. Next, the collection evaluates the collateral costs attached to the ongoing campaign to reduce regulations that protect consumers, workers, and the environment. Likewise, valuing America's narrow self-interests may also have effects internationally, where crime and violence may be tied to Trump's promotion of White nationalism, toleration of human rights violations, and denial of climate change. Lastly, criminal justice policies are examined, both in the early stages of Trump's presidency, which were marked by his get-tough rhetoric, along with the more recent support for the First Step Act.

The authors represent different perspectives in the discipline—critical/feminist and mainstream criminologists, quantitative and qualitative scholars, and students of both street and white-collar crime. Taken together, this book reflects a variety of criminological voices and advances immeasurably our understanding of the Trump administration's influence on crime and justice in America.

The chapters in this book were originally published as a special issue of *Victims & Offenders: An International Journal of Evidence-based Research, Policy, and Practice.*

Francis T. Cullen is Distinguished Research Professor Emeritus and Senior Research Associate in the School of Criminal Justice at the University of Cincinnati, USA. He is the past President of the American Society of Criminology and the Academy of Criminal Justice Sciences. He has published more than 400 works spanning criminological theory, correctional policy, and white-collar crime.

Amanda Graham is an Assistant Professor in the Department of Criminal Justice and Criminology at Georgia Southern University, Statesboro, USA. In 2019, she received her Ph.D. in criminal justice from the University of Cincinnati, USA. Her research focuses on police-community relations, measurement within criminology, and racial beliefs and criminal justice policy.

Crime and Justice in the Trump Era

Edited by
Francis T. Cullen and Amanda Graham

Routledge
Taylor & Francis Group
LONDON AND NEW YORK

First published 2020
by Routledge
2 Park Square, Milton Park, Abingdon, Oxon, OX14 4RN

and by Routledge
52 Vanderbilt Avenue, New York, NY 10017

Routledge is an imprint of the Taylor & Francis Group, an informa business

© 2020 Taylor & Francis

All rights reserved. No part of this book may be reprinted or reproduced or utilised in any form or by any electronic, mechanical, or other means, now known or hereafter invented, including photocopying and recording, or in any information storage or retrieval system, without permission in writing from the publishers.

Trademark notice: Product or corporate names may be trademarks or registered trademarks, and are used only for identification and explanation without intent to infringe.

British Library Cataloguing-in-Publication Data
A catalogue record for this book is available from the British Library

ISBN13: 978-0-367-90240-7

Typeset in Minion Pro
by codeMantra

Publisher's Note
The publisher accepts responsibility for any inconsistencies that may have arisen during the conversion of this book from journal articles to book chapters, namely the inclusion of journal terminology.

Disclaimer
Every effort has been made to contact copyright holders for their permission to reprint material in this book. The publishers would be grateful to hear from any copyright holder who is not here acknowledged and will undertake to rectify any errors or omissions in future editions of this book.

Contents

Citation Information

The chapters in this book were originally published in the *Victims & Offenders*, volume 14, issue 8 (November 2019). When citing this material, please use the original page numbering for each article, as follows:

Chapter 1
Defenders of Freedom or Perpetrators and Facilitators of Crimes? Beyond Progressive Retreatism in the Trump Era
Walter S. DeKeseredy
Victims & Offenders, volume 14, issue 8 (November 2019) pp. 925–939

Chapter 2
President or Predator? The Social Construction of Donald Trump in a Divided America
Teresa C. Kulig, Francis T. Cullen, and Murat Haner
Victims & Offenders, volume 14, issue 8 (November 2019) pp. 940–964

Chapter 3
Turning Back the Clock? Violence against Women and the Trump Administration
Dawn L. Rothe and Victoria E. Collins
Victims & Offenders, volume 14, issue 8 (November 2019) pp. 965–978

Chapter 4
Less Safe in the Ivory Tower: Campus Sexual Assault Policy in the Trump Administration
Leah C. Butler, Heejin Lee, and Bonnie S. Fisher
Victims & Offenders, volume 14, issue 8 (November 2019) pp. 979–996

Chapter 5
America First? Trump, Crime, and Justice Internationally
Ronen Ziv, Amanda Graham, and Liqun Cao
Victims & Offenders, volume 14, issue 8 (November 2019) pp. 997–1009

Chapter 6
"Murderers, Rapists, and Bad Hombres": Deconstructing the Immigration-Crime Myths
Cecilia Chouhy and Arelys Madero-Hernandez
Victims & Offenders, volume 14, issue 8 (November 2019) pp. 1010–1039

Chapter 7

Will Black Lives Matter to the Police? African Americans' Concerns about Trump's Presidency
Hannah D. McManus, Francis T. Cullen, Cheryl Lero Jonson, Alexander L. Burton, and Velmer S. Burton Jr.
Victims & Offenders, volume 14, issue 8 (November 2019) pp. 1040–1062

Chapter 8

Harming America: Corporate Crime in a Context of Deregulation
Michael L. Benson, William A. Stadler, and Henry N. Pontell
Victims & Offenders, volume 14, issue 8 (November 2019) pp. 1063–1083

Chapter 9

Justice, Not Jailbreak: The Context and Consequence of the First Step Act
Derek M. Cohen
Victims & Offenders, volume 14, issue 8 (November 2019) pp. 1084–1098

For any permission-related enquiries please visit:
http://www.tandfonline.com/page/help/permissions

Contributors

Michael L. Benson is a Professor in the School of Criminal Justice at the University of Cincinnati, USA.

Alexander L. Burton is a Doctoral Student in the School of Criminal Justice at the University of Cincinnati, USA.

Velmer S. Burton Jr. is the Sr. Vice Chancellor for University Strategy and Performance & Professor of Criminal Justice at the University of Arkansas at Little Rock, USA.

Leah C. Butler is an Assistant Professor in the School of Criminology and Criminal Justice at the University of Nebraska Omaha, USA.

Liqun Cao is a Professor in the Faculty of Science and Humanities at Ontario Tech University, Oshawa, Canada.

Cecilia Chouhy is an Assistant Professor in College of Criminology and Criminal Justice at Florida State University, Tallahassee, USA.

Derek M. Cohen is the Director of the Center for Effective Justice and Right on Crime at the Texas Public Policy Foundation, Austin, USA.

Victoria E. Collins is an Associate Professor in the School of Justice Studies at Eastern Kentucky University, Richmond, USA.

Francis T. Cullen is a Distinguished Research Professor Emeritus and Senior Research Associate in the School of Criminal Justice at the University of Cincinnati, USA.

Walter S. DeKeseredy is an Anna Deane Carlson Endowed Chair of Social Sciences, the Director of the Research Center on Violence, and a Professor of Sociology at West Virginia University, Morgantown, USA.

Bonnie S. Fisher is a Professor in the School of Criminal Justice at the University of Cincinnati, USA.

Amanda Graham is an Assistant Professor in the Department of Criminal Justice and Criminology at Georgia Southern University, Statesboro, USA.

Murat Haner is a Research Administration Faculty Fellow/Instructor of Criminology at the University of South Florida Sarasota-Manatee, USA.

Cheryl Lero Jonson is an Associate Professor in the Department of Criminal Justice at Xavier University, Cincinnati, USA.

Teresa C. Kulig is an Assistant Professor in the School of Criminology and Criminal Justice at the University of Nebraska at Omaha, USA.

Heejin Lee is a Doctoral Student in the School of Criminal Justice at the University of Cincinnati, USA.

Arelys Madero-Hernandez is an Assistant Professor in the Department of Criminal Justice at Shippensburg University, USA.

Hannah D. McManus is a Doctoral Candidate in the School of Criminal Justice at the University of Cincinnati, USA.

Henry N. Pontell is a Distinguished Professor at John Jay College of Criminal Justice, USA.

Dawn L. Rothe is a Professor in the School of Criminology and Criminal Justice at Florida Atlantic University, Boca Raton, USA.

William A. Stadler is an Assistant Professor in the College of Arts and Sciences at Saint Martin's University, Lacey, USA.

Ronen Ziv teaches in the Institute of Criminology at Faculty of Law at The Hebrew University, Jerusalem, Israel.

Introduction

Francis T. Cullen and Amanda Graham

On November 9, 2016, those Americans who had not stayed awake to learn the final election results were greeted in the morning with the stunning news that the impossible had occurred—Donald J. Trump would be the 45th President of the United States. Was it political ignorance or arrogance that blinded us to his electability—or both? Most of us derided the Republican Party for nominating such an ill-prepared celebrity to be their nominee. But we missed the reality that Trump had obliterated a field of established Republican candidates to capture the nomination. He had charisma, offered the prospect of change as a true outsider, and appealed to the emotional interests of a slice of the electorate who felt devalued by so-called liberal elites. We also likely underestimated the lack of enthusiasm for Hillary—a combination of Clinton fatigue, her receiving sustained and unfair Congressional scrutiny (e.g., the Benghazi incident), Russian-facilitated leaks of her emails, and James Comey's last-minute reopening of an FBI investigation that proved baseless, but damaging. A perfect storm had indeed coalesced and swept Trump into office. Many of us took solace that Hillary won the popular vote by nearly 3 million supporters. Yet even this oft-repeated opiate is deceptive. Take out the totals from California—where Clinton had more than a 4 million-vote advantage—and Donald Trump was supported by a majority of Americans in the rest of the nation.

Upon taking office, it seemed that President Trump would be kept in check by the former military generals he appointed, a seasoned oil company CEO, and perhaps Ivanka and Jared—even if an alleged White nationalist and a team of loyalists had offices close by. His advisors instructed him to curb the tweets and be more presidential. Now deep into his presidential term, Trump has banished all those who attempted to restrain his impulses, except for family members. The tweets are issued daily and, when Trump is under critique, they are discharged rapid fire and are littered with words, such as "vicious," "low IQ," "Pocahontas," "disgusting, rat and rodent infested mess," and "s-hole." President Trump controls the Republican Party, with an approval rating among its members that hovers near 90% and a congressional caucus afraid to cross him lest they be voted out of office by his loyal base.

In short, Trump is a force to be reckoned with, and his impact on American culture and well-being needs to be fully assessed. This volume is an important step in this direction. Indeed, the contributors have masterfully documented the Trump administration's victimization of the nation, undermining of justice, and influence on crime policy. Multi-faceted scholarship was needed for this purpose. Thus, this enterprise includes essays that not only report primary data and synthesize extant empirical research but also chronicle the details of Trump's policy initiatives and provide critical commentary illuminating the stakes at risk in his presidency. Further, the authors represent different perspectives in the discipline—critical/feminist and mainstream criminologists, quantitative and more qualitative scholars, and students of both street and white-collar crime. Taken together, these works reflect a variety of criminological voices and advance immeasurably our understanding of the Trump presidency's effects. The contributions are divided into three parts.

Given the president's rhetorical posturing and alleged personal attacks on individual females, Part I (*Harming Women*) reviews how women have been impacted by his election. At issue is not only whether President Trump is viewed as a sexual predator, or as guilty only of locker-room talk, but also how his administration's policies have affected the rights and safety of female Americans. In particular, violence against women, including sexual assault, receives special consideration.

In this regard, Walter DeKeseredy raises the broad proposition, largely confirmed by other contributors, that the Trump administration not only "commits crimes of the powerful" but also facilitates "interpersonal violence in private places." He uses the victimization of women to illustrate this thesis. As a critical criminologist, he is concerned with praxis. Adopting a new left realist perspective, he conveys practical strategies for avoiding "progressive retreatism" and advancing human rights. Feminist scholars Dawn Rothe and Victoria Collins echo these themes but then provide a framework for conceptualizing President Trump's impact. They carefully document how Trump attempts to "turn back the clock" in violence toward women through two kinds of attack—"lawfare," or using legal changes to undermine females' rights and protections, and "wordfare," or using rhetoric in speeches and tweets to bully and delegitimate female critics and victims. Leah Butler, Heejin Lee, and Bonnie Fisher flesh out this theme through a meticulous account of U.S. Secretary of Education Betsy DeVos's efforts to weaken Title IX protections against sexual and gender-based violence on college campuses. Their policy analysis reveals how the Trump administration has diverged from the "victim-centered goals of the Obama administration," potentially making women "less safe in the ivory tower." Finally, based on a national-level survey, Teresa Kulig, Francis Cullen, and Murat Haner show that more Americans see Trump as a "predator than as an innocent president." Still, how he is socially constructed depends on which political "tribe" earns a respondent's allegiance. The public is deeply polarized on whether the president engaged in serious crimes or just in bad behavior or nothing at all. Their beliefs are likely to shape their voting in the 2020 elections.

Part II (*Borders and Beyond*) considers the impact of the Trump administration at and beyond the nation's borders. From a global perspective, Ronen Ziv, Amanda Graham, and Liqun Cao observe how crime and violence may be tied to Trump's promotion of White nationalism, toleration of human rights violations in authoritarian regimes, and denial of climate change. They note that his "America First" policy departs from the vision of the nation as a "city upon a hill" first voiced by John Winthrop in 1630. Although popular in some nations, polls indicate that Trump's approval rating is generally low internationally and that his actions have attenuated the Unites States' standing as a global leader. President Trump has also made visible the contentious issue of whether immigrants—especially those who cross the border uninvited—pose a danger to the American citizenry. An important criminological task is to evaluate whether, in fact, they engage in crime at rates higher than U.S. residents. In a detailed review of the research, Cecilia Chouhy and Arelys Madero-Hernandez dispel the claim that immigrants pose a special criminogenic risk. Their findings call into question the Trump administration's attempt to justify restrictive immigration policies based on the myth of the dangerous "bad hombre."

Part III (*Affecting America*) examines how the Trump administration's rhetoric and policies have harmed and, through one important reform, helped Americans. Thus, Trump's presidency arguably has been a challenge for people of color. Fear of mistreatment, if not actual hate crime, is on the rise. Trump has asked the police, when handling suspects, to "please don't be too nice," and he has shown little concern for the plight of African Americans victimized by officer brutality and use of lethal force. His fear-mongering toward Muslims and his advocacy of cruelty toward immigrants at the U.S. southern border are palpable. Once heralded as a "nation of immigrants," he arguably seeks to turn the United States into a "nation of White nationalism." One crucial issue is how his election has impacted the African American community. Hannah McManus and colleagues show that a high percentage of their national sample of 1,000 Black respondents stated that Trump's presidency will expose African Americans to more hate from the public, police violence, and arrest and imprisonment.

Another potential harm has emerged from the Trump administration's corporate policies. Although promising to drain the swamp, Trump has placed business-friendly figures in charge of the nation's regulatory agencies—some of whom have already resigned under accusations of corruption. Beyond the president's own arguably criminal conduct, his administration has embarked on a systematic campaign to neutralize regulations that protect consumers, workers, and the environment. Climate change is deemed a hoax, and short-term economic profit is privileged over the wellness of Americans and their surroundings. Literally thousands are projected to become ill and perhaps die due to these harmful policies. In a fascinating tour of the regulatory state, Michael Benson, William Stadler, and Henry Pontell detail the diverse techniques used by the Trump administration to achieve this rampant deregulation. They argue that these actions pose serious dangers, likely creating "real physical, emotional, and financial harm to the lives of American workers and the general public."

The early stages of Trump's presidency were marked by his get-tough rhetoric on crime and by Attorney General Jeff Sessions's efforts to ratchet up federal punishments for drug and other offenses. At the same time, we would be remiss not to credit the Trump administration for an important federal reform—the First Step Act—that includes the assessment of offenders' risks and needs in sentencing decisions. Derek Cohen's essay provides an informative account of the origins and nature of this legislation. An important example of bipartisan cooperation, the act reflects a changing national context aimed at restraining mass imprisonment and finding ways to reintegrate offenders into society. This reform makes the next steps possible and merits praise.

In closing, the sobering reality is that the reelection of Donald Trump seems far more possible than did his initial election. As Walter DeKeseredy and others warn, this is no time for progressive retreatism; resistance is required. As scholars, we have the capability, if not obligation, to use our skills to illuminate the harms being perpetrated on the American public—especially in the areas of crime and justice. In so doing, we expose ourselves to the charge of "fake criminology"—of being a bunch of "vicious" Leftists out to destroy the people's president. But as the essays in this volume reveal, the dangers posed by Trump go far beyond partisan disagreement. Trump rules in ways that evaporate traditional political categories, which is why many serious Republicans have abandoned their party and now are among his most vociferous critics. Making America great again post-Trump will require a concerted effort by all of us—regardless of party or ideology. As the always-wise Jon Meacham observes, we are now engaged in a battle for the "soul of America." Let us work together to ensure that our "better Angels," as he calls them, might prevail.

Part I

Harming Women

Defenders of Freedom or Perpetrators and Facilitators of Crimes? Beyond Progressive Retreatism in the Trump Era

Walter S. DeKeseredy

ABSTRACT
Heavily influenced by broad definitions of crime developed by a few pioneering critical criminologists, the main objective of this article is to provide evidence showing that the current Trump administration is a regime that commits crimes of the powerful and facilitates some types of interpersonal violence in private places. Special attention is devoted to direct and in-direct state-perpetrated violent crimes against women.

Critical criminology views hierarchical social stratification and inequality along class, racial/ethnic, gender, and patriarchal lines as the primary sources of crime and as the key factors that shape societal reactions to violations of legal and social norms. Since the late 1960s, some of the most important movements in critical criminology were responses by progressive scholars to the criminogenic nature of governments and their complicity in the commission of individual acts of interpersonal violence in private places. We are now seeing a new critical criminological movement aimed at identifying and preventing the harms caused by Trumpism, populism, and a rising right (Brabazon, Redhead, & Chivaura, 2019; DeKeseredy & Currie, 2019), one with roots in the writings of pioneering critical criminologists like Elias (1986) and Schwendinger and Schwendinger (1975). These radical scholars influenced many contemporary progressive criminologists and activists to broaden the definition of crime to include such socially injurious behaviors as racism, poverty, unemployment, sexism, imperialism, inadequate social services (e.g., housing, child care, education, and medical care), and corporate and state wrong doings. Guided by their conceptual work, in the words of Barak (1990), the main objective of this article is to demonstrate that the Trump administration is "a criminogenic institution" that "not only violates the rights of individuals, but it contributes to the production of other forms of criminality as well" (p. 12). Special attention is devoted to what Collins (2016) refers to as direct and indirect forms state-perpetrated violence against women.

Direct forms of state-perpetrated violence against women: assaults on women's reproductive rights

If Trump and his Cabinet are "defenders of order" (Schwendinger & Schwendinger, 1975), it is an order that shores up "structural discrimination via attacks on women's reproductive rights, health care for pregnant women, implementing new forms of racialized discrimination against immigrants, and support for failed 'tough on crime' policies" (Dragiewicz, 2018, p. 334). Consider, too, the Trump government's efforts to eliminate the Affordable Health Care Act (also known as Obamacare), a major increase in military spending, large tax cuts for the wealthy coupled with equally large cuts in benefits for low-income Americans, major assaults on environmental regulations, moves to open public lands to private exploitation, and the elimination of the Obama administration's August 2016 order to phase out private prisons (DeKeseredy & Currie, 2019). These crimes are much more socially, physically, environmentally, and economically injurious than crimes on the streets, but they all cannot be addressed here. My focus in this section is on the Trump government's assault on women's reproductive rights, which is, as Chesney-Lind (2019) notes, "the most prominent anti-women initiative launched by the Trump administration … ." (p. 135).

Some feminist criminologists, such as Collins (2016), would contend that Trump's efforts to eliminate *Roe v. Wade* through the appointment of an anti-abortion judge (Neil Gorsuch) to the Supreme Court and other means are prime examples of direct forms of state-perpetrated violence. She reminds us that, "Women's bodies and their lives are subject to different types of violence than that of men" and "the state has historically sanctioned violence against women in various forms. Despite 'progress' over the centuries, the institution of law has been instrumental in normalizing gender relations that award rights to men and simultaneously deny the same rights to women" (p. 23).

Will the U.S. Supreme Court overturn *Roe v. Wade* during Trump's tenure as President? This is an empirical question that can only be answered empirically. Some observers predict that this court is more likely to "chip away" at this legal ruling rather than simply gut women's constitutional right to abortion (Liptak, 2019). Still, at the time of writing this article in June 2019, a few states passed laws that either directly ban abortion altogether or outlaw it after doctors detect a "fetal heartbeat," which generally happens around the sixth week of pregnancy. In May 2019, Alabama, for example, criminalized all abortions, even those resulting from rape and incest.

Some criminologists and human rights activists deem abortion bans as forms of state-perpetrated forced pregnancy. Forced pregnancy is often defined as one or more assaults on a woman with the intent to impregnate her (Goldstein, 1993). The exact number of Alabama rape and incest survivors who were specifically targeted by offenders for the purpose of forced pregnancy will never be known. The same can be said about the number of survivors forced by this state to bear children. What is definitely known, however, is that Alabama is forcing survivors to be pregnant and they will be "left with a permanent reminder of the sexual violence perpetrated against them, as well as tasked with providing for the child economically, financially, emotionally, and physically" (Collins, 2016, p. 75). Hopefully, as some predict (e.g., Liptak, 2019), lower courts will strike down Alabama's law and other states' bans.

Forced pregnancy is generally seen a war crime punishable by the International Criminal Court (Collins, 2016). Though Alabama and other states that ban abortion are technically not at war, some people claim that they have essentially declared a war on women (Crain, 2019), which many women actually support. Consider State Representative Terri Collins who sponsored Alabama's anti-abortion bill. She and the women who back her position are, from a radical feminist standpoint, *exonerators*. In other words, they are apologists for the patriarchal status quo, exculpate men who oppress them and other women, and turn women against each other (Daly, 1978; Dines, 2017). For radical feminists, the main causes of gender-inequality are: (1) the needs or desires of men to control women's sexuality and reproductive potential and (2) patriarchy (Beirne & Messserschmidt, 2014; MacKinnon, 1984). Indeed, there is ample evidence today in the U.S. and elsewhere of men's aggressive attempts to control women's reproductive rights and the recent laws banning abortion are major examples. As well, the gender structure of the U.S. and most countries in the world is patriarchal (Renzetti, 2013). The rates of sexual violence against female college students reported later in this article constitute just one of more than a thousand pieces of evidence.

On top of regarding total abortion bans as forced pregnancy, some radical feminists might consider them as torture (Wright, 2019). Catherine MacKinnon (2006) is a radical feminist legal scholar and her conceptualization is appropriate here. For her, the "generally recognized purpose of torture is to control, intimidate or eliminate those who challenge a regime … ." (p. 18). She further states that, "the abuse is systematic and known, the disregard is official and organized, and the effective governmental tolerance is a matter of law and policy" (p. 25). Support for defining total abortion bans as torture is provided by Juan Mendez (2013), the United Nations' (UN) Special Rapporteur on Torture, who asserts that the "denial of abortion services may constitute torture and/or cruel, inhuman or degrading treatment" (p. 1). Perhaps, then, the United Nations might call for Alabama and other states to change their abortion laws, given that in 2006, the UN Committee Against Torture called for Nicaragua to modify its ban. Since 2006, Nicaragua removed all exceptions to a ban on abortions, including medical procedures to save the lives of pregnant women (MADRE, 2010). The UN also called on other countries (e.g., Ireland and Honduras) to reform their restrictive abortion laws.

Radical feminists also identify some parallels between *The Handmaid's Tale* and abortion bans in the Trump era (DeKeseredy, DeKeseredy, & DeKeseredy, in press). Streamed on Hulu, *The Handmaid's Tale* is based on the best-selling novel by Canadian author Margaret Atwood (1985). The series is set in Gilead, a patriarchal dystopia in the U.S. governed by a male totalitarian regime. In Gilead, women are not permitted to participate in government, hold jobs or own property. Faced with a sharp decline in child births related to an environmental disaster, the few remaining fertile women are forced to become Handmaids to procreate for the Republic of Gilead. Those who refuse to do so are exiled to toxic waste sites or are harmed in other ways. Other women in Gilead serve as wives, trainers of Handmaids, or wives' servants.

This section is not solely a scholarly interpretation of *The Handmaid's Tale*. As Joseph Fiennes, who plays Commander Fred Waterford in the series stated on CBS News on July 24, 2018, "I think our writers like Margaret Atwood and Bruce Miller, or showrunner, have really tapped into something extraordinary, creatively, and tapping into the energy and psyche of society the way they do has sort of brought about a parallel between our show and what is happening" (cited in Park, 2018, p. 1). In fact, the series is specifically designed to mirror current events, especially those involving the oppression of women. For instance, Handmaids are unable to control their own bodies and are instead used for producing children. Those who resist or fail to bear children are punished. This is strikingly familiar to many women in the "real world." Note that during his campaign, Trump suggested that women who seek abortions should be subject to "some form of punishment" (White, 2016). Handmaids, like women seeking abortions in Alabama and some other states, are punished because they challenge *male sexual proprietariness*, which is "the tendency of [men]to think of women as sexual and reproductive 'property' they can own and exchange" (Wilson & Daly, 1992, p. 85). This is not a new problem. The social control of women's sexuality and reproduction has a very long history and is a major feature of patriarchal societies like the U.S. (Chesney-Lind, 2019; Renzetti, Curran, & Maier, 2012).

The Handmaid's Tale is so illustrative of current events that some people fear that the U.S. could turn into a regime similar to the one in Gilead (Bilton, 2017). Probably not entirely, but women's control over their bodies is definitely under siege and there is no sign that this type of oppression is going away in the U.S. and elsewhere. Keep in mind that 39% of the world's population lives in nations with very restrictive laws governing abortion (Chesney-Lind, 2019). Moreover, there is no evidence of a decline in many types of violence against women behind closed doors.

Indirect forms of state-perpetrated violence against women: interpersonal violence in private places

Over 40 years of rigorous survey research shows that women around the world are raped, beaten, and abused by men in numerous other ways in "numbers that would numb the mind of Einstein" (Lewis cited in Vallee, 2007, p. 22). For example, international studies show that no less than 30% of women worldwide are targets of intimate violence (Fitz-Gibbon, Walklate, McCulloch, & Maher, 2018). Some places are safer for women than others and many people share this vision of U.S. institutions of higher education:

> The vision, more or less, includes a beautiful, quiet rural setting, and in that setting is a small college with perfect buildings, and a kind of idyllic, peaceful environment for the pursuit of higher learning. The dorms are comfortable, each has its own dining room, laundry service, and sensitive and caring counselors. Professors, all of whom seem to like each other as well as the students, live in gingerbread houses near the gingerbread village. What could be better (Schuman & Olufs, 1995, p. 31)?

Numerous U.S. citizens also perceive colleges as peaceful sanctuaries from the "real world." They are commonly seen as places where students, faculty, administrators, and support staff strive constantly to provide "practical solutions to the problems of the day" (Strong-Boag, 1996, p. 105), while a growing number of people especially those who hold conservative values and beliefs, view postsecondary schools as little more than "ivory towers" or bastions of political correctness (Johnson & Taylor, 2017).

To some extent, all of these perceptions are correct. Some campuses are beautiful; some members of campus communities try to help policymakers, the media, and members of the general population come to terms with major social, cultural, and economic change. Moreover, some faculty, students, and administrators are strong proponents of political correctness. However, colleges consist of a diverse range of people, attitudes, and beliefs. In fact, the campus is a place where "everybody brings something different, seems to expect something different, and often reacts in different ways" (Schuman & Olufs, 1995, p. 17).

The campus and its immediate surroundings are also some of the most dangerous places for young women. as demonstrated by research dating back to the late 1950s (see Kirkpatrick & Kanin, 1957). Numerous recent surveys show that least one out of every four such students is victimized by some type of sexual assault and that approximately the same number is targeted by physical assault during their college careers (DeKeseredy, 2017). A few studies uncovered higher figures. DeKeseredy, Hall-Sanchez, and Nolan (2018) survey, for example, found that 34% of the women in their sample were victimized since these respondents enrolled at college. Moreover, the vast majority of perpetrators are not strangers. Rather, they are either male acquaintances, classmates, friends, "hookup" partners, boyfriends or former boyfriends (DeKeseredy, 2018a).

Violence against women on college campuses is now extensively discussed and debated, with many commentators asserting that U.S. colleges are experiencing a recent *epidemic* of woman abuse. Yet, again, such violence is not new. In fact, college campuses have long been fertile breeding grounds for high levels of male-to-female violence. Thus, the concept of epidemic is out of place here. To health officials, an epidemic is a disease that devastates a population before eventually subsiding. The reality is that woman abuse, as demonstrated by years of rigorous research, is deeply entrenched in the U.S. college population. Hence, if female victimization on college campuses is a disease, it is in its endemic phase, possibly to be compared with methamphetamine and opioid use among rural residents of West Virginia (DeKeseredy, 2017; McGreal, 2018).

Despite overwhelming evidence of high prevalence rates, there are (and always were), critics like Yoffe (2014) and Johnson and Taylor (2017) who contend that male-to-female physical and sexual violence survey data are misleading. They claim that female survivors are more likely to complete campus climate surveys and that their voices are not representative of the entire student population. Though recent studies show few significant differences in the characteristics of students who participate in campus climate surveys (Pritchard, DeKeseredy, Nolan, & Hall-Sanchez, 2018; Rosenthal & Freyd, 2018), their prominent detractors receive extensive publicity and exposure for their statements – despite having no background or expertise in the area, never having conducted a self-report or victimization survey on sexual assault, and never having revealed any knowledge of this complex field.

The Trump era is characterized by a rabid anti-feminist backlash and there is an enormous market in the media for material that belittles female survivors of male violence (Dragiewicz, 2018; Pritchard et al., 2018). Furthermore, DeKeseredy, Burnham, Nicewarner, Nolan, and Hall-Sanchez (in press) found that many people who dismiss or sharply criticize campus climate surveys belong to what Kimmel (2017) refers to as a "new breed of angry white men" who are experiencing *aggrieved entitlement*:

> It is that sense that those benefits to which you believed yourself entitled have been snatched away from you by unseen forces larger and more powerful. You feel yourself to be heir to a great promise, the American Dream, which has turned into an impossible fantasy for the very people who were *supposed* to inherit it (p. 18, emphasis in original).

One of the main strategies angry white men repeatedly use to deal with "their problems" is claim that they are the "real victims" and that rates of male-to-female sexual assault are greatly exaggerated (DeKeseredy, Fabricius, & Hall-Sanchez, 2015). A white, heterosexual, male undergraduate who participated in DeKeseredy, Burnham, et al.'s (in press) campus climate survey highlights this point:

> I would be greatly happy if this school would stop perpetuating the "rape culture" meme. There is no rape culture, and faulty statistics are used when talking about sexual assault. It is nowhere the epidemic academia has made it out to be. Rape is bad, yes, and should be punished to the fullest extent of the law. This enthusiastic consent BS is a load of crap,

> though. Most of our language is not verbal anyway. It is very obvious if someone does not want to have sex. I think that the social justice warriors have gotten the better of us.

A similar male respondent adds:

> Especially in cases of sexual assault/rape, I believe that the University is biased. When a woman reports that she was sexually assaulted by a male, the male is already seen as guilty before any evidence that shows that he actually did in fact commit the crime. Males are "guilty until proven innocent." I have a male friend who was wrongly accused of sexual assault/rape by his ex-girlfriend ... His ex-girlfriend is a person who seeks attention and will do so anyway she can get it, including lying about being raped. At first, it all started as physical abuse, and as the case went along, it increased to rape. Before this event, I did not know a person that is that delusional to lie about being sexually assaulted, but I am very surprised. Now, I am not saying that all women are lying to get attention because this is not the case at all. I just know that in this particular case, this girl was lying to get attention. Just wanted to throw it out there.

Trump and his Cabinet definitely heard these men's voices and those of other angry white men (DeKeseredy, 2019). In 2017, Education Secretary Betsy DeVos declared that the Obama administration went "too far" by protecting sexual assault survivors to the detriment of alleged perpetrators (Bolger & Brodsky, 2017). So, one of the Trump government's top priorities is to strengthen patriarchal oppression by introducing new rules that reduce the liability of colleges for investigating sexual assault claims and giving defendants the right to cross-examine survivors. Trump's "overhaul" of rules governing sexual assault on college campuses also call for a narrower definition of harassment, relieving schools of the responsibility to investigate off-campus sexual assaults, giving schools the "flexibility" to create higher evidentiary standards, and establishing an appeals process (Green, 2018).

These "rollbacks" would radically change how schools meet their obligations under Title IX, which is part of the U.S. Education Amendments Act of 1972. Title IX prohibits discrimination, denial, and exclusion based on gender in all schools and colleges. It is also supposed to protect college students victimized by sexual assault and sexual harassment (Wood, Sulley, Kammer-Kerwick, Follingstad, & Bush-Armendariz, 2017). Nevertheless, rather than prioritize female students' safety, the Trump administration, like many other governments around the world, is now a "collaborator and facilitator" of various types of violence against women (Fitz-Gibbon et al., 2018). Put differently, it "indirectly facilitates interactional, institutionalized and structural harms suffered by women" (Collins, 2016, p. 88).

According to DeKeseredy and Schwartz's (1993) modified male peer support model, the *absence of deterrence* will thus remain a major problem on college campuses. Before describing this element in their complex theory, it is first necessary to define *male peer support*. It is the attachments to male peers and the resources that these men provide that encourage and legitimate woman abuse (DeKeseredy, 1988). In patriarchal societies, with frequent online and offline messages offering excuses for the oppression, degradation and sexual victimization of women, many men are concerned and confused about their relations with women. Male peer support theory argues that when some men seek the advice of their peers, they are given both encouragement and advice on how to abuse women who "talk back" or do not provide sex on demand. Over 30 years of research shows that having friends who offer such advice is one of the most powerful determinants of whether a young male physically or sexually assaults female acquaintances or intimate partners (DeKeseredy, 2017; DeKeseredy & Schwartz, 2013a).

Returning to the problem of absence of deterrence, perpetrators' friends either overlook or actively support their behavior. Plus, it is rare for a male college student to be arrested for, and convicted of, sexual assault, and very few students are expelled for rape. What is more, when men are punished for abusing women, the penalties are mild (DeKeseredy & Schwartz, 2015; Germain, 2016). Few local prosecutors will push such cases, particularly against athletes (DeKeseredy, 2017), and one of the biggest problems on college campuses is that few sexual assaults are reported to the police. Many survivors are pressured not to report by other students, such as members of their sorority, while others are convinced that they would be publicly embarrassed, and a tremendous number believe what they have been told, that they are responsible for their assault because they were in a man's room, were drinking, or took drugs (DeKeseredy & Schwartz, 2013a).

Administrative negligence and disregard for the needs of sexual assault survivors are also common at colleges and many women with the courage to officially report their victimization experience these responses (Carrigan Wooten & Mitchell, 2016). For instance, the lead detective at a major state university explained in an interview with Martin Schwartz, "All of the claims of rape on this campus come from girls who are trying to get out of taking exams" (cited in DeKeseredy & Schwartz, 2013a, pp. 63–64). Similarly, in March 2006, I and Dr. William F. Flack Jr. met a lawyer at a small private university in the U.S. to discuss sexual assaults on his campus. He maintained that a recent study of unwanted sex at his school is flawed and, at best, reveals a high rate of "regretted sex." When I told him that unless his college developed an effective prevention plan, there is a strong likelihood that survivors' parents would sue, he replied that he was more worried about lawsuits filed by "alleged perpetrators." He presumed that false allegations of sexual assault are more significant problems than true ones. The reality is that less than 2% of campus rapes reported to the police are false allegations (DeKeseredy, Burnham, et al., in press).

The above two statements are prime examples of *institutional betrayal* (Freyd & Birrel, 2013). Such insensitive responses, according to leading psychologists in the field, "are experienced by victims as an especially acute form of disbelief and rejection because they come from social groups that victims often identify with and consider important parts of their self-concept" (Swartout & Flack, 2019, p. 291). Unfortunately, they are common and are likely to be more public if the Trump government makes the aforementioned legislative changes.

College proceedings, though often widely promoted as an effective alternative to criminal court (Swartout & Flack, 2019), commonly trivialize sexual assault cases (Germain, 2016). This lack of sanctions, male peer support theorists argue, explains why there are large groups of men on college campuses who are pro-abuse and who organize numerous pro-abuse activities (Sanday, 1990; Schwartz & DeKeseredy, 1997). If the key issue in preventing woman abuse is to get men to worry about what happens to their reputations if they were discovered as woman abusers, then it should be obvious why there is so much woman abuse. As a broad and general statement, most men on most campuses (not all men on all campuses) will not lose much if their violent conduct comes to the attention of campus officials. The reason, simply, is that on many of these campuses, school officials will not seriously punish men who batter and/or sexually abuse women.

Schwartz and Leggett (1999) conclude that in a society that in a society that accepts male aggression on women as normative:

> If too many men act like they can force sexual intercourse on a woman any time they wish on college campuses and get away with it, it is because it is too often true. In fact, they can often act with impunity … When approximately five percent of victimized women are reporting even forcible rape, there is very little reason for a rapist to fear any consequences of his action (pp. 266–267).

What is to be done?

In his commentary on the election of Donald Trump, Currie (2019) correctly points out that:

> Much of the established Democratic Party, and much of the liberal community, seemed oddly desensitized to the larger currents in American life that were bringing long-simmering and widely shared discontents to a boil – and that had helped to propel one of the most unqualified candidates ever to ascend the highest reaches of the political stage into the most powerful position on the planet (p. 212).

What is to be done? Many people, including numerous liberals and leftists, have simply given up. What Currie (2013) observed six years ago is directly relevant today:

> [T]here is a … sense that there is not much anybody can *do* about it … . There is a widespread sense that the *alternatives* to an out-of-control capitalism have also failed or a are simply irrelevant in this new global age. The result is a kind of deep resignation – a profound pessimism, even among many progressive people, about the possibilities for a better society (p. 3, emphasis in original).

Thousands of others are challenging Trump, but fail to recognize that "the master's tools will never dismantle the master's house" (Lorde, 1983, p. 94). They engage in what Currie (1992) defines as *progressive retreatism*, which involves embracing parts of conservative policies to win elections. Nancy Pelosi, Democrat Speaker of the U.S. House of Representatives embodies this approach, but this is not a new Democrat strategy. When Bill Clinton ran for President in 1992, "No Republican was going to 'out-tough' him on crime" (Chesney-Lind, 2007, p. 212). To emphasize this point, he interrupted his New Hampshire campaign to preside over the execution of Rickey Ray Rector in Arkansas (Sherrill, 2001). Therefore, it is erroneous to assume that radically progressive laws will be passed if a Democrat is elected President in 2020. As Winlow, Hall, and Treadwell (2019) put it, we cannot "in good conscience encourage millions of ordinary people, struggling to make ends meet, to vote for political parties that promise nothing other than the continued reproduction of what already exists" (p. 28). Keep in mind that rates of violence against women behind closed doors were also very high when Clinton and Barak Obama were President. This is why, as Currie (2019) emphasizes, we need to think "*systematically* – that is, of viewing recent political developments in terms of underlying national and global economic forces than simply the malign influence of particularly destructive personalities" (p. 216).

In this context, how can we move beyond the failed strategy of progressive retreatism in addressing the criminogenic and other harmful impacts of the Trump administration? The first step toward solving the problems identified in this article, as well as others spawned by neo-liberalism and patriarchy, is to create solidarity among various factions of the political left (Currie, 2019; Winlow et al., 2019). Structured social inequality thrives on fragmentation and divisions (DeKeseredy & MacLeod, 1997). Hence, rather than going down the well-worn path of shouting down progressives who do not share other progressives' viewpoints, it is vital to develop "an alliance of broader constituencies" (Currie, 2013, p. 11). This entails working closely with women's groups, civil liberties associations, labor groups, LGBTQ coalitions, and a host of other progressive collectives (DeKeseredy & Schwartz, 2013b). There must be a sincere effort to create "a new politics of sameness," a type of politics that recognizes that a diverse range of people, regardless of their gender, sexual identity, or race/ethnicity, are subordinated to the capitalist, patriarchal, and racist motives of neo-liberalism (Winlow et al., 2019).

Once solidarity is achieved, it is then necessary to recognize that radical change will not occur in the near future and that a new left realist agenda is required. In the early days, left realists in the United Kingdom and in North America focused the bulk of their intellectual and political energy on proposing progressive, short-term strategies aimed at reducing predatory street crime (Currie, 1985; Lea & Young, 1984), in an attempt to fill the vacuum of thinking on the left about such crime that existed through the 1980s. This allowed little time to pay attention to crimes of the powerful. Things are slowly changing and one example is the creation of policies aimed at the highly injurious effects of the electronic corporate distribution of adult pornography (DeKeseredy, 2018b; DeKeseredy & Corsianos, 2016). Nevertheless, their critics are correct in suggesting that left realists need to do more work on developing initiatives aimed at reducing human rights violations like abortion bans. However, left realists devote considerable attention to male-to-female acts of interpersonal violence (DeKeseredy & Schwartz, 2018), which can also be equated with violations of human rights (DeKeseredy & MacLeod, 1997). There are various definitions of human rights, but the one offered here is put forth by feminist scholar Bumiller (2008): "[H]uman rights are universal ethical standards that affirm the equality and dignity of all individuals. These rights can be applied either supranationally or to groups and individuals within states" (p. 132).

Scholars, activists, and practitioners working in the international gender and development field do not treat forced pregnancy and intimate violence against women as unique social problems, but rather connect them to other forms of violence and structural violations against women (DeKeseredy & Corsianos, 2016; Fisher, 2011). This human rights perspective is exemplified below in an excerpt from a United Nations (1995) report prepared for the Fourth World Conference on Women, held in Beijing, China in September 1995:

> Violence against women both violates and impairs or nullifies the enjoyment by women of human rights and fundamental freedoms. Taking into account the Declaration on the Elimination of Violence against Women and the work of the special Rapporteurs, gender-based violence, such as battering and other domestic violence, sexual abuse, sexual slavery and exploitation, and international trafficking in women and children, forced prostitution and sexual harassment, as well as violence against women, resulting from cultural prejudice, racism and racial discrimination, xenophobia, pornography, ethnic cleansing, armed conflict, foreign occupation, religious and anti-religious extremism, and terrorism are incompatible with the dignity and the worth of the human person and must be combatted and eliminated (p. 85).

The human rights approach grew out of post-World War II attempts to use international law to curb crimes against humanity, such as genocidal rape. International law carries much weight because the longer a nation has been a party to the 1979 Convention on the Elimination of All forms of Discrimination against Women (CEDAW), the lower the rates of gender inequality and female HIV. Additionally, such a country has better legal protections against male-to-female intimate violence. On the other hand, nations that have reversed out of CEDAW's Article 2 have weaker sexual assault and domestic violence legislation (Richards & Haglund, 2015).

A new left realist human rights agenda should emphasize multifaceted preventive measures that move beyond a focus on individual acts of violence to a broader emphasis on improving the position of women in society (DeKeseredy & Corsianos, 2016; DeKeseredy & MacLeod, 1997). A manual prepared for the United Nations (1993) by an international group of experts includes the following measures that might be used in a prevention strategy:

- reforming the law to foster equality;
- reforming the law to prohibit corporal punishment;
- promoting equal opportunities and human rights;
- combatting stereotypes in the media;
- offering economic opportunities to ensure economic independence;
- providing affordable housing;
- providing child support; and
- improving social policies (p. 85).

Additionally, an effective human rights prevention strategy involves "men changing men" (True, 2012). Efforts to do so are not new and there many models to choose from, but all feminist male violence preventionists agree that men must take an active role in stopping violence against women and other forms of patriarchal control and domination throughout society (DeKeseredy, Dragiewicz, & Schwartz, 2017). Actually, it is more than an active role. Feminist men place the responsibility for woman abuse squarely on men. One widely cited assertion is that "since it is men who are the offenders, it should be men – not women – who change their behavior" (Thorne-Finch, 1992, p. 236).

Stephen Fisher's (2011) curriculum is a valuable teaching aid. He worked with the Fiji Women's Crisis Center to develop the *Male Advocates for Women's Human Rights Handbook*, which is particularly relevant to the issues covered in this article. There are also feminist men's curricula and men's groups in other countries, and the most common activities of feminist men involve protesting patriarchal laws and policies, giving lectures and workshops, lobbying for services, and confronting men who make sexist comments, abuse women, and who engage in other patriarchal practices (DeKeseredy & Corsianos, 2016).

Left realism always went beyond progressive retreatism thanks to the efforts of Currie (1992) and others working in the realist tradition (e.g., Matthews, 2014). It must also, especially during Trump's tenure as President, constantly challenge left-wing scholars and activists who advance *progressive minimalism.* This involves minimizing or denying the seriousness of what Currie (2016) calls *ordinary violence* and other types of street crime (e.g., illegal drug use and dealing). We are now experiencing what he sees as a "new brand of idealist complacency" that not only denies the realities of gun violence in major cities like Chicago, Baltimore and St. Louis (p. 24), but also involves many liberals labeling those who call for a progressive response to predatory street crimes in economically disadvantaged communities as "alarmists," "un-American," and "intrinsically racist" (Currie, 2019, p. 62).

As was the case in the 1980s when Ronald Reagan was President of the U.S. and when Margaret Thatcher was the Prime Minister of the United Kingdom, the political and academic left's failure to take ordinary violence in both urban and rural communities seriously will continue to give politicians like Trump much room to generate ideological support for harsh "law and order" policies, and establish in the minds of the general public that conservatives are the only experts on crime control (DeKeseredy & Schwartz, 2013b). And so progressives must always treat crimes at the top and at the bottom as equally worrying. To be sure, the more vulnerable a person is politically and economically, the more likely it is that a person will be victimized from all directions; by corporate and white-collar crime, state crime, street crime, unemployment and poverty, and a host of other social ills (Lea & Young, 1984). There is much more work to do and progressive minimalists need to now come to grips with what Currie (1992) said nearly 30 years ago: "We are now a generation further down the road and we are, indeed, in worse trouble. So it is already past the time to put the half-forgotten realist agenda back in the center of the public debate" (p. 93).

Acknowledgments

I would like to thank Francis T. Cullen, Elliott Currie, Joseph F. Donnermeyer, and Peter Kraska for their comments and support.

Disclosure statement

No potential conflict of interest was reported by the authors.

References

Atwood, M. (1985). *The handmaid's tale*. Toronto, ON: McClelland and Stewart.

Barak, G. (1990). Crime, criminology and human rights: Towards and understanding of state criminality. *The Journal of Human Justice*, *2*(1), 11–28. doi:10.1007/BF02637528

Beirne, P., & Messserschmidt, J. W. (2014). *Criminology: A sociological approach* (6th ed.). New York, NY: Oxford University Press.

Bilton, N. (2017, June 23). Is *The Handmaid's Tale* the allegory of the *Trump* era? *Vanity Fair*. Retrieved from https://www.vanityfair.com/news/2017/06/handmaids-tale-trump-era-inside-the-hive-podcast

Bolger, D., & Brodsky, A. (2017, September 8). Betsy DeVos' Title IX interpretation is an attack on sexual assault survivors. *The Washington Post*. Retrieved from https://www.washingtonpost.com/news/posteverything/wp/2017/09/08/betsy-devoss-title-ix-interpretation-is-an-attack-on-sexual-assault-survivors/?utm_term=.5821d6e0c7f0

Brabazon, T., Redhead, S., & Chivaura, R. S. (2019). *Trump studies: An intellectual guide to why citizens vote against their interests*. Bingley, UK: Emerald.

Bumiller, K. (2008). *In an abusive state: How neoliberalism appropriated the feminist movement against sexual violence*. Durham, NC: Duke University Press.

Carrigan Wooten, S., & Mitchell, R. W. (2016). Introduction. In S. Carrigan Wooten & R. W. Mitchell (Eds.), *The crisis of campus sexual violence: Critical perspectives on prevention and response* (pp. 1–11). London, UK: Routledge.

Chesney-Lind, M. (2007). Epilogue: Criminal justice, gender and diversity: A call for passion and public criminology. In S. L. Miller (Ed.), *Criminal justice research and practice: Diverse voices from the field* (pp. 210–220). Boston, MA: Northeastern University Press.

Chesney-Lind, M. (2019). Abortion politics and the persistence of patriarchy. In W. S. DeKeseredy & E. Currie (Eds.), *Progressive justice in an age of repression: Strategies for challenging the rise of the right* (pp. 134–152). London, UK: Routledge.

Collins, V. E. (2016). *State crime, women and gender*. London, UK: Routledge.

Crain, A. (2019, May 16). On the front lines of the war on women: In Alabama, the supermajority always wins. *The New York Times*. Retrieved from https://www.nytimes.com/2019/05/16/opinion/alabama-abortion-women.html

Currie, E. (1985). *Confronting crime: An American challenge*. New York, NY: Pantheon.

Currie, E. (1992). Retreatism, minimalism, realism: Three styles of reasoning on crime and drugs in the United States. In J. Lowman & B. D. MacLean (Eds.), *Realist criminology: Crime control and policing in the 1990s* (pp. 88–97). Toronto, ON: University of Toronto Press.

Currie, E. (2013). The sustaining society. In K. Carrington, M. Ball, E. O'Brien, & J. Tauri (Eds.), *Crime, justice and social democracy: International perspectives* (pp. 3–15). New York, NY: Palgrave Macmillan.

Currie, E. (2016). The violence divide: Taking "ordinary" crime seriously in a volatile world. In R. Matthews (Eds.), *What is to be done about crime and punishment? Towards a 'public criminology'* (pp. 9–30). New York, NY: Palgrave Macmillan.

Currie, E. (2019). Epilogue: Pitfalls and possibilities. In W. S. DeKeseredy & E. Currie (Eds.), *Progressive justice in an age of repression: Strategies for challenging the rise of the right* (pp. 212–221). London, UK: Routledge.

Daly, M. (1978). *Gyn/ecology: The metaethics of radical feminism*. Boston, MA: Beacon Press.

DeKeseredy, W. S. (1988). Woman abuse in dating relationships: The relevance of social support theory. *Journal of Family Violence*, *3*(1), 1–13. doi:10.1007/BF00994662

DeKeseredy, W. S., Fabricius, A., & Hall-Sanchez, A. (2015). Fueling aggrieved entitlement: The contribution of women against feminism. In W. S. DeKeseredy & L. Leonard (Eds.), *Crimsoc report 4: Gender, victimology & restorative justice* (pp. 3–33). Sherfield Gables, UK: Waterside Press.

DeKeseredy, W. S., & Schwartz, M. D. (2015). Male peer support theory. In F. T. Cullen, P. Wilcox, J. L. Lux, & C. Lero Jonson (Eds.), *Sisters in crime revisited: Bringing gender into criminology* (pp. 302–322). New York, NY: Oxford University Press.

DeKeseredy, W. S. (2017). Explaining campus violence against women: Unhealthy masculinity and male peer support. In C. Kaukinen, M. Hughes Miller, & R. A. Powers (Eds.), *Addressing violence against women on college campuses* (pp. 65–77). Philadelphia, PA: Temple University Press.

DeKeseredy, W. S., & Schwartz, M. D. (2018). Left realism: A new look. In W. S. DeKeseredy & M. Dragiewicz (Eds.), *Routledge handbook of critical criminology* (2nd ed., pp. 30–42). London, UK: Routledge.

DeKeseredy, W. S. (2018a). Sexual assault on the college campus. In P. Lussier & E. Beauregard (Eds.), *Sexual offending: A criminological perspective* (pp. 204–219). London, UK Routledge.

DeKeseredy, W. S. (2018b). Confronting adult pornography. In W. S. DeKeseredy & M. Dragiewicz (Eds.), *Routledge handbook of critical criminology* (2nd ed., pp. 455–464). London, UK: Routledge.

DeKeseredy, W. S. (2019). But why this man? Challenging hegemonic masculinity in an age of repression. In W. S. DeKeseredy & E. Currie (Eds.), *Progressive justice in an age of repression: Strategies for challenging the rise of the right* (pp. 11–25). London, UK: Routledge.

DeKeseredy, W. S., DeKeseredy, A., & DeKeseredy, P. (in press). Understanding The Handmaid's Tale: The contribution of radical feminism. In J. A. Grubb & C. Posick (Eds.), *Streaming criminology: Theory and justice through the lens of popular TV shows*. New York, NY: New York University Press.

DeKeseredy, W. S., Burnham, K., Nicewarner, R., Nolan, J., & Hall-Sanchez, A. (in press). Aggrieved entitlement in the ivory tower: Qualitative results from a large-scale campus climate survey. *Journal of Qualitative Criminal Justice and Criminology*.

DeKeseredy, W. S., & Corsianos, M. (2016). *Violence against women in pornography*. London, UK: Routledge.

DeKeseredy, W. S., & Currie, E. (Eds.). (2019). *Progressive resistance in an age of repression: Strategies for challenging the rise of the right.* London, UK: Routledge.

DeKeseredy, W. S., Dragiewicz, M., & Schwartz, M. D. (2017). *Abusive endings: Separation and divorce violence against women.* Oakland, CA: University of California Press.

DeKeseredy, W. S., Hall-Sanchez, A., & Nolan, J. (2018). College campus sexual assault: The contribution of peers' proabuse informational support and attachments to abusive peers. *Violence Against Women, 24*(8), 922–935. doi:10.1177/1077801217724920

DeKeseredy, W. S., & MacLeod, L. (1997). *Woman abuse: A sociological story.* Toronto, ON: Harcourt Brace.

DeKeseredy, W. S., & Schwartz, M. D. (1993). Male peer support and woman abuse: An expansion of DeKeseredy's model. *Sociological Spectrum, 13*(4), 393–413. doi:10.1080/02732173.1993.9982041

DeKeseredy, W. S., & Schwartz, M. D. (2013a). *Male peer support & violence against women: The history & verification of a theory.* Boston, MA: Northeastern University Press.

DeKeseredy, W. S., & Schwartz, M. D. (2013b). Confronting progressive retreatism and minimalism: The role of a new left realist approach. *Critical Criminology, 21*(3), 275–286. doi:10.1007/s10612-013-9192-5

Dines, G. (2017, May 1). *The Handmaid's Tale* offers a terrifying warning, but the hijacking of feminism is just as dangerous. *Feminist Current.* Retrieved from https://www.feministcurrent.com/2017/05/01/the-handmaids-tale-offers-a-terrifying-warning-but-hijacking-feminism-just-as-dangerous/

Dragiewicz, M. (2018). Antifeminism and backlash: A critical criminological imperative. In W. S. DeKeseredy & M. Dragiewicz (Eds.), *Routledge handbook of critical criminology* (2nd ed., pp. 334–347). London, UK: Routledge.

Elias, R. (1986). *The politics of victimization: Victims, victimology and human rights.* New York, NY: Oxford University Press.

Fisher, S. (2011). *Male advocates for women's human rights handbook.* Suva, Fiji: Fiji Women's Crisis Center.

Fitz-Gibbon, K., Walklate, S., McCulloch, J., & Maher, J. (2018). Introduction: Intimate partner violence, risk and security – Securing women's lives in a global world. In K. Fitz-Gibbon, S. Walklate, J. McCulloch, & J. Maher (Eds.), *Intimate partner violence, risk and security: Securing women's lives in a global world* (pp. 1–15). London, UK: Routledge.

Freyd, J. J., & Birrel, P. (2013). *Blind to betrayal: Why we fool ourselves we aren't being fooled.* Hoboken, NJ: Wiley.

Germain, L. J. (2016). *Campus sexual assault: College women respond.* Baltimore, MD: Johns Hopkins University Press.

Goldstein, A. T. (1993). *Recognizing forced impregnation as a war crime under international law.* New York, NY: Centre for Reproductive Law & Policy.

Green, E. L. (2018, May 16). Sex assault rules under DeVos bolster defendants' rights and ease college liability. *The New York Times.* Retrieved from https://www.nytimes.com/2018/11/16/us/politics/betsy-devos-title-ix.html

Johnson, K. C., & Taylor, J. S. (2017). *The campus rape frenzy: The attack on due process at America's universities.* New York, NY: Encounter Books.

Kimmel, M. (2017). *Angry white men: American masculinity at the end of an era.* New York, NY: Nation Books.

Kirkpatrick, C., & Kanin, E. J. (1957). Male sex aggression on a university campus. *American Sociological Review, 22*(1), 52–58. doi:10.2307/2088765

Lea, J., & Young, J. (1984). *What is to be done about law and order?* New York, NY: Penguin.

Liptak, A. (2019, May 15). Alabama aims squarely at Roe, but the Supreme Court may prefer glancing blows. *The New York Times.* Retrieved from https://www.nytimes.com/2019/05/15/us/politics/supreme-court-abortion.html?action=click&module=RelatedCoverage&pgtype=Article&region=Footer

Lorde, A. (1983). *The master's tools will never dismantle the master's house.* New York, NY: Penguin.

MacKinnon, C. A. (1984). Not a moral issue. *Yale Law and Policy Review, 2*(2), 32–145.

MacKinnon, C. A. (2006). *Are women human?* Cambridge, MA: Harvard University Press.

MADRE. (2010, May 20). *UN committee against torture calls for an end to Nicaragua's life-threatening abortion ban*. Retrieved from https://www.madre.org/press-publications/press-release/un-committee-against-torture-calls-end-nicaraguas-life-threatening

Matthews, R. (2014). *Realist criminology*. New York, NY: Palgrave Macmillan.

McGreal, C. (2018). *American overdose: The opioid tragedy in three acts*. New York, NY: PublicAffairs.

Mendez, J. (2013). *Denial of abortion services and the prohibition of torture and cruel, inhuman and degrading treatment*. Retrieved from https://www.ohchr.org/Documents/Issues/Women/WG/AmicusBrazil.pdf

Park, A. A. (2018, July 24). Joseph Fiennes on how *The Handmaid's Tale* mirrors real life. *CBS News*. Retrieved from https://www.cbsnews.com/news/joseph-fiennes-on-how-the-handmaids-tale-mirrors-real-life/

Pritchard, A. J., DeKeseredy, W. S., Nolan, J., & Hall-Sanchez, A. (2018). Who speaks first? Analyzing response waves in a large-scale campus climate survey. *Journal of Aggression, Maltreatment & Trauma*. doi:10.1080/10926771.2018.1468374

Renzetti, C. M. (2013). *Feminist criminology*. London, UK: Routledge.

Renzetti, C. M., Curran, D. J., & Maier, S. L. (2012). *Women, men, and society*. Boston, MA: Pearson.

Richards, D. L., & Haglund, J. (2015). *Violence against women and the law*. Boulder, CO: Paradigm Publishers.

Rosenthal, M. N., & Freyd, J. J. (2018). Sexual violence on campus: No evidence that studies are biased due to self-selection. *Dignity: A Journal on Sexual Exploitation and Violence*, *3*(1), 1–12. doi:10.23860/dignity

Sanday, P. R. (1990). *Fraternity gang rape*. New York: New York University Press.

Schuman, D., & Olufs, D. (1995). *Diversity on campus*. Boston, MA: Allyn & Bacon.

Schwartz, M. D., & DeKeseredy, W. S. (1997). *Sexual assault on the college campus: The role of male peer support*. Thousand Oaks, CA: Sage.

Schwartz, M. D., & Leggett, M. S. (1999). Bad dates or emotional trauma? The aftermath of campus sexual assault. *Violence Against Women*, *5*(3), 251–271. doi:10.1177/10778019922181211

Schwendinger, H., & Schwendinger, J. (1975). Defenders of order or guardians of human rights. In I. Taylor, P. Walton, & J. Young (Eds.), *Critical criminology* (pp. 113–146). London, UK: Routledge & Kegan Paul.

Sherrill, R. (2001, January 8). Death trip: The American way of execution. *Nation*. Retrieved from http://www.thenation.com/doc/20010108/sherill

Strong-Boag, V. (1996). Too much is not enough: The paradox of power for feminist academics working community feminists on issues related to violence. In C. Stark-Adamec (Ed.), *Violence: A collective responsibility* (pp. 105–115). Ottawa: Social Science Federation of Canada.

Swartout, K. M., & Flack, W. F., Jr. (2019). Campus sexual assault. In W. S. DeKeseredy, C. M. Rennison, & A. K. Hall-Sanchez (Eds.), *The Routledge international handbook of violence studies* (pp. 286–295). London, UK: Routledge.

Thorne-Finch, R. (1992). *Ending the silence: The origins and treatment of male violence against women*. Toronto, ON: University of Toronto Press.

True, J. (2012). *The political economy of violence against women*. New York, NY: Oxford University Press.

United Nations. (1993). *Strategies for confronting domestic violence: A resource manual*. New York, NY: Author.

United Nations. (1995). *Focus on women: Violence against women*. Report prepared for the Fourth World Conference on Women, Action for Equality, Development and Peace, Beijing, Author.

Vallee, B. (2007). *The war on women: Elly Armour, Jane Harshman, and criminal violence in Canadian homes*. Toronto, ON: Key Porter Books.

White, D. (2016, June 16). Donald Trump on abortion: "I'm saying women punish themselves". *Time*. Retrieved from http://time.com/4340358/donald-trump-womn-abortions-punish/well-being

Wilson, M., & Daly, M. (1992). Till death do us part. In J. Radford & D. E. H. Russell (Eds.), *Femicide: The politics of women killing* (pp. 83–98). New York, NY: Twayne.

Winlow, S., Hall, S., & Treadwell, J. (2019). Why the left must change: Right-wing populism in context. In W. S. DeKeseredy & E. Currie (Eds.), *Progressive justice in an age of repression: Strategies for challenging the rise of the right* (pp. 26–41). London, UK: Routledge.

Wood, L., Sulley, C., Kammer-Kerwick, M., Follingstad, D., & Busch-Armendariz, N. (2017). Climate surveys: An inventory of understanding sexual assault and other crimes of interpersonal violence at institutions of higher education. *Violence Against Women*, *23*(10), 1249–1267. doi:10.1177/1077801216657897

Wright, J. (2019, May 16). Why Alabama's abortion ban is akin to torture. *Harper's Bazzar*. Retrieved from https://www.harpersbazaar.com/culture/politics/a27484973/alabama-abortion-law-rape-incest-explained/

Yoffe, E. (2014, December 7). The college rape overcorrection. *Slate*. Retrieved from http://www.slate.com/articles/double_x/doublex/2014/college_rape_campus_sexual_assault_is_a_serious_problem_but_the_efforts.html

President or Predator? The Social Construction of Donald Trump in a Divided America

Teresa C. Kulig, Francis T. Cullen, and Murat Haner

ABSTRACT
During the presidential election, numerous women accused Donald Trump of sexual harassment and/or assault. Then a presidential candidate, he denied these complaints and said the women were all untruthful – a position he has continued to espouse. To explore "who the public believes," we commissioned YouGov to conduct an opt-in online survey of a national sample of 1,000 Americans. Notably, half of Americans (51.0%) believed that "the women are telling the truth when they reported that Mr. Trump sexually harassed or assaulted them" versus 23.1% who sided with the president. Nearly two-thirds (64.9%) stated that it was unlikely that all the women were lying, and 3 in 5 Americans (60.5%) supported President Trump's impeachment by the U.S. Congress if these accusations could be proven. Informed by research on political psychology (especially Haidt's *The Righteous Mind*), the data are explored to see why Americans embrace divergent moral narratives – with some seeing Mr. Trump as a truthful president and others seeing him as a predator unworthy of the office he holds.

During the early 1980s, 38-year-old Jessica Leeds was a traveling businesswoman for a paper company when she reported boarding a plane to New York (Twohey & Barbaro, 2016). Leeds was originally seated in coach, but a flight attendant invited her to upgrade to an empty seat in first class. Her upgrade placed her next to Donald Trump – who was flying commercial airlines because he had yet to own a fleet of private aircraft (Twohey & Barbaro, 2016). Leeds stated that Trump introduced himself and shook her hand. Her conversation with Trump, which extended through the in-flight meal, started off with pleasantries and moved on to questions about her marital status. Once the trays were cleared, Leeds alleged that Trump raised the armrest, encroached on her space, and groped her, including putting his hands on her breasts and up her skirt (Kurtzleben, 2016; Twohey & Barbaro, 2016). She described Trump as being "like an octopus" because his hands were all over her in a matter of moments (Twohey & Barbaro, 2016). In response to his unwanted advances, she stood up and returned to her original seat in coach.

Leeds said that she did not speak of the incident because unwanted advances from men were something that women were blamed for at the time. It was not until Trump started his campaign for president that she began telling friends about what happened out of a sense of obligation to illuminate his behavior. She was one of the first women to share her story publicly – along with another accuser, Rachel Crooks – in an article published in *The New York Times* on October 12, 2016 (Twohey & Barbaro, 2016).

In response to Jessica Leeds's accusations of sexual misconduct, Donald Trump has adamantly denied the event ever occurred. A day after *The New York Times* broke the story, Trump discussed the incident in a speech in Florida:

> Now, today the same two discredited writers, who should've been fired from *The New York Times* for what they did, tell another totally fabricated and false story, that supposedly took place on an airplane more than 30 years ago. Another ridiculous tale, no witnesses, no nothing. ("Transcript: Donald Trump's speech," 2016)

He threatened to sue the newspaper for false reporting, but there is no evidence that a formal lawsuit has been filed to date (Keneally, 2018a). A couple of days later at a rally in North Carolina, he retold the story again and implied that she was not an attractive target by stating, "believe me, she would not be my first choice" (McCaskill, 2016).

Jessica Leeds's account of her interaction with Donald Trump may have been considered an anomaly had it not been for the multiple women who also came forward to share their own stories. Depending on the source, there have been between 13 and 24 women who have accused Trump of varying types of inappropriate sexual behavior since the 1980s (Ford, 2017; Graves & Morris, 2017; Kelly, 2017; Keneally, 2018a; North, 2019a; Relman, 2019). These allegations include Trump walking into locker rooms where women were dressing or naked, making sexually harassing or suggestive comments, engaging in forcible kissing, groping women's breasts or buttocks, pressing women against walls, and putting his hands up women's skirts. The most recent allegation asserts that Trump raped one woman in a department store dressing room (Carroll, 2019). He has repeatedly denied that any of these incidents took place (e.g., Keneally, 2018a; Kessler & Kelly, 2018; Relman, 2019) and stated that "these vicious claims about me of inappropriate conduct with women are totally and absolutely false" (Transcript: Donald Trump's speech, 2016). In his responses, he has called the accusers liars, insinuated that some women were too unattractive to assault, and speculated whether the Clinton campaign was behind the stories (McCaskill, 2016).

Although there were earlier reports of sexually inappropriate behavior by Trump (e.g., Barbaro & Twohey, 2016), the flurry of accusations during the 2016 campaign seem to have been prompted, in part, by the release of the *Access Hollywood* recording (e.g., Stoynoff, 2016; Twohey & Barbaro, 2016). The tape – originally documented in 2005 – surfaced in an exposé by *The Washington Post* days before the presidential debate in October 2016 (Fahrenthold, 2016). In the video footage, Trump is heard on a microphone speaking with Billy Bush on a bus as they were making their way to the set of the television program *Days of Our Lives*. The video features crude language and illustrates tactics that Trump admits to using to advance sexually with women. As stated by Trump in the conversation, he had attempted to have sexual intercourse with a married woman:

> You know and I moved on her, actually. You know, she was down on Palm Beach. I moved on her, and I failed. I'll admit it. I did try and fuck her. She was married ... She wanted to get some furniture. I said, "I'll show you where they have some nice furniture." I took her out

> furniture – I moved on her like a bitch. But I couldn't get there. And she was married. ("Transcript: Donald Trump's taped comments," 2016)

The recording continued with dialog between Trump and Billy Bush as they prepared to exit the bus to greet their female set escort:

> *Trump:* I better use some Tic Tacs just in case I start kissing her. You know, I'm automatically attracted to beautiful – I just start kissing them. It's like a magnet. Just kiss. I don't even wait. And when you're a star, they let you do it. You can do anything.
>
> *Bush:* Whatever you want.
>
> *Trump:* Grab 'em by the pussy. You can do anything.

The vivid language used by Trump to describe sexually assaultive behavior resulted in a mass outcry by Americans and politicians (e.g., "Leaked tape captures Trump," 2016; Powers, 2016; "Republicans react to Donald," 2016). Shortly after the footage was released, Trump provided a statement apologizing for his language (Haberman, 2016). Within that statement, he highlighted that his words were not as offensive as Bill and Hillary Clinton's behavior:

> I've never said I'm a perfect person, nor pretended to be someone that I'm not. I've said and done things I regret, and the words released today on this more than a decade-old video are one of them. Anyone who knows me knows these words don't reflect who I am. I said it, I was wrong, and I apologize ... I pledge to be a better man tomorrow and will never, ever let you down ... I've said some foolish things, but there's a big difference between the words and actions of other people. Bill Clinton has actually abused women, and Hillary has bullied, attacked, shamed, and intimidated his victims. ("Transcript of Donald Trump's videotaped apology," 2016)

On the eve of the second presidential debate, he went on to host a panel with four of Bill Clinton's accusers to distance his language from Clinton's actions (Stokols & Conway, 2016). At the debate, Trump dismissed the *Access Hollywood* conversation as something that, though not proud of, was just "locker room talk" (White, 2016). He further stated that he has "tremendous respect" for women and that he has never kissed or groped women without their consent.

In addition to the sexual misconduct allegations, Trump has faced continuous scrutiny for his conduct and behavior toward women before and after his election. In particular, he has insulted various women's appearances and called them names such as "pig", "horse-face", "slob", and "dog" (Keneally, 2018c; Shear & Sullivan, 2018; Strum & Fears, 2015). He also admitted to funding at least one non-disclosure agreement with pornographic actress Stephanie Clifford (otherwise known as Stormy Daniels), with whom he was accused of having an affair (e.g., Feuer, 2018; Forsythe, 2018; Neely & Montanaro, 2018). Former Playboy model Karen McDougall alleges that she also had an affair with Trump; her story was purchased but never published by a media company (e.g., Palazzolo, Hong, Rothfeld, O'Brien, & Ballhaus, 2018; Rutenberg, 2018). Trump has continued to deny that either affair ever happened (Feuer, 2018; Palazzolo et al., 2018). Furthermore, he has publicly defended men who have been accused of assaulting women, including Bill O'Reilly (news anchor), Roy Moore (politician), and Brett Kavanaugh (judge) (Keneally, 2018b). In the high-profile U.S. Supreme Court confirmation hearing for Judge

Kavanaugh, Trump went so far as to publicly mock Kavanaugh's accuser – Christine Blasey Ford – during a rally in Mississippi (Garber, 2018).

These events have spurred significant reactions (e.g., Cohen, 2017). On January 21, 2017 – the day after Donald Trump was inaugurated as the 45th President of the United States – between 800,000 and 1.2 million Americans were estimated to have gathered in Washington, DC to participate in the Women's March protesting Trump's election despite his offensive behavior toward women (Women's March, 2017). Hundreds of corresponding marches were held across the nation and worldwide (Chenoweth & Pressman, 2017). Protesters have gathered annually to show their continued disapproval of Trump's anti-female conduct and policies (Wines & Stockman, 2019). A larger campaign to raise awareness about the pervasiveness of sexual harassment and sexual assault also earned prominence: the #MeToo movement. Originally started in 2006, this initiative achieved national momentum in 2017 after multiple reports from women detailed sexual misconduct allegations against film executive Harvey Weinstein (Farrow, 2017; Kantor & Twohey, 2017; Parker, 2017; Remnick, 2018). Weinstein was eventually arrested on charges of rape, criminal sex act, sex abuse, and sexual misconduct; he pleaded not guilty (Levenson & Moghe, 2018; Samuelson, 2018). The shift to publicly denounce inappropriate sexual behavior affected hundreds of powerful men, including Charlie Rose (television host), Matt Lauer (news anchor), Al Franken (senator), Louis C. K. (comedian), and Kevin Spacey (actor) (Carlsen et al., 2018).

Trump responded to the #MeToo movement at a rally where he said it is a "very scary time for young men in America" who could be falsely accused (Griffiths, 2018). Regardless of data suggesting that sexual assaults are prevalent, underreported, and rarely result in false accusations (e.g., Fisher, Cullen, & Turner, 2000; Lisak, Gardinier, Nicksa, & Cote, 2010), he further voiced concern that people are condemned as guilty instead of assumed as innocent until otherwise proven (Scott, 2018). Notably, a record number of women were elected to office during the 2018 midterm elections – many of whom ran on platforms that resisted Trump's presidency (Gaudiano, 2018).

These movements highlight broader concerns of Americans regarding the sexual misconduct of individuals – particularly men – and their social status. In the midst of these social actions, Donald Trump has been at the center of various controversies for his alleged sexually inappropriate behavior with women – all of which he has denied (Folmer, 2019; Kessler & Kelly, 2018). Despite this turmoil, he was elected as the President of the United States by securing support from more than 60 million Americans ("2016 presidential election results," 2016). Commentators often take some solace in the fact that Trump lost the popular vote to Hillary Clinton. Still, Clinton's advantage was based substantially on her decisive victory in California (Jackson, 2016). Elsewhere across the United States, a majority of the electorate voted for Donald Trump to be the nation's president in the 2016 election despite allegations that he engaged in sexually inappropriate behavior with multiple women.

Notably, there appears to be a divide in how the U.S. citizenry perceives Trump and his alleged sexual behavior – with some individuals protesting him and others endorsing him (Gstalter, 2018; Kew, 2017). Given the divergent reactions to Trump, the current study seeks to illuminate "who the public believes" regarding the sexual misconduct allegations against him. This issue is probed through a 2017 national survey of 1,000 respondents conducted by YouGov America, Inc. We hypothesize that some Americans view Trump as an innocent *president*, whereas others view him as a dangerous *predator* who assaulted multiple women. We argue that these responses are rooted in oppositional worldviews that are shaped by moral foundations (Haidt, 2012). The potential sources of these views are described more fully below.

The divide in America?

Surveys support the notion that Americans are deeply divided on their opinions about Trump – including at the time our survey was conducted. For example, a telephone survey of 805 adults conducted by Monmouth University Poll in August 2017 – a little more than a year after the *Access Hollywood* tape was publicized – found that, of the respondents who approved of Trump, most (61%) indicated that they could not see him doing anything that would make them disapprove of him. For respondents who disapproved of the president, a majority (57%) said there was nothing Trump could do, other than resign, that would make them approve of the job he was doing. The permanency of their position suggests that some individuals will support or oppose Trump no matter what – nothing is going to sway them.

Surveys also provide valuable insights into factors related to a divide on the sexual misconduct allegations against Trump. In particular, political party affiliation seems to be important when distinguishing support for or resistance to Trump. For example, *Politico* surveyed 1,955 registered voters in December 2017 (Shepard, 2017). Half of the respondents (50%) viewed the allegations against Trump as credible. When examined by party affiliation, 62% of Democrats viewed the allegations as credible compared to only 38% of Republicans. Among self-identified Trump voters, 39% thought the charges were credible as opposed to 37% who thought they were not credible (24% reported that they did not know or had no opinion). This finding suggests that some individuals who voted for Trump did not believe his accusers, whereas others discounted the importance of their victimization. Another poll was conducted with 1,230 voters in December 2017 by Quinnipiac University (Malloy & Smith, 2017). Half of American voters surveyed believed Trump should resign because of the sexual allegations against him. Additional breakdowns indicated that these opinions were pervasive among Democrats (85%) and women (59%). Comparatively, only 41% of men said Trump should resign. Republicans were more likely to indicate that he should *not* resign (92%) – only 7% indicated that he should resign (1% of the sample reported that they did not have an opinion).

One explanation for this potential divide involves the moral foundations that guide our lives. In his book *The Righteous Mind*, Haidt (2012) argues that there are at least six moral foundations or intuitions that underlie the way people organize the world: (1) care/harm; (2) fairness/cheating; (3) loyalty/betrayal; (4) authority/subversion; (5) sanctity/degradation; and (6) liberty/oppression. Haidt (2012) contends that political orientation is a product of moral foundations with which we identify. Although all political ideologies (left, right, and center) care about each of these foundations to an extent, some moral guidelines seem more salient than others depending on an individual's ideological allegiance. These moral guidelines can also be interpreted differently depending on the "tribe."

The political left, he contends, aligns most with the care/harm and liberty/oppression principles – facets that promote social justice, compassion for the poor, and solidarity to fight oppression. Fairness/cheating is also endorsed by liberals, but this alignment can be discarded when it conflicts with compassion or a desire to fight oppression (Haidt, 2012, p. 214). In this way, liberals are considered to have "bleeding hearts" for individuals who could be harmed by policies or actions that disproportionately affect the vulnerable. It is the government's job to protect these populations at the risk of other objectives. In the context of the sexual misconduct allegations against Trump, it is instructive that individuals who identified as Democrats in the aforementioned surveys viewed these accusations more seriously than individuals who identified as Republicans. The females who alleged the behavior also documented substantial harm that they experienced during and after these events occurred (e.g., Twohey & Barbaro, 2016). In this way, the political left would be more sensitive to the harm caused to the women, especially by someone in a position of authority.

Conversely, the political right tends to emphasize all six of the moral foundations, with the liberty/oppression ideal viewed as one of the most prominent. Conservatives "hold more traditional ideas of liberty as the right to be left alone" and to be free from any government interference (Haidt, 2012, p. 212). Haidt (2012) argues that the protections for vulnerable populations or the environment put forth by liberals tend to result in resentment by conservatives. Accordingly, hard work should be compensated and not penalized by giving away resources to those who are not seen as deserving. Although the political right taps into all six moral foundations, the care/harm foundation is seen as more expendable. Conservatives are generally more willing than liberals to "let some people get hurt in order to achieve their many other moral objectives" (p. 214). Thus, harm to others could be seen as collateral damage to achieve the bigger picture. When considering the sexual misconduct allegations against Trump, the alleged harm exhibited by the individuals who came forward could be seen as less important than other moral foundations – and related interests and policies – that Trump might advance for conservatives.

Within this framework of moral foundations, the current study examines whether the public is more likely to believe Donald Trump or his female accusers – again, using a national sample of 1,000 respondents. Although this analysis is not able to control for Haidt's (2012) moral foundations directly, there are measures of the respondents' political ideology and political affiliation as proxy indicators. In addition to other sociodemographic characteristics associated with Trump voters (e.g., White, male, no college degree), these political indicators are likely key variables to tap into the moral values that contribute to any divide (Tyson & Maniam, 2016). Thus, four questions guide the current analysis: (1) To what extent does the American public believe the women who accused Trump of sexual misconduct? (2) Is the view of Trump mixed or do respondents fall into distinct tribes? (3) What predicts views toward Trump? And (4) do opinions about Trump affect self-reported voting in the 2016 election beyond political indicators?

Method

Sample

The data for this study come from a survey administered to 1,000 respondents by YouGov America, Inc. between October 17 and 24, 2017. YouGov is an international market research company that administers surveys on topics including politics, products, and current social issues (YouGov, 2018a). It has more than 6 million panelists internationally, with 2 million respondents located in the United States (YouGov, 2018b). These panelists are voluntary participants who "opt-in" or agree to complete online surveys. In return, participants earn points that can be redeemed for gift cards for brands such as Amazon, Target, Old Navy, and Nike (YouGov, 2016). Note that opt-in surveys are becoming a standard measure in the social sciences, including crime-related research (Thielo, Graham, & Cullen, in press).

YouGov's strategy does not remove all sampling biases, but it does employ a multi-stage matching process to maximize the representativeness of the sample (see also Thielo, 2017). The process used to obtain the current sample is outlined below:

> YouGov interviewed 1099 respondents who were then matched down to a sample of 1000 to produce the final dataset. The respondents were matched to a sampling frame on gender, age, race, education, party identification, ideology, and political interest. The frame was constructed by stratified sampling from the full 2010 American Community Survey (ACS) sample with selection within strata by weighted sampling with replacements (using the person weights on the public use file). Data on voter registration status and turnout were matched to this frame using the November 2010 Current Population Survey. Data on interest in politics and party identification were then matched to this frame from the 2007 Pew Religious Life Survey. The matched cases were weighted to the sampling frame using propensity scores. The matched cases and the frame were combined and a logistic regression was estimated for inclusion in the frame. The propensity score function included age, gender, race/ethnicity, years of education, region, voter registration status, and ideology. The propensity scores were grouped into deciles of the estimated propensity score in the frame and post-stratified according to these deciles. The weights were post-stratified on a four-way stratification of gender, age, race, and education, and on 2016 presidential vote choice. (YouGov, 2017, p. 1)

Respondents who "opt-in" to take YouGov surveys answer a standard set of socio-demographic items (e.g., gender, race, birth year, education) that are updated regularly. They comprise YouGov's "core profile" and are provided for each study. In addition to the core demographic variables, respondents answered 10 items developed for this study on their opinions regarding the sexual misconduct allegations against Donald Trump. The completed survey responses to all items were delivered by YouGov in weighted and unweighted form. The weighted data are used in the current analyses to increase the representativeness of the sample. As outlined in Table 1, the sample was split nearly evenly by gender, about two thirds of respondents were White (67.5%), and the average age was approximately 46 (standard deviation [SD] = 17.2). Relevant to the current study, about one-third of the sample self-reported as being conservative (34.3%), and about one-fourth identified themselves as Republican (25.2%).

Dependent variables

Sexual misconduct opinions

The 10 Trump-related items presented to the respondents started with the following instructions:

> During the presidential election, at least 10 women came forward and disclosed that Donald Trump had used force to kiss them, had grabbed or groped them sexually, or had otherwise engaged in behavior that might have been viewed as a sexual assault. Then a presidential candidate, Donald Trump denied these complaints and said that all the women were

Table 1. Descriptive statistics of key covariates (N = 1,000).

Variable	Percent/Mean (SD)	Min	Max
Political Ideology		0	1
Conservative	34.3		
Other	65.7		
Political Affiliation		0	1
Republican	25.2		
Other	74.8		
Gender		0	1
Male	48.0		
Female	52.0		
Age	46.7 (17.2)	18	92
Race		0	3
White	67.5		
Black	11.8		
Hispanic	13.6		
Other	7.1		
Education	3.2 (1.5)	1	6
Marital Status		0	3
Married	43.6		
Divorced	10.6		
Never Married	35.2		
Other	10.6		
Child Under 18 in Household		0	1
Yes	24.7		
No	75.3		
Employment Status		0	5
Employed (full/part)	46.4		
Unemployed	10.6		
Retired	18.9		
Homemaker	7.9		
Student	4.4		
Other	11.8		
Born Again		0	1
Yes	34.4		
No	65.6		
Religiosity	2.9 (1.1)	1	4

> untruthful. He said that he had never engaged in any of these behaviors. Given that Donald Trump is now the President of the United States, we wanted to understand how the American public feels about this matter.

The directions continued by indicating that the respondents should select the answer that most closely represents their views even if it does not match exactly. The subsequent sexual misconduct items asked the respondents to answer whether they viewed Trump favorably or unfavorably. The respondents were asked whether they believed Trump or his female accusers, including questions about what should happen if the accusations are true. Furthermore, the respondents were asked about the significance of the *Access Hollywood* tape recording, whether Trump is worse than Hillary Clinton, perceptions on Trump defending Bill O'Reilly, and how Trump treats women more generally. Each item is reviewed in more detail below when discussed in the Results section.

Again, the survey went into the field on October 17, 2017. Although it was not possible to administer the survey immediately after the accusations were publicized, the survey was released approximately one year after the *Access Hollywood* tape was made public. This time difference gave ample opportunity for the respondents to learn about the multiple accusations from women and Trump's subsequent responses declaring his innocence (e.g., Transcript: Donald Trump's speech, 2016).

Voting in 2016 election

As part of YouGov's "core profile" items, sample members were asked to indicate who they voted for in the 2016 Presidential election. The respondents reported that they did not vote (37.4%), voted for Hillary Clinton (30.0%), voted for Donald Trump (28.8%), or voted for another candidate (3.8%). The responses were dichotomized where 1 = "voted for Donald Trump" (28.8%) and 0 = "other vote" (71.2%) for subsequent analyses to determine characteristics of those who were most likely to vote for Trump.

Key covariates

Political moral foundations

Two variables were used to evaluate political moral foundations: political ideology and political affiliation (Haidt, 2012). *Political ideology* was assessed by asking respondents how they would describe their political viewpoints (0 = other; 1 = conservative). *Political affiliation* asked respondents to indicate if they were a Democrat, Republican, Independent, or other (0 = other; 1 = Republican). Due to "not sure" responses for ideology (n = 94) and affiliation (n = 68), the measures were dichotomized to avoid the need to delete individuals making this response and losing cases in the analyses (see, e.g., Shelley et al., 2017).

Control variables

Several sociodemographic characteristics were also included in the models to identify sources of any potential divides in opinions. Basic demographic characteristics included *gender* (0 = female; 1 = male), *age* (in years), and *race* (0 = White; 1 = Black; 2 = Hispanic; 3 = other). *Education* asked respondents the highest level of education that they have completed. The values ranged from 1 = "no high school" to 6 = "post-grad," with higher values indicating greater levels of education. Additional variables were included to assess respondents' *marital status* (0 = married; 1 = divorced; 2 = never married; 3 = other), whether *children under 18* were in the home (0 = no; 1 = yes), and *employment* (0 = employed; 1 = unemployed; 2 = retired; 3 = homemaker; 4 = student; 5 = other). The respondents also provided details on whether they were religious or spiritual. *Born again* asked respondents if they would describe themselves as born-again or an evangelical Christian (0 = no; 1 = yes). The respondents were also asked about their *religiosity*. Response categories were on a 4-point scale (1 = "not at all important" to 4 = "very important"), where higher values indicate that religion is important to them.

Analytic strategy

There were relatively few missing data points in the current analyses, with only missing values for some of the 10 sexual misconduct opinion questions. At most, there were 33 responses missing for at least one of these items. Thus, the current analysis used information from all available observations. As previously noted, all analyses included weighted data to increase the representativeness of the sample. All independent variables were examined for potential issues with multicollinearity. The variance inflation factor (VIF) values did not exceed 1.88 with the exception of age (VIF = 2.58), and the condition index was below the recommended cutoff of 30, with a value of 19.78 (Belsley, Kuh, & Welsch, 1980; Fox, 1991; Wooldridge, 2009). These findings indicate that multicollinearity was not a concern in the current analyses.

The analyses were carried out in four stages. First, we review the response patterns of participants to glean their opinions regarding the sexual misconduct allegations against Donald Trump. Second, we conduct a latent class analysis (LCA) to examine whether respondents fall into different "tribes" based on the 10 sexual misconduct opinion questions. LCA is generally able to recover hidden groups most commonly through variables with binary indicators (Nylund-Gibson & Choi, 2018; Oberski, 2016). Although there were some missing values on these opinion-related items, Stata 15 uses maximum likelihood methods with missing values for LCA (estimated using *gsem*), which means that more observations can generally be incorporated on an equation-by-equation basis (StataCorp, 2017). In this context, the full information maximum likelihood method was able to incorporate all available observations without implementing listwise techniques so that the entire sample of 1,000 respondents was retained for all estimations. Third, we use latent class regression techniques to predict opinions about the sexual misconduct allegations against Donald Trump. Finally, we apply logistic regression methods to determine whether sexual misconduct opinions – using the unconditional predicted posterior probability for each group classification – predict self-reported voting in the 2016 election beyond the political moral foundation variables.

Results

Sexual misconduct opinion responses

Table 2 provides an overview of the 10 sexual misconduct opinion items. The following descriptions are divided into four themes: (1) views about accusations (Items 1 through 5); (2) Trump and women (Items 6 and 7); (3) Trump compared to Hillary Clinton (Item 8); and (4) feelings about Trump (Items 9 and 10). In addition to the overall level of agreement with each response category, the findings are also broken down by gender for comparison (see Table 2).

Views about accusations

Several items focused on how the respondents perceived the women and their accusations. Most significant, Item 1 asked who they believed regarding the sexual misconduct allegations – Donald Trump or the multiple women. Was he a president or a predator? Notably, half of the respondents (51.0%) believed that the female accusers were telling the truth when they disclosed that they were sexually harassed or assaulted. Conversely, only about a quarter (23.1%) of the sample believed that Trump did not engage in any sexual misconduct. However, another quarter of the respondents (25.9%) stated that Trump may have done something wrong but that it was not sexual assault – suggesting that they were uncertain about the severity of the specific incidents but aware that something inappropriate may have occurred. Similarly, a substantial portion of Americans doubted that Trump was being truthful about the *Access Hollywood* tape (Item 2). Here, a majority of respondents viewed his statements on the tape as admitting sexual assault

Table 2. Opinions about Donald Trump's involvement in sexual misconduct.[a]

	Percentages		
Items	Overall	Male	Female
1. Which of the following statements best represents your view of claims that Donald Trump engaged in unwanted sexual conduct with a number of women? (n = 993)			
a. I believe that Mr. Trump is telling the truth and that he said that he did not harass or sexually assault any of the women (f)	23.1	29.5	17.2
b. Mr. Trump might have done something inappropriate but it was minor and not a sexual assault (f)	25.9	26.4	25.4
c. I believe that the women are telling the truth when they reported that Mr. Trump sexually harassed or assaulted them (un)	51.0	44.1	57.4
2. During the presidential campaign, a video tape was released of Donald Trump telling television host Billy Bush that he often grabbed women sexually. Mr. Trump said: "I don't even wait. And when you're a star, they let you do it. You can do anything … grab 'em by the pussy." What do you think about this incident? (n = 988)			
a. Mr. Trump was engaging in "locker room" talk that all guys do, so it was no big deal (f)	42.4	47.8	37.4
b. Mr. Trump was admitting that he sexually assaulted women, just as the 10 women who accused him of doing to them (un)	57.6	52.2	62.6
3. Finally, remember that 10 women accused Donald Trump of sexual misconduct. What is the likelihood that all of them are lying? (n = 997)			
a. Highly Likely (f)	12.2	16.5	8.1
b. Likely (f)	22.9	25.9	20.2
c. Unlikely (un)	31.9	30.4	33.3
d. Highly Unlikely (un)	33.0	27.2	38.4
4. One criticism of Donald Trump's accusers was that many of the alleged acts occurred years ago and they never reported them to their bosses or the police. What is your view of this? (n = 994)			
a. Because the women did not file a report when the act supposedly occurred, I am more likely to believe Mr. Trump that nothing ever occurred (f)	37.1	45.2	29.7
b. Women who are sexually harassed or assaulted by powerful men, like Mr. Trump, do not report incidents to authorities because they are afraid and think that nothing will be done (un)	62.9	54.8	70.3
5. Let us assume that the 10 women who accused Mr. Trump of sexual misconduct are telling the truth. If this were proven to be the case, which of the following statements best represents your view? (n = 985)			
a. Mr. Trump should be impeached by the U.S. Congress and forced to resign as President (un)	60.5	55.2	65.2
b. Mr. Trump should remain as president (f)	39.5	44.8	34.8
6. Donald Trump has claimed that he will be the best president ever for women – he has "tremendous respect" for women and he will do more for women than any other president. To what extent do you agree with this statement? (n = 1,000)			
a. Strongly Agree (f)	11.9	16.4	7.8
b. Agree (f)	16.6	19.8	13.7
c. Agree a Little (f)	13.6	13.5	13.7
d. Disagree a Little (un)	10.9	11.0	10.7
e. Disagree (un)	9.4	7.1	11.5
f. Strongly Disagree (un)	37.6	32.2	42.6
7. The day after Donald Trump was inaugurated as president of the United States, there was a Women's March across the United States and around the world. Which of the following statements best describes how you felt? (n = 992)			
a. The size of the Women's March was exaggerated by the fake news and it made no difference anyway (f)	43.2	44.6	41.9
b. The Women's March showed that hundreds of thousands, if not millions, of women were upset with Donald Trump and with the sexual assaults that females often experience (un)	56.8	55.4	58.1
8. To what extent do you agree with this statement: "Even if Donald Trump did something wrong, Hillary Clinton was more immoral, is a crook, and should be locked up." (n = 998)			
a. Strongly Agree (f)	23.6	29.4	18.1
b. Agree (f)	13.3	14.4	12.2
c. Agree a Little (f)	12.9	13.2	12.6

(*Continued*)

Table 2. (Continued).

Items	Percentages		
	Overall	Male	Female
d. Disagree a Little (un)	10.3	8.6	12.0
e. Disagree (un)	13.6	13.1	14.1
f. Strongly Disagree (un)	26.3	21.3	31.0
9. Which of the following statements best describes how you felt the day after Donald Trump was elected president? (n = 991)			
a. I was happy because I thought he would be a great president and make America great again (f)	46.6	52.6	41.1
b. I was depressed because I could not believe that my fellow Americans could elect a sexual predator to the presidency of the country I love (un)	53.4	47.4	58.9
10. Recently, Bill O'Reilly was forced out of Fox News Channel because of allegations of sexual harassment of women. Donald Trump commented that he thought that Mr. O'Reilly was "a good person" and that "I don't think Bill did anything wrong." What is your reaction to Mr. Trumps' comments? (n = 966)			
a. It was a case of one sexual predator defending another sexual predator (un)	54.6	52.2	56.8
b. It was a case of one falsely accused public figure defending another public figure he felt was being falsely accused (f)	45.4	47.8	43.2

Sample sizes vary due to missing data. Survey items were originally presented to respondents in the following item order: 1, 4, 2, 8, 5, 6, 9, 7, 10, 3.

[a]The response categories recoded as "favorable Trump responses" are labeled with (f) and responses recoded as "unfavorable Trump responses" are labeled with (un).

(57.6%) rather than as mere locker room talk (42.4%). Taken together, these findings indicate that Americans are more likely to suspect that Trump is a sexual predator than to see him as an innocent president.

Importantly, Item 3 asked the respondents how likely it was that all 10 of the women were lying. More than 6 in 10 indicated that it was unlikely (31.9%) or highly unlikely (33.0%). About the same proportion rejected the view that failure to notify anyone about Trump's alleged misconduct was evidence that the incident did not occur. Thus, when asked why the women waited to report their experiences with Trump to bosses or the police (Item 4), many respondents stated that women who are harassed or assaulted by powerful men do not report out of fear or because they think nothing will be done (62.9%). This finding has implications beyond President Trump, showing that a majority of Americans in the #MeToo era reject the idea that the non-reporting of a past incident means it did not occur.

A clear majority of the sample also believed that if the allegations could be substantiated, the president should be forced to relinquish his office. Item 5 asked if the women were telling the truth, then what should happen to Trump. About three-fifths of the sample (60.5%) indicated that he should be impeached if the women are telling the truth. Still, a group of respondents existed who believed that he should remain president even if he had engaged in sexual harassment or assault (39.5%).

Trump and women

The second theme within the questions assessed public perceptions of Trump's relationship with women more generally, which the data suggest is problematic. Item 6 asked whether participants believed that Trump has "tremendous respect" for women; a majority of the sample disagreed with this statement (57.9%). When asked about the significance of the Women's March (Item 7), a similar percentage (56.8%) of the respondents indicated that this protest showed that women were upset with Trump and with the sexual assaults that females often experience.

Trump compared to Hillary Clinton

Within the sexual misconduct opinion questions, one item assessed whether the respondents believed Trump was better or worse than Hillary Clinton (Item 8). The sample was divided on this issue, with about half agreeing (49.8%) and disagreeing (50.2%) that Hillary was "more immoral, is a crook, and should be locked up." Some tolerance of Trump's indiscretions may be linked to this apparent belief in the moral equivalence between Hillary Clinton and Donald Trump – that he was no worse than she was.

Feelings about Trump

Finally, two items assessed how the respondents felt about Trump personally. One question asked the respondents how they felt the day after the election (Item 9). More of the sample stated that they felt depressed (53.4%) as opposed to happy (46.6%), but this difference was modest. Item 10 asked how Trump's defense of Bill O'Reilly was perceived. Again, a bit more than half of the sample (54.6%) reported that it was one predator defending another. These results show that President Trump has his firm supporters but also faces a substantial segment within the American public – likely over half – who oppose him, doubt his veracity, or see him as capable of sexual misconduct.

Gender breakdowns

In general, females selected less favorable responses toward Trump compared to males across each of the items (see Table 2). For example, women (57.4%) were more likely to believe the women were telling the truth about the accusations against Trump compared to men (44.1%), χ^2 = (2, N = 993) 6.60, $p < .01$ (Item 1). A majority of women (70.3%) also believed that females do not report sexual misconduct by powerful men because they believe nothing will happen compared to 54.8% of men, χ^2 (1, N = 994) = 13.66, $p < .01$ (Item 4). Bivariate tests (i.e., chi-square, t-test) indicated that there was a significant relationship between gender and each of the survey items with two exceptions. Neither Item 7 (view of the Women's March; χ^2 [1, N = 992] = 0.39, $p > .05$) nor Item 10 (comments on Bill O'Reilly; χ^2 [1, N = 966] = 1.14, $p > .05$) was significantly related to gender (all bivariate analyses are available upon request). Females likely evaluate the allegations brought against Trump differently than males given that they are disproportionately the targets of sexual assaults and misconduct (e.g., Black et al., 2011; Fisher et al., 2000). Perhaps unsurprisingly, these findings support the notion that gender is an important factor when assessing the divide in the American public.

Existence of "tribes"

The next stage of analysis was to assess whether the respondents fell into distinct "tribes" based on their responses to the sexual misconduct opinions or whether the response patterns were indistinguishable. Prior to LCA, the original survey items were recoded into binary categories where 1 = "in favor of Trump" and 0 = "not in favor of Trump" (see Table 2 for coding classifications by item). Table 3 provides the model fit statistics for the different number of classes estimated. Indices with lower values on the Bayesian Information Criterion (BIC) and Akaike Information Criterion (AIC) indicate better model fit; values closer to 1 on the entropy statistic indicate a better classification of individuals into classes (Nylund-Gibson & Choi, 2018). Most of the model fit statistics greatly improved from one and two classes to three classes, with the exception of entropy from two to three classes. Although the log-likelihood and AIC indices improved with the four-class solution, the BIC increased and the entropy decreased from the three-class model. Thus, the three-class solution was identified as the best model fit overall (Nylund-Gibson & Choi, 2018). In sum, the LCA confirmed that there were, in fact, different "tribes" based on the 10 sexual misconduct opinion responses reported in Table 2.

As outlined in Table 3, Class 1 was labeled as "unfavorable Trump responses" because the mean values across items were close to zero (overall $\overline{x}$ = .04; range: .01 – .12). Conversely, the mean values for items in Class 3 – labeled as "favorable Trump responses" – were unanimously close to one and illustrated great support for Trump (overall $\overline{x}$ = .94; range: .85 – .99). Finally, Class 2 mean values ranged from .33 to .69, which indicated that respondents supported Trump on some items more than others (overall $\overline{x}$ = .54). This class was labeled as "mixed responses" because individuals could be swayed in one direction or another, whereas respondents in the other classes had consistent opinions about Trump. Approximately 46%, 23%, and 31% of the sample were predicted to fall into Class 1 ("unfavorable Trump responses"), Class 2 ("mixed responses"), and Class 3 ("favorable Trump responses"), respectively.

Predicting opinions about Trump

After identifying the different classes of responses based on the LCA, the goal then was to analyze what predicted membership to these groups. In particular, the effect of political

Table 3. Latent class analysis three-class solution (N = 1,000).

Model Fit Statistics by Number of Classes	1 Class	2 Classes	3 Classes	4 Classes
Log likelihood	−6,725.26	−3,784.24	−3,448.47	−3,398.98
Degrees of freedom	10	40	70	92
AIC	13,470.53	7,648.48	7,036.94	6,981.96
BIC	13,519.61	7,844.79	7,380.48	7,433.47
Entropy	–	.97	.92	.80

	Class 1		Class 2		Class 3	
	Unfavorable Trump Responses		Mixed Responses		Favorable Trump Responses	
Three-Class Solution Estimates	Mean	SE	Mean	SE	Mean	SE
Q1: Belief about sexual misconduct claims	.07	.02	.66	.07	.99	.002
Q2: Thoughts about *Access Hollywood* tape	.03	.01	.48	.06	.99	.02
Q3: Likelihood all accusers are lying	.03	.01	.33	.05	.85	.04
Q4: Delayed reporting of accusations	.02	.01	.37	.07	.91	.03
Q5: Outcome if accusers are truthful	.05	.01	.48	.06	.86	.03
Q6: Whether he has tremendous respect for women	.02	.02	.49	.08	.97	.02
Q7: View of the Women's March	.03	.02	.57	.06	.94	.03
Q8: Whether Clinton is more immoral	.12	.03	.69	.07	.93	.03
Q9: Feelings day after election	.01	.01	.66	.08	.99	.003
Q10: Comments on Bill O'Reilly	.04	.01	.65	.07	.97	.01
Overall mean	.04		.54		.94	
Class probabilities	.46		.23		.31	

Survey items were recoded where 1 = "favorable responses toward Trump" and 0 = "unfavorable responses toward Trump" so higher values indicate greater support for Donald Trump (see Table 2 for coding classifications by response category). AIC = Akaike Information Criterion; BIC = Bayesian Information Criterion.

moral foundations – again, measured here as being conservative or Republican – was assessed in addition to several other covariates. Table 4 presents the findings from the latent class regression model; the unfavorable Trump responses group was the reference category.

In support of the moral foundations framework, being conservative or Republican increased the likelihood of having mixed or favorable responses compared to individuals who were identified as having unfavorable responses (see Table 4). Respondents who were conservative and who were Republican had 4.11 and 9.18 greater odds of endorsing mixed responses than unfavorable ones, respectively. These effects were stronger for individuals identified as being more favorable toward Trump, with conservatives and Republicans having 9.93 and 21.22 greater odds of being classified in this group rather than the respondents in the unfavorable group, respectively.

Additional key covariates were also identified as important when examining group membership (see Table 4). Individuals who were older and who had higher levels of education had .97 and .74 times the odds of being in the mixed group rather than the unfavorable group, respectively. The effect of education was similar for the favorable group (Odds Ratio [OR] = .79). Compared to married respondents, participants who never married had .38 lower odds of responding as mixed than unfavorable toward Trump. Finally, compared to those who were employed, respondents who identified as

Table 4. Latent class regression predicting views on Trump (N = 1,000).

	Mixed Responses			Favorable Trump Responses		
	b	SE	OR	*b*	SE	OR
Conservative	1.41**	0.44	4.11	2.30***	0.39	9.93
Republican	2.22***	0.40	9.18	3.06***	0.39	21.22
Male	0.17	0.30	1.19	1.37***	0.31	3.92
Age	−0.03*	0.01	0.97	0.02	0.02	1.02
Race						
White (ref)	–	–	–	–	–	–
Black	−0.25	0.44	0.78	−2.22**	0.81	0.11
Hispanic	−1.17	0.60	0.31	−1.80***	0.52	0.17
Other	−0.77	0.65	0.47	−0.07	0.44	0.93
Education	−0.30**	0.09	0.74	−0.23*	0.09	0.79
Marital Status						
Married (ref)	–	–	–	–	–	–
Divorced	0.45	0.39	1.57	0.05	0.39	1.05
Never Married	−0.97*	0.39	0.38	−0.47	0.46	0.63
Other	−0.03	0.55	0.97	0.001	0.44	1.00
Child Under 18	−0.46	0.32	0.63	−0.28	0.39	0.75
Employment						
Employed (ref)	–	–	–	–	–	–
Unemployed	0.11	0.46	1.12	0.79	0.48	2.19
Retired	−0.91	0.48	0.40	−0.51	0.51	0.60
Homemaker	−1.23	0.80	0.29	0.27	0.51	1.31
Student	−0.11	0.73	0.90	0.12	0.75	1.13
Other	−1.01*	0.51	0.36	−0.95*	0.47	0.39
Born Again	0.05	0.36	1.05	−0.43	0.37	0.65
Religiosity	0.25	0.14	1.28	0.45**	0.14	1.56
Constant	1.04	0.89		−3.12**	1.04	
Log Likelihood	−3,448.47					
AIC	7,036.94					
BIC	7,380.48					

The reference dependent variable is "unfavorable Trump responses." Model was estimated with robust standard errors. OR = Odds Ratio; AIC = Akaike Information Criterion; BIC = Bayesian Information Criterion.

having other employment had .36 and .39 times the odds of responding as mixed and favorable than unfavorable, respectively.

Individuals within the favorable response group also had several unique predictors. Respondents who identified as being male (OR = 3.92) or having higher levels of religiosity (OR = 1.56) were significantly more likely to be classified in the favorable group than the unfavorable group. However, compared to White individuals, Black and Hispanic respondents had 0.11 and 0.17 times the odds of responding with favorable opinions than unfavorable opinions toward Trump, respectively.

Predicting voter preference in 2016 election

The final stage of the analysis was to determine what variables predicted self-reported voting in the 2016 election. Although causal ordering could not be established by surveying respondents prior to and after the election, the sexual misconduct allegations were publicized nationally before voting began. Albeit speculative, we assume that the publicity of the accusations likely affected opinions about Trump and that those opinions, in turn, influenced who respondents voted for. In this way, we would not anticipate Americans to vote and *then* make judgments about the candidates; those judgments are likely formed before heading to the polls. Supplemental checks indicated that multicollinearity was still not a concern with all variables (Max. VIF excluding age = 1.90 [age VIF = 2.61]; Condition Index = 20.77). Table 5 presents the results from two logistic regression models predicting whether respondents voted for Donald Trump. Model 1 includes all previously noted variables, whereas Model 2 adds a variable representing the sexual misconduct opinion group classifications.

Model 1 findings

As presented in Model 1, being conservative (OR = 3.41) and being Republican (OR = 4.50) increased the likelihood of voting for Trump (see Table 5). Compared to White respondents, Black and Hispanic individuals had .09 and .21 lower odds of supporting Trump at the polls, respectively. Additionally, those who had never been married (OR = .44; compared to married individuals) and who had other employment (OR = .22; compared to employed individuals) were significantly less likely to vote for Trump.

Model 2 findings

Model 2 was estimated to determine whether opinions about the sexual misconduct allegations against Trump predicted voting behavior beyond sociodemographic and political characteristics (see Table 5). Importantly, compared to individuals who provided unfavorable responses toward Trump, those in the mixed (OR = 14.93) and in the favorable (OR = 97.16) groups had greater odds of voting for him. Although individuals who identified as Republicans had 2.43 greater odds of voting for Trump, being conservative was no longer significant in the model. Compared to Whites, Blacks had .24 lower odds of voting for Trump. Additionally, those with higher levels of education had 1.49 greater odds of selecting him as the next president. The effects for individuals who were never married (OR = .45) and who engaged in some other employment (OR = .19) were similar to Model 1.

Table 5. Logistic regression predicting voting for Donald Trump in the 2016 election (N = 1,000).

	Model 1			Model 2		
	b	SE	OR	*b*	SE	OR
Sexual Misconduct Opinions						
Unfavorable of Trump (ref)	–	–	–	–	–	–
Mixed	–	–	–	2.70***	0.52	14.93
Favorable of Trump	–	–	–	4.58***	0.52	97.16
Conservative	1.23***	0.24	3.41	0.34	0.32	1.40
Republican	1.50***	0.27	4.50	0.89**	0.34	2.43
Male	0.42	0.23	1.53	−0.16	0.29	0.85
Age	0.02	0.01	1.02	0.01	0.01	1.01
Race						
White (ref)	–	–	–	–	–	–
Black	−2.41***	0.51	0.09	−1.42*	0.62	0.24
Hispanic	−1.56**	0.49	0.21	−1.05	0.57	0.35
Other	−0.08	0.38	0.92	−0.29	0.50	0.75
Education	0.14	0.07	1.15	0.40***	0.11	1.49
Marital Status						
Married (ref)	–	–	–	–	–	–
Divorced	−0.14	0.36	0.87	−0.21	0.44	0.81
Never Married	−0.82*	0.35	0.44	−0.81*	0.40	0.45
Other	−0.52	0.43	0.60	−0.73	0.49	0.48
Child Under 18	−0.17	0.29	0.84	−0.18	0.42	0.83
Employment						
Employed (ref)	–	–	–	–	–	–
Unemployed	−0.51	0.55	0.60	−1.11	0.61	0.33
Retired	−0.10	0.36	0.90	0.11	0.47	1.11
Homemaker	−0.30	0.39	0.74	−0.56	0.54	0.57
Student	−0.87	0.86	0.42	−0.88	0.83	0.42
Other	−1.52**	0.49	0.22	−1.65**	0.58	0.19
Born Again	0.17	0.27	1.18	0.51	0.36	1.67
Religiosity	0.22	0.13	1.25	−0.01	0.16	0.99
Constant	−3.17***	0.79		−5.29***	1.11	
Model $\chi 2$ (df)		191.10 (19)***			170.01 (21)***	
McFadden's R^2		0.29			0.47	
Nagelkerke R^2		0.47			0.67	

The reference dependent variable is "other" vote. Models were estimated with robust standard errors. OR = Odds Ratio.
*p < .05; **p < .01; ***p < .001

Because education only became significantly related to voting preference once the sexual misconduct opinions were included, two supplemental checks were done to assess the relationship between these variables. First, eta-squared indicated that sexual misconduct opinions only explained 1.3% of the variation among respondents in terms of their education levels. Second, another model was estimated that excluded education. The direction of estimates and significance levels were generally consistent with the full model – Hispanic respondents were also less likely to vote for Trump once education was excluded (OR = .25, $p < .05$). Furthermore, the effect sizes were similar to the full model with the exception of being marginally reduced for the misconduct opinions (Mixed: OR = 9.87; Favorable of Trump: OR = 63.98). Thus, the exclusion or inclusion of the education measure does not seem to affect the substantive findings of Model 2.

Discussion

Since Donald Trump started his campaign for the presidency, he has been beloved and detested by the American people – with the response varying depending on who is asked. On the one hand, he has been nominated for the Nobel Peace Prize and praised for his efforts to try to develop relationships with North Korea (Fouche, 2019). He continues to draw enthusiastic crowds to his political speeches, with the audience proudly wearing their "Make America Great Again" (MAGA) caps. On the other hand, he has been the subject of ongoing impeachment efforts and protests since the day he was elected (Gopnik, 2019). Although he certainly is not the first president to provoke debate, his abrasive and sometimes vulgar retorts have ushered in a new era of presidential controversy. Depending on the source, these actions can also be viewed as a major reason for his success. In this way, some Americans applaud his willingness to cast aside political correctness and to say what he thinks regardless of the cost (Blake, 2017). However, there is another side to his presidency where other Americans actively push against him by championing legislative reforms, joining protests, and running for office (e.g., Chenoweth & Pressman, 2017; Gaudiano, 2018).

At the center of this debate are the sexual misconduct allegations that have been brought forth by multiple women (e.g., Ford, 2017; Kelly, 2017; Relman, 2019). Similar to other controversies, the American people seem to be divided on whether to side with Trump or to side with the accusers. But how can one person elicit such diverse reactions given the seriousness of the claims? In this way, we argue that Donald Trump is socially constructed based on the underlying moral foundations that guide people more generally (Haidt, 2012). There is, of course, an objective reality to his words, behavior, and agenda. The purpose of this study was to examine whether Americans have different narratives that contribute to a broader division in the United States as they relate to the sexual misconduct allegations. In particular, we sought to determine whether the respondents viewed him as a sexual *predator* or as an innocent and respectable *president*. The current analysis identified four important implications for consideration.

First, many Americans believe that Trump did something inappropriate – even if it was not a sexual assault specifically. Recall that all but one of the female accusers have not alleged that they were raped; they reported being subjected to sexually suggestive comments, forcible kissing, and groping. In this context, half of the sample reported that they trusted the female accusers, with only a small subsample believing Trump was completely innocent. And one-quarter of the respondents suspected that he might have done something wrong but that it was not a sexual assault, indicating that they are less likely to give credence to the more serious accusations. Thus, Trump was viewed as a *predator* more than an innocent president. Although there was some variation in the remaining survey items, approximately half to two-thirds of the sample cast doubt on Trump and viewed him unfavorably. It is likely that the absence of definitive proof of the misconduct (e.g., photos, videotape) – which is common among sexual misconduct incidents more generally – contributes to uncertainty about his behavior even if his words suggest he has sexually assaulted women (i.e., *Access Hollywood* tape).

Note, however, that were proof of sexual misconduct to be uncovered, a majority of respondents indicated that President Trump should be impeached by Congress. The survey did not probe whether such proof would prompt sample members to welcome the president's criminal indictment or, in any event, whether they favor current civil suits against Trump (e.g., the case of Summer Zervos) (Nir, 2019). Given the opinions expressed by the respondents, it seems that support for such actions is likely.

Second, consistent with Haidt's (2012) moral foundations theory, individuals can be divided into "tribes" based on their opinions about the sexual misconduct allegations.

Many respondents always viewed Trump favorably, whereas others always viewed him unfavorably. Those in each group consistently supported or denounced Trump, which could mean that these respondents are unlikely to change their stance (see also Monmouth University Poll, 2017). Importantly, the latent class analysis also identified a "mixed" group whose members responded more favorably to some items than others. These respondents appeared to be swayed for or against the president depending on content of the item – a variability that was not present in the other identified groups who functioned more as warring tribes. With others' minds already made up, the individuals in the "mixed" group will likely influence the results of the next election depending on whether they swing for or away from Donald Trump.

Third, certain factors increased the likelihood of having favorable views toward Trump – despite the sexual misconduct allegations. In particular, being conservative, Republican, male, White, and religious increased the likelihood of providing more favorable responses toward Trump than unfavorable responses. These findings are consistent with the profile usually attributed to the president's "base" of supporters (Tyson & Maniam, 2016). Being conservative and Republican also increased the odds of having mixed responses than unfavorable ones. Thus, Haidt's (2012) political moral foundations – examined here with conservative and Republican serving as proxies for moral foundations – seem to be important indicators when tapping into this divide and likely suggest a deeper underlying process that contributes to group polarization.

Fourth, the respondents who believed Trump or neutralized the sexual misconduct allegations against him were more likely to vote for him. Although it is not surprising that those who favored Trump were more likely to select him as their next president, it was instructive that the respondents with mixed views were also more likely to vote for him. Thus, the mixed attitudes about the sexual misconduct allegations did not limit some individuals' voting preferences. If anything, admitting that Trump's indiscretions did not rise to the level of a serious incident may have served as a technique of neutralization that allowed individuals to vote for Trump despite their awareness of, if not concern about, his alleged victims' allegations (Sykes & Matza, 1957). Additionally, although those who were Republican were more likely to vote for Trump, the analysis showed that being conservative was no longer significantly related to voter preference once sexual misconduct opinions were included. As Haidt (2012) would predict, the voters acted like tribes, internalizing beliefs that either justified or allowed them to cast a vote for an innocent future president or against a known sexual predator.

In sum, the social construction of Trump and the sexual misconduct allegations against him matter. Individuals who viewed Trump more favorably were more likely to vote for him in spite of the allegations against him and this finding extended to respondents with mixed views. It is unclear, however, how the prevailing context will affect the public in the time ahead. Members of the public could become more aware of the nature and prevalence of sexual misconduct due to ongoing social movements attempting to illuminate these issues (e.g., #MeToo, Women's March). For example, the Public Religion Research Institute between August and September 2018 examined whether Americans would be willing to vote for someone accused of sexual harassment (N = 1,856). Approximately 60% of Americans would not consider supporting candidates accused of sexual harassment by multiple people, whereas only 32% said they would still be open to voting for candidates if they agreed with them on the issues (Vandermaas-Peeler et al., 2018). Although it is unclear how Americans would have responded to this survey prior to the allegations against Trump or whether views expressed in an opinion poll would actually influence behavior, most individuals viewed accusations from multiple people as a political "deal-breaker."

Another possibility, however, is that people could become desensitized to such accusations as news outlets become overwhelmed with new headlines (Burmila, 2017; North, 2019b). For example, a more recent survey conducted by YouGov in June 2019 examined public perceptions of the allegations against Trump (N = 1,000; Huffington Post, 2019). One of the items assessed whether the respondents had heard about the most recent accusation of assault on E. Jean Carroll (Carroll, 2019). Only a fraction of respondents (11%) had "heard a lot" about this allegation; more than half (53%) had "heard nothing at all." Thus, even though more than 20 women – and counting – have accused Trump of sexual misconduct, it is no longer considered a major scandal worthy of undivided media attention. When asked about the victim's credibility more broadly, the respondents were divided between "they are credible" (41%), "they are *not* credible" (29%), and "haven't heard enough to say" (21%). Importantly, many participants believed that Trump should be "disqualified" as president if the accusations are true (40%) – a slight dip from 44% in 2016 (Edwards-Levy, 2019). Another 24% of the sample believed that it is relevant but does not disqualify him as president; 21% of respondents believed that the accusations (if truthful) are not relevant to his position as president. The remaining participants reported that they were "not sure" what should happen if the allegations are true (15%). In this way, these recent estimates suggest an ongoing divide in how the American public views Trump.

The seriousness with which sexual misconduct accusations are viewed today is due, in part, to the results of the 2016 election. As previously noted, allegations of this type have recently resulted in the fall from grace of particularly powerful men (e.g., Carlsen et al., 2018). Thus, the social reaction to the election of Donald Trump could usher in a new phase where sexual misconduct allegations could have more serious repercussions for the accused. Of course, it remains to be seen whether these opinions will affect President Trump's political future. Trump's base seems unshakable in their loyalty, but the American public also contains a large tribe that abhors him and other citizens who could be influenced by emerging circumstances. If the responses to this survey are an accurate barometer, then any definitive proof of sexual misconduct committed by Trump could result in support for his impeachment or votes for his opponent in the 2020 presidential election.

Acknowledgments

The authors wish to thank Christopher J. Sullivan for his comments on this manuscript.

Disclosure statement

No potential conflict of interest was reported by the authors.

ORCID

Murat Haner http://orcid.org/0000-0002-9988-3848

References

2016 presidential election results. (2016, December 13). *Politico*. Retrieved from https://www.politico.com/2016-election/results/map/president/

Barbaro, M., & Twohey, M. (2016, May 14). Crossing the line: How Donald Trump behaved with women in private. *The New York Times*. Retrieved from https://www.nytimes.com/2016/05/15/us/politics/donald-trump-women.html

Belsley, D. A., Kuh, E., & Welsch, R. E. (1980). *Regression diagnostics: Identifying influential data and sources of collinearity*. New York, NY: John Wiley.

Black, M. C., Basile, K. C., Breiding, M. J., Smith, S. G., Walters, M. L., Merrick, M. T., … Stevens, M. R. (2011). *The national intimate partner and sexual violence survey: 2010 summary report*. Atlanta, GA: National Center for Injury Prevention and Control of the Centers for Disease Control and Prevention.

Blake, A. (2017, April 3). 'I don't regret anything': President Trump is completely un-humbled. *The Washington Post*. Retrieved from https://www.washingtonpost.com/news/the-fix/wp/2017/04/03/president-trump-is-completely-un-humbled/?utm_term=.4bbd9fe02329

Burmila, E. (2017, December 14). The year of being completely overwhelmed by Trump. *Rolling Stone*. Retrieved from https://www.rollingstone.com/politics/politics-features/the-year-of-being-completely-overwhelmed-by-trump-202135/

Carlsen, A., Salam, M., Miller, C. C., Lu, D., Ngu, A., Patel, J. K., & Witchter, Z. (2018, October 29). #Metoo brought down 201 powerful men. Nearly half of their replacements are women. *The New York Times*. Retrieved from https://www.nytimes.com/interactive/2018/10/23/us/metoo-replacements.html

Carroll, J. E. (2019, June 21). Hideous men: Donald Trump assaulted me in a Bergdorf Goodman dressing room 23 years ago. But he's not alone on the list of awful men in my life. *The Cut*. Retrieved from https://www.thecut.com/2019/06/donald-trump-assault-e-jean-carroll-other-hideous-men.html#_ga=2.82011606.1387733870.1563653594-289793144.1563653594

Chenoweth, E., & Pressman, J. (2017, February 7). This is what we learned by counting the women's marches. *The Washington Post*. Retrieved from https://www.washingtonpost.com/news/monkey-cage/wp/2017/02/07/this-is-what-we-learned-by-counting-the-womens-marches/?utm_term=.032a60e5e362

Cohen, C. (2017, July 14). Donald Trump sexism tracker: Every offensive comment in one place. *The Telegraph*. Retrieved from https://www.telegraph.co.uk/women/politics/donald-trump-sexism-tracker-every-offensive-comment-in-one-place/

Edwards-Levy, A. (2019, June 25). Trump was accused of assault again. Half of American had no idea. *HuffPost*. Retrieved from https://www.huffpost.com/entry/e-jean-carroll-trump-sexual-assault-poll_n_5d12a515e4b0aa375f551aaf

Fahrenthold, D. A. (2016, October 8). Trump recorded having extremely lewd conversation about women in 2005. *The Washington Post*. Retrieved from https://www.washingtonpost.com/politics/trump-recorded-having-extremely-lewd-conversation-about-women-in-2005/2016/10/07/3b9ce776-8cb4-11e6-bf8a-3d26847eeed4_story.html?utm_term=.33e9edfbc87e

Farrow, R. (2017, October 23). From aggressive overtures to sexual assault: Harvey Weinstein's accusers tell their stories. *The New Yorker*. Retrieved from https://www.newyorker.com/news/news-desk/from-aggressive-overtures-to-sexual-assault-harvey-weinsteins-accusers-tell-their-stories

Feuer, A. (2018, August 27). What we know about Trump's $130,000 payment to Stormy Daniels. *The New York Times*. Retrieved from https://www.nytimes.com/2018/08/27/nyregion/stormy-daniels-trump-payment.html

Fisher, B. S., Cullen, F. T., & Turner, M. G. (2000). *The sexual victimization of college women.* Washington, DC: National Institute of Justice.

Folmer, K. (2019, June 23). President Trump denies sexual assault allegation. *ABC News.* Retrieved from https://abcnews.go.com/Politics/president-trump-denies-sexual-assault-allegation/story?id=63895448

Ford, M. (2017, December 7). The 19 women who accused president Trump of sexual misconduct. *The Atlantic.* Retrieved from https://www.theatlantic.com/politics/archive/2017/12/what-about-the-19-women-who-accused-trump/547724/

Forsythe, J. S. (2018, May 3). Timeline of the Donald Trump-Stormy Daniels saga. *Wall Street Journal.* Retrieved from https://www.wsj.com/articles/timeline-of-the-donald-trump-stormy-daniels-saga-1525373930

Fouche, G. (2019, February 18). No need for Shinzo Abe: Trump already nominated for Nobel peace prize. *Reuters.* Retrieved from https://www.reuters.com/article/us-nobel-prize-peace/no-need-for-shinzo-abe-trump-already-nominated-for-nobel-peace-prize-idUSKCN1Q71IS

Fox, J. (1991). *Regression diagnostics.* Newbury Park, CA: Sage.

Garber, M. (2018, October 3). The most striking thing about Trump's mockery of Christine Blasey Ford. *The Atlantic.* Retrieved from https://www.theatlantic.com/entertainment/archive/2018/10/trump-mocks-christine-blasey-ford/572005/

Gaudiano, N. (2018, November 6). New 'year of the woman'? Over 100 female candidates set to win seats in Congress, make history. *USA Today.* Retrieved from https://www.usatoday.com/story/news/politics/elections/2018/11/06/women-candidates-midterms/1845639002/

Gopnik, A. (2019, March 18). The pros and cons of impeaching Trump. *The New Yorker.* Retrieved from https://www.newyorker.com/magazine/2019/03/18/the-pros-and-cons-of-impeaching-trump

Graves, L., & Morris, S. (2017, November 29). The Trump allegations. *The Guardian.* Retrieved from https://www.theguardian.com/us-news/ng-interactive/2017/nov/30/donald-trump-sexual-misconduct-allegations-full-list

Griffiths, B. D. (2018, October 10). Trump mocks 'rules' of #metoo during rally. *Politico.* Retrieved from https://www.politico.com/story/2018/10/10/trump-mocks-metoo-during-rally-892057

Gstalter, M. (2018, April 17). Image projected on Trump hotel: 'There's a rapist in the White House'. *The Hill.* Retrieved from https://thehill.com/blogs/blog-briefing-room/news/383541-theres-a-rapist-in-the-white-house-projected-on-trump-dc-hotel

Haberman, M. (2016). Donald Trump's apology that wasn't. *The New York Times.* Retrieved from https://www.nytimes.com/2016/10/08/us/politics/donald-trump-apology.html?module=inline

Haidt, J. (2012). *The righteous mind: Why good people are divided by politics and religion.* New York, NY: Vintage.

Huffington Post. (2019). *Huffpost: Assault allegations.* Retrieved from https://big.assets.huffingtonpost.com/athena/files/2019/06/25/5d12a68fe4b0a394186a25da.pdf

Jackson, D. M. (2016, November 23). Clinton's popular vote lead passes the 2 million mark. *USA Today.* Retrieved from https://www.usatoday.com/story/news/politics/onpolitics/2016/11/23/donald-trump-hillary-clinton-2-million-popular-vote/94339510/

Kantor, J., & Twohey, M. (2017, October 5). Harvey Weinstein paid off sexual harassment accusers for decades. *The New York Times.* Retrieved from https://www.nytimes.com/2017/10/05/us/harvey-weinstein-harassment-allegations.html?_r=0

Kelly, M. (2017, November 22). President Trump and accusations of sexual misconduct: The complete list. *The Washington Post.* Retrieved from https://www.washingtonpost.com/news/fact-checker/wp/2017/11/22/president-trump-and-accusations-of-sexual-misconduct-the-complete-list/?utm_term=.28a03a7ad1aa

Keneally, M. (2018a, February 22). List of Trump's accusers and their allegations of sexual misconduct. *ABC News.* Retrieved from https://abcnews.go.com/Politics/list-trumps-accusers-allegations-sexual-misconduct/story?id=51956410

Keneally, M. (2018b, September 22). 6 men Trump has defended amid accusations of assault or misconduct. *ABC News.* Retrieved from https://abcnews.go.com/beta-story-container/US/men-trump-defended-amid-assault-accusations/story?id=53045851

Keneally, M. (2018c, October 17). 'Horseface, 'crazy,' 'low IQ': Trump's history of insulting women. *ABC News*. Retrieved from https://abcnews.go.com/Politics/trumps-long-history-calling-women-crazy-attacking-appearances/story?id=48348956

Kessler, G., & Kelly, M. (2018, September 26). Fact-checking President Trump's statements about sexual misconduct allegations. *The Washington Post*. Retrieved from https://www.washington post.com/politics/2018/09/27/fact-checking-president-trumps-statements-about-sexual-miscon duct-allegations/?utm_term=.ce231eae8583

Kew, B. (2017, April 28). Making America great again: Donald Trump's 100 days' success. *Breitbart*. Retrieved from https://www.breitbart.com/politics/2017/04/28/making-america-great-again-donald-trumps-100-day-success/

Kurtzleben, D. (2016, October 20). 1 more woman accuses Trump of inappropriate sexual conduct. Here's the full list. *NPR Politics*. Retrieved from http://www.npr.org/2016/10/13/497799354/a-list-of-donald-trumps-accusers-of-inappropriate-sexual-conduct

Leaked tape captures Trump in crude rant with tv host. (2016, October 7). *Fox News*. Retrieved from https://www.foxnews.com/politics/leaked-tape-captures-trump-in-crude-rant-with-tv-host

Levenson, E., & Moghe, S. (2018, July 9). Harvey Weinstein pleads not guilty to additional sex crime charges. *CNN*. Retrieved from https://www.cnn.com/2018/07/09/us/harvey-weinstein-arraign ment/index.html

Lisak, D., Gardinier, L., Nicksa, S. C., & Cote, A. M. (2010). False allegations of sexual assault: An analysis of ten years of reported cases. *Violence against Women*, *16*, 1318–1334. doi:10.1177/ 1077801210387747

Malloy, T., & Smith, P. (2017, December 19). *U.S. voter economic outlook hits all-time high, Quinnipiac University national poll finds: But voters disapprove of Trump's handling of economy*. Hamden, CT: Quinnipiac University.

McCaskill, N. D. (2016, October 14). Trump suggests his accusers are too unattractive to assault. *Politico*. Retrieved from https://www.politico.com/story/2016/10/trump-jessica-leeds-accusations-229805

Monmouth University Poll. (2017, August 15). *National: Trump temperament consequences*. West Long Beach, NJ: Monmouth University.

Neely, B., & Montanaro, D. (2018, May 2). Trump admits to authorizing Stormy Daniels payoff, denies sexual encounter. *NPR*. Retrieved from https://www.npr.org/2018/05/02/607943366/giu liani-says-trump-did-know-about-stormy-daniels-payment

Nir, S. M. (2019, March 14). Trump can be sued for defamation by Summer Zervos, 'Apprentice' contestant, court rules. *The New York Times*. Retrieved from https://www.nytimes.com/2019/03/ 14/nyregion/summer-zervos-trump-defamation-lawsuit.html

North, A. (2019a, February 27). A woman has made a new sexual misconduct allegation against Trump. *Vox*. Retrieved from https://www.vox.com/policy-and-politics/2019/2/25/18239678/ trump-alva-johnson-sexual-misconduct-allegations-post

North, A. (2019b, June 24). Why E. Jean Carroll's assault accusation against Trump wasn't front-page news. *Vox*. Retrieved from https://www.vox.com/identities/2019/6/24/18715459/e-jean-car roll-trump-new-york-magazine

Nylund-Gibson, K., & Choi, A. Y. (2018). Ten frequently asked questions about latent class analysis. *Translational Issues in Psychological Science*, *4*, 440–461. doi:10.1037/tps0000176

Oberski, D. (2016). Mixture models: Latent profile and latent class analysis. In J. Robertson & M. Kaptein (Eds.), *Modern statistical methods for HCI* (pp. 275–287). New York, NY: Springer.

Palazzolo, J., Hong, N., Rothfeld, M., O'Brien, R. D., & Ballhaus, R. (2018, November 9). Donald Trump played central role in hush payoffs to Stormy Daniels and Karen McDougal. *Wall Street Journal*. Retrieved from https://www.wsj.com/articles/donald-trump-played-central-role-in-hush-payoffs-to-stormy-daniels-and-karen-mcdougal-1541786601

Parker, N. (2017, December 6). Who is Tarana Burke? Meet the woman who started the me too movement a decade ago. *The Atlanta Journal-Constitution*. Retrieved from https://www.ajc.com/ news/world/who-tarana-burke-meet-the-woman-who-started-the-too-movement-decade-ago/ i8NEiuFHKaIvBh9ucukidK/

Powers, K. (2016, October 17). Trump's misogyny platform. *USA Today*. Retrieved from https://www.usatoday.com/story/opinion/2016/10/17/donald-trump-sexual-assault-locker-room-poll-women-kirsten-powers-column/92017072/

Relman, E. (2019, June 21). The 24 women who have accused Trump of sexual misconduct. *Business Insider*. Retrieved from https://www.businessinsider.com/women-accused-trump-sexual-misconduct-list-2017-12

Remnick, D. (2018, October 10). One year of #metoo. *The New Yorker*. Retrieved from https://www.newyorker.com/news/news-desk/one-year-of-metoo

Republicans react to Donald Trump's vulgar remarks caught on tape. (2016, October 7). *ABC7*. Retrieved from https://abc7chicago.com/politics/republicans-react-to-donald-trumps-vulgar-remarks/1545075/

Rutenberg, J. (2018, April 18). Ex-playboy model, freed from contract, can discuss alleged Trump affair. *The New York Times*. Retrieved from https://www.nytimes.com/2018/04/18/us/politics/karen-mcdougal-american-media-settlement.html

Samuelson, K. (2018, May 25). Harvey Weinstein arrested on charges of rape, sex abuse and more. *Time*. Retrieved from http://time.com/5291392/harvey-weinstein-arrested/

Scott, E. (2018, October 3). Trump says men don't feel safe from false persecution. That's not a new feeling—For black men. *The Washington Post*. Retrieved from https://www.washingtonpost.com/politics/2018/10/03/trump-says-men-dont-feel-safe-false-persecution-thats-not-new-feeling-black-men/?utm_term=.36ad3db173e3

Shear, M. D., & Sullivan, E. (2018, October 16). 'Horseface,' 'lowlife,' 'fat, ugly': How the president demeans women. *The New York Times*. Retrieved from https://www.nytimes.com/2018/10/16/us/politics/trump-women-insults.html?login=email&auth=login-email

Shelley, W. W., Pickett, J. T., Mancini, C., McDougle, R. D., Rissler, G., & Cleary, H. (2017). Race, bullying, and public perceptions of university safety. *Journal of Interpersonal Violence*. Advance online publication. doi:10.1177/0886260517736272

Shepard, S. (2017, December 13). Half of voters say sexual misconduct accusations against Trump are credible. *Politico*. Retrieved from https://www.politico.com/story/2017/12/13/republicans-senate-moore-alabama-293096

StataCorp. (2017). *Stata structural equation modeling reference manual: Release 15*. College Station, TX: Stata Press Publication.

Stokols, E., & Conway, M. (2016, October 9). Trump hosts surprise panel with Bill Clinton's accusers. *Politico*. Retrieved from https://www.politico.com/story/2016/10/donald-trump-bill-clinton-accusers-229441

Stoynoff, N. (2016, October 12). Physically attacked by Donald Trump—A People writer's own harrowing story. *People*. Retrieved from https://people.com/politics/donald-trump-attacked-people-writer/

Strum, B., & Fears, D. (2015, August 8). Trump: Megyn Kelly had 'blood coming out of her wherever'. *New York Post*. Retrieved from https://nypost.com/2015/08/08/trump-megyn-kelly-had-blood-coming-out-of-her-wherever/

Sykes, G. M., & Matza, D. (1957). Techniques of neutralization: A theory of delinquency. *American Sociological Review*, *22*, 664–670. doi:10.2307/2089195

Thielo, A. J. (2017). *Redemption in an era of penal harm: Moving beyond offender exclusion* (Unpublished doctoral dissertation). University of Cincinnati, Cincinnati, OH.

Thielo, A. J., Graham, A., & Cullen, F. T. (in press). Opt-in internet surveys. In J. C. Barnes & D. R. Forde (Eds.), *The encyclopedia of research methods and statistical techniques in criminology and criminal justice*. New York, NY: Wiley.

Transcript of Donald Trump's videotaped apology. (2016, October 8). Retrieved from https://www.nytimes.com/2016/10/08/us/donald-trump-apology-statement.html

Transcript: Donald Trump's speech responding to assault accusations. (2016, October 13). Retrieved from https://www.npr.org/2016/10/13/497857068/transcript-donald-trumps-speech-responding-to-assault-accusations

Transcript: Donald Trump's taped comments about women. (2016, October 8). Retrieved from https://www.nytimes.com/2016/10/08/us/donald-trump-tape-transcript.html

Twohey, M., & Barbaro, M. (2016, October 12). Two women say Donald Trump touched them inappropriately. *The New York Times*. Retrieved from https://www.nytimes.com/2016/10/13/us/politics/donald-trump-women.html

Tyson, A., & Maniam, S. (2016, November 9). Behind Trump's victory: Divisions by race, gender, education. *Pew Research Center*. Retrieved from http://www.pewresearch.org/fact-tank/2016/11/09/behind-trumps-victory-divisions-by-race-gender-education/

Vandermaas-Peeler, A., Cox, D., Najle, M., Fisch-Friedman, M., Griffin, R., & Jones, R. P. (2018). *Partisanship trumps gender: Sexual harassment, woman candidates, access to contraception, and key issues in 2018 midterms*. Washington, DC: Public Religion Research Institute.

White, D. (2016, October 10). Watch Donald Trump explain the lewd video at the second debate. *Time*. Retrieved from http://time.com/4524406/presidential-debate-donald-trump-locker-room-talk-video/

Wines, M., & Stockman, F. (2019, January 19). Smaller crowds turn out for third annual women's march events. *The New York Times*. Retrieved from https://www.nytimes.com/2019/01/19/us/womens-march-2019.html

Women's March. (2017). *Women's march annual report 2017*. Retrieved from https://static1.squarespace.com/static/5c3feb79fcf7fdce5a3c790b/t/5c422af80e2e725f8f0ea8f8/1547840252450/2017%2BWM%2BAnnual%2BReport_LoRes.pdf

Wooldridge, J. M. (2009). *Introductory econometrics: A modern approach* (4th ed.). Mason, OH: Cengage.

YouGov. (2016). *Survey procedures: Information related to the treatment of human subjects*. Redwood City, CA: Author.

YouGov. (2017). *Trump survey: Variable map and codebook*. Redwood City, CA: Author.

YouGov. (2018a). *Frequently asked questions*. Retrieved from https://today.yougov.com/about/faqs/

YouGov. (2018b). *Our panel*. Retrieved from https://today.yougov.com/about/about-the-yougov-panel/

Turning Back the Clock? Violence against Women and the Trump Administration

Dawn L. Rothe and Victoria E. Collins

ABSTRACT
The Trump Administration has engaged in a systematic rolling back of protections, regulations, and a host of other social safety net programs for vulnerable people, leaving over half of the population in dismay while others celebrate archaic triumphs. In this context, our focus is limited to the Trump Administration's efforts—through law and words—to turn back the clock for women. We examine the reinforcement of overt forms of inequality rooted in patriarchy through domestic law as well as Trump's misogynistic attitude and language toward women. Given that his words hold a greater significance now that he is President of the United States, he has a "gold-plated" pulpit to share and spread his misogynistic hostile rhetoric and propaganda: anti-women objectification, devaluing, and demonization through hegemonic "wordfare" while feeding and fueling sexism across the country. We conclude by suggesting that Trump's rhetoric and that of other leading political figures are contributing to a darker time for those not in the white elite hetero-normative order with short and long term implications and harm. We caution that the current dangers posed by these attacks are entering us into an endemic misogynist normal: retroactively moving the Country back in time at a dangerous speed.

Following the election of Trump, there has been a marked increase in the implementation of neoconservative agendas across the United States, leaving over half of the population in dismay while others celebrate archaic triumphs. In addition to rollbacks of corporate and environmental regulations and protections at the federal and state levels, the Trump presidency has inaugurated an agenda of draconian, neoconservative social rollbacks that threaten women, people of color, people with disabilities, and those who violate hetero-normative understandings of gender (i.e., LGBTQ) – all aimed at ensuring the continuation of an inept, violent status quo benefiting a White, wealthy power elite. All of these social rollbacks are important and deserve attention. However, due to the inordinate number of policies and their consequential harms, our focus here is limited to the Trump Administration's efforts, through both law and words, to turn back the clock for women to a time when rights were even more limited, women were mere property and when patriarchal order was rarely contested.

This discussion focuses on two forms used by the Trump Administration to attack women. First, we argue that the neoliberal carceral state's use of the United States domestic legal system to roll back the advancements of women's rights should be thought of as "lawfare." We expand upon the concept of "lawfare" to invoke the metaphor of using law for fighting against an "enemy." Second, we examine Trump and his allies' use of "wordfare" to demean women. This includes but is not limited to, tweets and other forms of discourse to those challenging Trump on political, economic, or gender issues where women are demonized while their victimizers, men, are portrayed as *the* victims. Taken together, these forms of warfare have created dark times for vulnerable populations with long-term implications. They contain the dual risk of fatalistic acceptance of current developments or the false optimism that the effects of Trump will soon pass without long term implications.

The spectacle of political "lawfare"

Dating back to the 1950s, the term lawfare was used in discussions of divorce law, colonialism, and courtroom advocacy. It was later used to refer to national law as a weapon of conflict where lawfare referred to the U.S.'s use of legalized international institutions to achieve strategic ends. In 2001, Colonel Charles Dunlap further popularized the concept of lawfare, where he used the term to refer to the "use of law as a weapon of war" (Lawfare, 2019). The latter definition of the term seems to allegorically characterize the Trump Administration's processes of implementing neoconservative agendas across the United States at the expense of the majority – and, for our point here, women. Domestically and globally the Trump Administration is significantly impacting and harming women, resulting in the rollback of rights that have slowly been gained over more than a century. One of the first official indicators of this attack was reflected in the president's twitter response to the Women's March on January 20, 2018, where he states: "Beautiful weather all over our great country, a perfect day for all Women to March … Get out there now to celebrate the historic milestones" (Trump, 2018a). What he does not say or admit is that women needed "to celebrate what we gained" as he slowly, and in many cases quietly, planned to dismantle this progress.

For example, through the promotion of a pro-life ideology, the Trump Administration has employed a national and global systemic campaign against reproductive health and rights during the last 18 months of his presidency. It began with the reinstatement and expansion of a global gag rule to prohibit foreign non-profits that receive any United States global health assistance from using private, non-United States funding to provide abortion services or advocate abortion policy reform. The Administration blocked all funding for the United Nations Population Fund that supports reproductive health, including maternal health programs across 150 nations (Barot, 2017). In addition to targeting women's reproductive health and freedom to decide the outcome of their own bodies, the Trump Administration has taken every opportunity to disavow women's right to breastfeed. The 2018 United Nations-affiliated World Health Assembly had expected the resolution supporting breastfeeding and breast milk for infants to receive overwhelming support from the hundreds of government delegates attending the meeting. This resolution reduces the reliance on corporatized synthetic infant formulas in favor of breastmilk. The Trump Administration's delegate opposed the resolution refusing to support language that promotes breast milk as being the healthiest option for infant children. When other countries, such as Ecuador, refused to support the United States in its endeavors, the Administration threatened to punish these countries through trade measures and withdrawal of military aid (Jacobs, 2018). Furthermore, the Trump Administration's pro-life stance has limited abortion services, increased freedom for businesses to deny "no-cost" birth control, and promoted abstinence-only sex education. Many of these changes have been made under Title X (Zaldivar & Crary, 2018), the federal grant program that is solely focused on family planning and related services.

In addition, Trump has assembled one of the "most anti-abortion cabinets in history," stacking "federal courts and the Supreme Court with anti-abortion judges who could serve for the next several decades" (Bassett, 2018). This includes Vice President Mike Pence who, before joining Trump's campaign, led the Republican Party's fight against legal abortion in the House of Representatives for over five years. Given Pence's historical efforts to dismantle women's rights, his ongoing efforts in this regard as Vice President should come as no surprise. Likewise, Trump's nominees for federal judges are almost all pro-life, including now-confirmed Supreme Court Justice Brett Kavanaugh. In 2018, 66 judges were approved by a Republican-dominated upper chamber, many of whom are white (76%) and in their mid-30s to 40s, taking on lifetime judicial positions (Zhou, 2018). As argued by Daniel Goldberg, the legal director for the Alliance for Justice, "long after Donald Trump leaves the seat, his fingerprints will still be on our justice system – two, three, four decades from now" (quoted in Zhou, 2018).

Trump also quietly signed a bill that would give states the power to withhold federal funds from centers that provide abortion services, such as Planned Parenthood. This action would lead to a million United States teenagers and millions more impoverished women not having access to sex education programs or reproductive health services from pap smears to birth control. In April 2017, Trump signed an executive order, HJ Resolution #43, giving states permission to defund Planned Parenthood (White House). This order reversed the requirement that states pass along family planning grants to all groups regardless if they offer abortion services to prevent states from withholding grants from any organization for reasons other than their ability to provide Title IX services. In addition, the Administration cut more "than $200 million in federal grants to 81 teen pregnancy prevention programs around the country, leaving an estimated 580,000 students without access to comprehensive sex education" (Scott, 2017). An "abstinence" ideology is supposed to be used rather than sex education or sexual reproductive health education. Trump also rolled back the requirement that birth control coverage by insurers – at no out of pocket cost to 62 million women – be guaranteed (Scott, 2017). He further reinstated a "global gap rule" policy which restricts government funding for international organizations that provide abortion services. And, he became the first sitting president to give a speech at a March for Life rally (Siddiqui, 2018), an annual march for the purposes of ending abortion

Additionally, through Executive orders, changes in policies, and laws, the Administration is making it harder for women to report sexual discrimination, much less attempt to fight against it. For example, Trump reversed the 2014 Fair Pay Act signed by former President Obama that forbids federal contractors from keeping secret or hushing sexual harassment and discrimination cases (Revocation Executive Order 13673, 13683, 13738, 2017, White House, 2017). Specifically, as it relates to women's rights, the rescindment of The Fair Pay order will no longer require paycheck transparency and continues the draconian practice of forced or mandatory arbitration clauses for sexual harassment, sexual assault, or discrimination claims – one of Trump's signature attempts to obfuscate his victims' abilities to speak out. These clauses legally forbid victims to sue their employer. This prohibition was upheld by the Supreme Court in a March 2018 ruling. Now hundreds of thousands or more claims from women will remain "hidden," once again suppressing their voices as has historically been the case.

In addition, the Administration rescinded the campus sexual assault guidance for ensuring compliance with Title IX. In essence, this decision undoes the power of the Office of Civil Rights tasked with tackling sexual assault. Such a move was rationalized as a "response" to an undue burden on accused students that must defend themselves under the previous order (O'Hara, 2017). Siding with men's rights groups, Trump's Secretary of Education Betsy Devos has doubled down on this justification by arguing the need for equal treatment of victims and perpetrators in sexual assault cases. Specifically, Devos has reversed the Obama-era guidelines that implemented a lowered burden of proof in campus sexual assault cases – that of a preponderance of the evidence. Devos, as well as the Trump administration more broadly, has become a heroic figure for the families (particularly the mothers) of sons on college campuses who have been accused of rape and sexual assault (Collins & Dunn, 2018).

The Trump Administration has also used the United States budget to reduce resources for victims of domestic abuse and rape into the 2018/2019 fiscal year. The Administration's budget funds for the Violence Against Women Act was reduced to $100 million below what Congress authorized. As noted by The National Coalition Against Domestic Violence (2018),

> Rather than showing a commitment to decreasing gender-based violence by investing tax-payer money in VAWA, the budget pays for the entirety of VAWA with a transfer from the Crime Victims Fund, a fund that is financed by fines and penalties paid by convicted federal offenders, not from tax dollars. This transfer is anticipated to decrease funding available to shelters and other direct service providers by up to almost 26% … The proposed cuts to important social safety net programs upon which victims and survivors rely to regain self-sufficiency will add barriers to victims seeking safety.

As a result, the National Coalition Against Domestic Violence has publicly denounced the budget.

The spectacle of "wordfare"

Unfortunately, we could go on with examples of significant and possibly long-term devastating rollbacks and lawfare through legislation and Executive Orders and Resolutions. Doing so, however, would obscure the more dangerous and damaging impact of the misogynist political discourse that constructs negative narratives of women, further fueling fear, hate, and a particular archaic heteronormative patriarchal viewpoint. To us, the deadly combination of lawfare and wordfare make this moment in time precarious at best. After all, politics and political discourse are the essential elements of persuasion. As Jeffrey Engel, Director of the Center for Presidential History at Southern Methodist University, so succinctly states:

> There is so much hue and cry and rending of cloth over the truly outlandish statements that no previous president would ever make publicly … that we are missing the fact that the

> tweets are the ripples on top of the water. The big, impactful currents are well below. (quoted in Page, 2018)

It is this discourse that builds a narrative to confirm and/or convince his base audience of the "truth" of the order, where the big, impactful currents will be felt.

Notably, Trump's personal disdain and poor treatment of women are not something new, nor should it be shocking given that his treatment of women as objects and "less than" has a long-standing historical pattern. For example, during George H. W. Bush Presidency in 1991, Trump spoke to *Esquire* magazine about his media coverage: "You know, it doesn't really matter what [they] write as long as you've got a young and beautiful piece of ass" (quoted in Cohen, 2017). The following year in an interview with *New York Magazine*, Trump told readers how women *have* to be treated: "You have to treat 'em like shit" (Gass, 2015). More recent examples include the now-infamous *Access Hollywood* recording of Trump (2005) where he states:

> I moved on her like a bitch … You know, I'm automatically attracted to beautiful – I just start kissing them. It's like a magnet. Just kiss. I don't even wait. And when you're a star, they let you do it. You can do anything … Grab 'em by the pussy. You can do anything.

It should not be unexpected then that as many as 23 women have accused Trump of sexual assault, all of which he denies and dismisses (Relman, 2019). On October 17, 2016, he tweeted: "Can't believe these totally phony stories, 100% made up by women (many already proven false) and pushed big time by press, have impact! They are 'fake news': false accusations and fabricated stories of women who I don't know and/or have never met" (Trump, 2016). Trump's misogynistic views extend to his own daughters as objects of pleasure. In a 1994 interview, host Robin Leach asked Trump and his former wife which physical traits Tiffany Trump inherited from them both. He stated: "She's a really beautiful baby, and she's got Marla's legs." Then, pointing to his chest making reference to her breasts, he continued: "We don't know whether she's got this part yet, but time will tell" (Trump, 1994). More recently he objectified Ivanka when speaking on *The View*, saying she has "a very nice figure and if Ivanka weren't my daughter, perhaps I'd be dating her" (Trump, 2006).

While the above examples, by far limited here, highlight the preponderance of Trump's misogynistic historical attitude toward women, his words hold a greater significance now that he occupies the United States presidency. The office provides him with a "gold-plated" pulpit to share and spread his misogynistic hostile rhetoric and propaganda – marked by anti-women objectification, devaluing attacks, and demonization through hegemonic "wordfare" while feeding and fueling sexism across the country.[1] After all, the presidential office carries a symbolic power and shapes public discourse as political speech does not exist in a vacuum or as an abstract realm separate from society and culture. Here, we draw from the concept of lawfare, meaning the use of law in a "war" against some position, ideology, or polity. "Wordfare," therefore, is the use of words to conduct a "war" against the advancement of women in society as equals in value and essence. This term seems especially fitting to use in a Gramscian frame, where words/language are at the center of the relationship between coercion and consent (Ives, 2004). In addition, language should not be analyzed as an "inert object, as a corpse on the dissecting table … it comes to life again" (Gramsci, 1999, p. 83), bringing with it the underlying currents. In this sense, Trump is using his platform to spread a political misogynist "wordfare" that reproduces and maintains asymmetrical power relations and returns society to a more draconian patriarchal society.

Trump's misogynistic "wordfare" has continued following his election as president. Indeed, he has expanded efforts to demoralize and demonize women beyond his historical fetishism of the "perfect" female body (parts) and as sexual objects. For example, on June 25, 2018, Trump tweeted:

> Congresswoman Maxine Waters, an extraordinarily low IQ person, has become, together with Nancy Pelosi, the Face of the Democrat Party. She has just called for harm to supporters, of which there are many, of the Make America Great Again movement. Be careful what you wish for Max! (Trump, 2018c)

In reference to Omarosa Newman, his former presidential aide, he tweeted on August 14, 2018: "When you give a crazed, crying lowlife a break, and give her a job at the White House, I guess it just didn't work out. Good work by General Kelly for quickly firing that dog!" (Keneally, 2018). His nasty wordfare seems endless. He called Stormy Daniels, his ex-mistress, "horseface" (Keneally, 2018). He labeled MSNBC personality Mika Brzezinski "crazy" and claimed she was "bleeding badly from a face-lift ... off the wall, a neurotic and not very bright mess," "very insecure" and "crazy" (Keneally, 2018) And in reference to Carly Fiorina, his only female rival for the GOP presidential nomination in 2016, he stated: "Look at that face! Would anyone vote for that?" (Keneally, 2018). After the GOP primary debate on CNN, Trump said in reference to Megyn Kelly: "There was blood coming out of her eyes, blood coming out of her wherever" (Keneally, 2018). Trump also attacked Senator Gillibrand, tweeting:

> Lightweight Senator Kirsten Gillibrand, a total flunky for Chuck Schumer and someone who would come to my office 'begging' for campaign contributions not so long ago (and would do anything for them), is now in the ring fighting against Trump. Very disloyal to Bill & Crooked-USED! (Trump, 2017b)

To be sure, men have also been subject to Trump's ire and bashed by him on twitter. Still, when his target is a woman, his tone can be characterized as mocking, patronizing, and belittling, casting insults that are sexist, such as those that focus on a women's menstrual cycle, her appearance, or her mental health. Such language has been, and still is, often associated with larger gender myths that frame women as being too emotional, weaker than men, and sexual objects. Again, this is not surprising given Trump's long recorded history of objectifying and sexualizing women and their bodies.

We have previously mentioned the rollbacks of women's rights through the national budget, law, and executive orders, but the moral and ethical significance of this Administration's support of men accused of domestic violence, sexual assault or rape is equally troubling. The president's public support of perpetrators of violence against women sends a rippling effect through to his audience as he narrates a story that invalidates and undermines women's claims of abuse, assault, and their victimization. The Trump Administration and other Republican politicians continue to support those that have committed domestic violence and abuse, framing allegations as "fake news" or outright denying them until they no longer can. In this use of wordfare against women, the abusers are touted as "good men" that are having their lives shattered and their careers ruined. Consider Trump's tweet in response to White House staff secretary Rob Porter and speechwriter David Sorensen, both accused of intimate partner abuse:

> Peoples [*sic*] lives are being shattered and destroyed by a mere allegation. Some are true and some are false. Some are old and some are new. There is no recovery for someone falsely accused – life and career are gone. Is there no such thing any longer as Due Process? (Trump, 2018b)

Or his enduring support for his confidants such as Roger Ailes – ousted from *Fox News* amidst multiple allegations of sexual harassment:

> I can tell you that some of the women that are complaining, I know how much he's helped them … And now, all of a sudden, they're saying these horrible things about him … It's very sad because he's a very good person. I've always found him to be just a very, very good person … So I feel very badly. (quoted in Dickinson, 2018)

He gave the same support to Bill O'Reilly. "He's a good person," Trump told the *New York Times*. "I think he shouldn't have settled … I know Bill. Bill's a good person … . I don't think Bill would do anything wrong" (Dickinson, 2018).

Trump, his allies, and a host of male Republican politicians' denouncements of claims of sexual harassment and rape broadcast a loud message to those coming forward: Shut-up and go away. More troubling is the production and use of a renewed narrative that moves beyond demeaning women and supporting Republican men and personal acquaintances, to one of fear and "conspiracy." As noted by Potter (in press), the "conspiracy framework also plays well because it draws on a long-standing American social tradition, which has seen conspiracies as the source of many of America's problems … the concept of conspiracy seems to play well in American politics, making it a most useful tool." In addition, it is well known that fear is a common political tactic used to spread a particular hegemonic ideology and to garner consent without explicitly coercing the population. Conspiracy coupled with fear, are then deployed to garner public support for those who have been accused of the horrific crimes against women. This tactic is not a new, but one that has been used whenever there are challenges to the existing heteronormative patriarchal social order. For example, days after the 9/11 attacks, Jerry Falwell (2001) commented over the air on the *700 Club* show:

> I really believe that the pagans, and the abortionists, and the feminists, and the gays and the lesbians who are actively trying to make that an alternative lifestyle, the ACLU, People For the American Way – all of them who have tried to secularize America – I point the finger in their face and say "you helped this happen."

While these views have always existed in the United States, they have mostly resided on the political and religious fringe. Given Trump's elevated platform as president, however, his words have a greater impact on his base and reach a larger audience than evangelicals or other individuals/groups have enjoyed in the past.

The power of his language and discourse as it relates to the dismissal of violence against women was especially evident when Christine Blasey-Ford made public her allegation that then-Supreme Court nominee Brett Kavanaugh sexually assaulted her at a party when they were teenagers. This disclosure led to a very public testimony during Kavanaugh's Senate Judiciary hearings. In response to the Kavanaugh hearings, the Trump Administration – quickly followed by other media pundits, politicians, and others – spun a tale of how scary a time it is now for young men.

> It's a very scary time for young men in America when you can be guilty of something that you may not be guilty of. You can be somebody that was perfect your entire life and somebody could accuse you of something ... and you're automatically guilty" (Trump, 2018d).

At a rally in Southaven Mississippi, Trump not only mocked Ford's testimony but used the "appeal-to-emotions" tactic of warning his supporters, "Think of your son ... Think of your husband" (Trump, 2018e). Likewise, Donald Trump, Jr. reacted to the sexual allegations against Brett Kavanagh by telling the *Daily Mail TV* that "I've got boys, and I've got girls. And when I see what's going on right now, it's scary." With a follow-up question regarding which of his five children he worries more about, he stated, "Right now, I'd say my sons" (Trump, 2018). This kind of remark not only implies the allegations are false and negates Christine Ford's victimization but also makes a larger statement about the motivations are truthfulness of rape and sexual assault victims; they lie. Likewise, Senate Majority John Cornyn stated on the Senate Floor: "A vote against Kavanaugh is a 'yes' vote for more of these despicable tactics being used time and time again in the future" (Cornyn, 2018). This common misrepresentation of rape victims as being motivated by revenge and implying that the perpetrator is the *real* victim is not new. This attempt to delegitimate the victim occurs despite consistent findings that false reporting for rape and sexual assault is very low and no greater than false reports for other criminal offenses (Lisak, Gardiner, Nicksa, & Cote, 2010).

Despite this empirical reality, such fear and conspiratorial narratives spread – including on *Fox News*, an outlet widely known to be a pro-Trump and neoconservative in its orientation. Heather Mac Donald, a Manhattan Institute fellow, told FOX News' Tucker Carlson: "Feminism has ambitions to take over civilization and when that happens you can say goodbye to civilization. They're trying to disappear males ... Feminism is really at odds with the civilizational legacy that we have inherited, that we have to preserve at all costs." She continued with "they are simply seizing power, and are in a manic rage to efface males" (Mac Donald, 2018). In agreement, Tucker then responded to his audience with the claim that "institution after institution has been taken over by feminists and the absurd diatribes that are launched against males, and that's the only conclusion you can reach" (Carlson, 2018). During the April 2, 2019 *Tucker Carlson Tonight* show, he belittled Chris Hayes, host of MSNBC's *All In* in the following sexist terms: "Chris Hayes is what every man would be if feminists ever achieved absolute power in this country: apologetic, bespectacled, and deeply, deeply concerned about global warming and the patriarchal systems that cause it" (Carlson, 2019). In short, the false information and demonization being spewed here, as with all other historical forms of demonizing the "other," misrepresent feminism, invalidate rape victimization, and eventually bends toward violence.

We believe the underlying currents are stretching widely as Trump's misogynistic views and "wordfare" have emboldened similar remarks by other politicians (nationally and globally), media pundits, judges, doctors, and CEOs to voice their sexist and derogatory views in the public arena. We are not saying misogynistic views are "new" or because of Trump, given the historical and current levels of sexism and misogynism throughout society. Likewise, we are fully aware of the ongoing misogyny that dominates many platforms of social media (see, e.g., Faludi, 2007; Jane, 2014, 2017; Richardson-Self, 2018). However, as we previously stated, given that the President of the United States regularly tweets misogynistic posts and supports men accused of violence and harms against women, his platform emboldens and increases the objectification and demonization of women in general.

For example, Oklahoma State Representative Justin Humphrey stated the following during a state legislature debate of a bill that would mandate a woman to have written permission from the man they had sex with before a legal abortion:

> I understand that they feel like that is their body. I feel like it is a separate – what I call them is, is you're a "host." And you know when you enter into a relationship you're going to be that host and so, you know, if you pre-know that then take all precautions and don't get pregnant. So that's where I'm at. I'm like, hey, your body is your body and be responsible with it. But after you're irresponsible then don't claim, well, I can just go and do this with another body, when you're the host and you invited that in. (quoted in Smith, 2017)

In addition, on September 21, 2018, South Carolina Republican congressional representative Ralph Norman opened a debate with the comment: "Did y'all hear this latest late-breaking news from the Kavanaugh hearings? Ruth Bader Ginsburg came out that saying she was groped by Abraham Lincoln." And consider the following Facebook post by Republican candidate Courtland Sykes: "I want to come home to a home-cooked dinner at six every night – one that she fixes and one that I expect one day to have daughters learn to fix after they become traditional homemakers and family wives" (quotes in Shugerman, 2018). He continued by portraying feminists as:

> career obsessed banshees who forego home life and children and the happiness of family to become nail-biting manophobic [*sic*] hell-bent feminist she devils who shriek from the tops of a thousand tall buildings they think they could have leaped over in a single bound – had men not "suppressing them." (quoted in Shugerman, 2018)

Consider as well, Laura Ingraham's comments on *Fox News* regarding the newly elected Congresswomen Ayanna Pressley, Rashida Tlaib, Ilhan Omar, and Alexandria Ocasio-Cortez. She called them the "four horsewomen of the apocalypse" and went on to say that Pressley is "a leftist on the war path against white men" (quoted in Leah, 2018).

Regretfully, there is no shortage of examples of misogynistic, hateful discourse propagated by politicians and media pundits (both men and women) that demonizes women. However, the discussion and empirical evidence of the patriarchal hegemonic discourse touted from the highest levels of government, reinforcing women as objects, property, and liars-undermining and discrediting their lives, experiences and voice across the country represent the surface of what is occurring. From the examples above, we suggest one can see not only the ripples on top of the water as Engel (quoted in Page, 2018) has stated but also the big and impactful currents that are causing a riptide effect well below.

Conclusion

Nothing changes instantaneously: in a gradually heating bathtub you'd be boiled to death before you knew it.

The Handmaids Tale (Atwood, 1986, p. 56)

"The rhetorical power of the presidency has a ripple effect that lasts longer than one's term in office. The implications for the present are clear" (Heer, 2018). Moreover, as the opening quote for this section suggests, nothing changes instantly, though, given

Trump's leading misogynistic wordfare and lawfare efforts, we see the bathtub gradually heating. Or as stated by Jacob Levy (2018, emphasis in original):

> "Ignore the tweets, ignore the language, ignore the words" is advice that affects a kind of sophistication: don't get distracted by the circus, keep your eye on what's going on behind the curtain. This is *faux* pragmatism, ignoring what is being communicated to other countries, to actors within the state, and to tens of millions of fellow citizens. It ignores *how all those actors will respond to the speech*, and how norms, institutions, and the environment for policy and coercion will be changed by those responses.

Ironically, while Trump and those now emboldened to use the same demonizing "wordfare" continue debasing women, he simultaneously, along with his daughter Ivanka, have started the Women's Global Development and Prosperity Initiative with $50 million (White House News, 2019). We are already seeing the currents below as the politically divisive and hateful discourse is increasingly playing out in society as a whole where private misogyny is becoming public as people become more and more emboldened. Consider Dr. Gary Tigges's (2018) comments in the *Dallas Medical Journal* (2018):

> Female physicians do not work as hard and do not see as many patients as male physicians … This is because they choose to, or they simply don't want to be rushed, or they don't want to work the long hours. Most of the time, their priority is something else … Family, social, whatever.

Also instructive are the cases of two men accused of sexually abusing women on airplanes, something that was later revealed to be an increasing problem. The FBI notes that sexual assaults on planes have increased at an alarming rate, with 63 investigations being launched into sexual assaults in 2017 alone (Diego, Jimenez, Marsh, & Summers, 2018). While we are not making a direct causative claim, the connection to and impact of Trump's "wordfare" to incidents such as these is creating an environment where the harassment, violence, and harm perpetrated against women is increasingly normalized, trivialized, and justified. Trump's language and actions are more often used to justify gender-based violence as a defense against the perpetrator's actions. Consider, for example, a Florida man accused of groping a woman's breast on a Southwest Airlines flight. He defended his alleged behavior by noting that "the president of the United States says it's OK to grab women by their private parts" (Fox2 Now, 2018). In addition, in a poll by the Morning Consult Survey National Tracking Poll (October 4–8, 2018), it was found that 57% of adults that responded said they equally worried about women facing sexual assault and the men "facing false accusations." This level of moral equivalence occurred after the "wordfare" of Trump and others aimed at protecting men accused of violence and sexual assault or rape. Note that as a group, Republican men expressed more concerned about men and false accusations than about women facing sexual assault (86%).

Overall, we see increases in hate crimes, racism, anti-immigration, and anti-religious choices. Although such ideologies and hatred have long existed, the rhetoric of Trump and other leading political figures is lending to darker times for those not in the White elite heteronormative order (Eligon, 2018; NAACP, 2018). It is important to recognize the very real risk that misogyny will be fatalistically accepted as normal as sustained political efforts are made to move backwards from the hard-won rights and protections afforded the nation's vulnerable populations. Blind optimism that all will be restored once the Trump Administration ends will get us nowhere. The rapidly mounting danger posed by the lawfare and wordfare against women will continue to have a ripple effect moving back to a draconian era.

Thus, we give a cautionary note to all citizens, critical criminologists, and women in particular, with a quote by Bob Dylan (1965), “You don’t need a weatherman to know which way the wind blows” as we are in the midst of a “wordfare” aimed at rolling back women’s rights, value, and essence. We close with a dystopian warning, we believe is very appropriate for the topic on hand in the novel, *The Slave and the Free* by Suzy Charnas (1974, p. 4):

> These men will enslave us if we let them: They tried to convince the others … The men heard and they rejoiced to find an enemy they could conquer at last … They pulled all the women together, and harangued them, saying, remember that you caused the wasting. It was a Black female’s refusal to sit in the back of the bus that sparked the rebellion … female terrorists made bombs side by side with our own rebel sons, whose mothers had brought them up to be half-men; female vermin of all kinds spewed our millions of young to steal our food supplies and our living space! Females themselves brought on the Wasting of the world … (And so) the men, armed with staves and straps, reminded them and saw to it that these things were not forgotten again.

Soon all that was remembered were the “evil races, youths who repudiated their fathers’ ways … and most of all the men’s cunning, greedy females” (p. 4).[2]

Note

1. We use the term “propaganda” to mean the information given through political discourse that is “intended to persuade an audience to accept a particular idea or cause, often by using biased material or by stirring up emotions” (author unknown, n.d.).
2. We use the term “propaganda” to mean the information given through political discourse that is “intended to persuade an audience to accept a particular idea or cause, often by using biased material or by stirring up emotions” (author unknown, n.d.).

Disclosure statement

No potential conflict of interest was reported by the authors.

References

Atwood, M. (1986). *The handmails tale*. Boston, MA: Houghton Mifflin Company.

Barot, B. (2017). When antiabortion ideology turns into foreign policy: How the global gag rule erodes health, ethics, and democracy. *Guttmacher Policy Review*. Retrieved from https://www.guttmacher.org/gpr/2017/06/when-antiabortion-ideology-turns-foreign-policy-how-global-gag-rule-erodes-health-ethics

Bassett, L. (2018, January 20). In one year, Trump dismantled reproductive rights around the world. *Huffington Post*. Retrieved from https://www.huffingtonpost.com/entry/in-one-year-trump-dismantled-reproductive-rights-around-the-world_us_5a623b94e4b074ce7a080152

Carlson, T. (2018). *Fox news interview with Tucker Carlson*. Retrieved from https://www.mediamatters.org/video/2018/12/06/tucker-carlson-and-guest-claim-feminists-are-destroying-civilization-and-trying-disappear-males/222253

Carlson, T. (2019), *Tucker Carlson tonight, Fox news*. Retrieved from https://www.youtube.com/watch?v=SOVtdm7Smo4

Charnas, S. M. (1974). *The slave and the free*. New York, NY: Tom Doharty Associates Book.

Cohen, C. (2017, July 14). Donald Trump sexism tracker: Every offensive comment in one place. *The Telegraph*. Retrieved from https://www.telegraph.co.uk/women/politics/donald-trump-sexism-tracker-every-offensive-comment-in-one-place/

Collins, V. E., & Dunn, M. (2018). The invisible/visible claims to justice: Sexual violence and the university camp(us). *Contemporary Justice Review*, *21*(4), 371–395. doi:10.1080/10282580.2018.1531717

Cornyn, J. (2018). *Senate judiciary committee on Kavanaugh nomination hearing*. Retrieved from https://www.c-span.org/video/?452378-1/us-senate-debates-brett-kavanaugh-nomination-faa-reauthorization

Dickinson, T. (2018, February 23). A history of sex and abuse in the Trump Administration: From Ivana and Marla to pussygate and Porter, a timeline of domestic abuse and sexual misconduct allegations against Trump and his inner circle. *Rolling Stone*. Retrieved from https://www.rollingstone.com/politics/politics-news/a-history-of-sex-and-abuse-in-the-trump-administration-202833/

Diego, J. D., Jimenez, O., Marsh, R., & Summers, J. (2018, June 20). FBI: Sexual assaults on flights increasing 'at an alarming rate'. *CNN politics*. Retrieved from https://www.cnn.com/2018/06/20/politics/fbi-airplane-sexual-assault/index.html

Dylan, B. (1965). Subterranean homesick blues. In *Bringing it all back home*. New York City, NY: Columbia.

Eligon, J. (2018, November 13). Hate crimes increase for the third consecutive year, F.B.I. reports. *New York Times*. Retrieved from https://www.nytimes.com/2018/11/13/us/hate-crimes-fbi-2017.html

Executive Order, Revocation 13673, 13683, 13738. (2017, March 27). *Presidential executive order on the revocation of federal contracting executive orders*. Retrieved from https://www.whitehouse.gov/presidential-actions/presidential-executive-order-revocation-federal-contracting-executive-orders/

Faludi, S. (2007). *The terror dream: Myth and misogony in an insecure America*. New York, NY: Henry Holt.

Falwell, J. (2001, September 13). *Christian broadcasting network's TV program "700 Club"*. Retrieved from https://www.cbsnews.com/news/falwell-i-blew-it/

Fox 2 Now, St. Louis. (2018, October 23). Accused in-flight groper claims the president 'says it's OK to grab women'. *Tribune Media*. Retrieved from https://fox2now.com/2018/10/23/man-cites-trump-defense-after-being-accused-of-groping-woman-on-flight/

Gass, N. (2015, December 8). The 15 most offensive things that have come out of Trump's mouth. *Politico*. Retrieved from https://www.politico.com/story/2015/12/trump-hte-216539

Gramsci, A. (1999). *Selections from the prison notebooks*. London, England: The Electric Book Company. Retrieved from http://abahlali.org/files/gramsci.pdf (Original published between 1929 and 1935).

Heer, J. (2018, February 12). President's words can be lasting deeds. *The New Republic*. Retrieved from https://newrepublic.com/article/147033/presidents-words-can-lasting-deeds

Ives, P. (2004). *Language and hegemony in Gramsci*. Ann Arbor, MI: Pluto Press.

Jacobs, A. (2018, July 8). Opposition to breast-feeding resolution by U.S. stuns World Health Officials. *New York Times*. Retrieved from https://www.nytimes.com/2018/07/08/health/world-health-breastfeeding-ecuador-trump.html

Jane, E. (2014). 'Back to the kitchen, cunt': Speaking the unspeakable about online misogyny. *Journal of Media & Cultural Studies*, *4*, 558–570. doi:10.1080/10304312.2014.924479

Jane, E. (2017). *Misogyny online: A short (and brutish) history*. Thousand Oaks, CA: Sage.

Keneally, M. (2018, October 17). 'Horseface,' 'crazy,' 'low IQ': Trump's history of insulting women. *ABS News*. Retrieved from https://abcnews.go.com/Politics/trumps-long-history-calling-women-crazy-attacking-appearances/story?id=48348956

Lawfare. (2019, April 11). *Author unknown*. Retrieved from https://www.lawfareblog.com/about-lawfare-brief-history-term-and-site

Leah, R. (2018, November 14). Laura Ingraham slams new diverse roster of congresswomen as the "four horsewomen of the apocalypse". *Salon*. Retrieved from https://www.salon.com/2018/11/14/

laura-ingraham-slams-new-diverse-roster-of-congresswomen-as-the-four-horsewomen-of-the-apocalypse/

Levy, J. (2018). The weight of the words. *Niskanen Center*. Retrieved from https://niskanencenter.org/blog/the-weight-of-the-words/

Lisak, D., Gardiner, L., Nicksa, S. C., & Cote, A. M. (2010). False allegations of sexual assault: An analysis of ten years of reported cases. *Violence Against Women, 16*, 1318–1334. doi:10.1177/1077801210387747

Mac Donald, H. (2018). *Fox News interview with Tucker Carlson*. Retrieved from https://www.mediamatters.org/video/2018/12/06/tucker-carlson-and-guest-claim-feminists-are-destroying-civilization-and-trying-disappear-males/222253

Morning Consult. (2018), *National tracking Poll #181011*. Retrieved from https://morningconsult.com/wpcontent/uploads/2018/10/181011_crosstabs_METOO_Adults_v1_.pdf

NAACP. (2018, June 29). *NAACP Sees continued rise in hate crimes, legacy of Trump's racism*. Retrieved from https://www.naacp.org/latest/naacp-sees-continued-rise-hate-crimes-legacy-trumps-racism/

The National Coalition Against Domestic Violence. (2018, February 20). NCADV Denounces President Trump's FY'19 Budget Request. *NCADV Bog*. Retrieved from https://ncadv.org/blog/posts/ncadv-denounces-president-trumps-fy19-budget-request

O'Hara, M. (2017, April 3). Trump pulls back Obama-era protections for women workers. *NBC News*. Retrieved from https://www.nbcnews.com/news/us-news/trump-pulls-back-obama-era-protections-women-workers-n741041

Page, S. (2018, January 18). A consequential president: Trump's tweets have overshadowed the impact of his policies at one year in. *USA Today*. Retrieved from https://www.usatoday.com/story/news/2018/01/18/consequential-president-trumps-tweets-have-overshadowed-impact-his-policies-one-year/1033731001/

Potter, G. (in press). Organized crime and the sociological imagination. In D. Rothe & V. Collins (Eds.), *Explorations in critical criminology in honor of William J. Chambliss* (pp. 28–43). Leiden, Netherlands: Brill.

Relman, E. (2019, February 25). The 23 Women who have accused Trump of sexual misconduct. *Business Insider*. Retrieved from https://www.businessinsider.com/women-accused-trump-sexual-misconduct-list-2017-12

Richardson-Self, L. (2018). Woman hating: On misogyny, sexism, and hate speech. *Wiley Online Library*. Retrieved from https://onlinelibrary.wiley.com/doi/abs/10.1111/hypa.12398

Scott, B. (2017). Shea-Porter to Trump: Hands off women's birth control. Media. Press Release. *Education & Labor Committee*. Retrieved from https://edlabor.house.gov/media/press-releases/shea-porter-to-trump-hands-off-womens-birth-control

Shugerman, E. (2018, January 25). Republican senate candidate on feminism: 'I want to come home to a home-cooked dinner at six every night'. *Independent*. Retrieved from https://www.independent.co.uk/news/world/americas/us-politics/courtland-sykes-republican-senate-candidate-missouri-feminism-dinner-womens-rights-a8178516.html

Siddiqui, S. (2018, January 18). How has Donald Trump's first year affected women? *The Guardian*. Retrieved from https://www.theguardian.com/us-news/2018/jan/18/how-has-donald-trumps-first-year-affected-women

Smith, J. (2017, February 13). Oklahoma lawmakers want men to approve all abortions. *The Intercept*. Retrieved from https://theintercept.com/2017/02/13/oklahoma-lawmakers-want-men-to-approve-all-abortions/

Tigges, G. (2018). Women in medicine. *Dallas Medical Journal, 104*(9), 10. Retrieved from http://www.dcms.branchmediapro.com/2018/09September/page_1.html

Trump, D. J. (1994). Interview with the lifestyles of the rich and famous. *Video in Ashley Collman, Daily Mail*. Retrieved from https://www.dailymail.co.uk/news/article-3528887/Donald-Trump-talks-infant-daughter-Tiffany-s-breasts-uncovered-interview-1994.html

Trump, D. J. (2005). Interview. *Access Hollywood*. Retrieved from https://www.bbc.com/news/election-us-2016-37595321

Trump, D. J. (2006). Interview. *The View*. Retrieved from https://www.youtube.com/watch?v=diMp241gAcw

Trump, D. J. (2016, October 17). *Real Donald Trump twitter account*. Retrieved from https://twitter.com/realdonaldtrump/status/787990502415167488?lang=en

Trump, D. J. (2017b, December 12). *Real Donald Trump twitter account*. Retrieved from https://twitter.com/realdonaldtrump/status/940567812053053441

Trump, D. J. (2018a, January 20). *Real Donald Trump twitter account*. Retrieved from https://twitter.com/realdonaldtrump/status/954788467069870081

Trump, D. J. (2018b, February 10). *Real Donald Trump twitter account*. Retrieved from https://twitter.com/realdonaldtrump/status/962348831789797381?lang=en

Trump, D. J. (2018c, June 25). *Real Donald Trump twitter account*. Retrieved from https://twitter.com/realdonaldtrump/status/1011295779422695424?lang=en

Trump, D. J. (2018d). *News conference*. Retrieved from https://www.vogue.com/article/donald-trump-very-scary-time-for-young-men-in-america

Trump, D. J. (2018e, October 2). *Speech given at the make America great again rally at landers center, Southhaven Mississippi*. Retrieved from https://www.c-span.org/video/?c4753153/president-trump-think-son-husband

Trump Jr., D. (2018). Trump Jr. says he fears more for his sons than daughters. *GeoBeats*. Retrieved from https://www.msn.com/en-ca/video/news/trump-jr-says-he-fears-more-for-his-sons-than-daughters/vi-BBNNij7

Unknown Author. (n.d.). Visual essay: The impact of propaganda. *Facing History and Ourselves*. Retrieved from https://www.facinghistory.org/holocaust-and-human-behavior/chapter-6/visual-essay-impact-propaganda

White House. (2017). *President Donald J. Trump signs H. J. Res. 43 into law.statements and releases*. Retrieved from https://www.whitehouse.gov/briefings-statements/president-donald-j-trump-signs-h-j-res-43-law/

White House News. (2019, February 7). *Briefing statements*. Retrieved from https://www.whitehouse.gov/briefings-statements/ivanka-trump-empower-women-to-foster-freedom/

Zaldivar, R., & Crary, D. (2018, January 18). How the Trump administration is remaking federal policy on women's reproductive health. *PBS Broadcasting*. Retrieved from https://www.pbs.org/newshour/politics/how-the-trump-administration-is-remaking-federal-policy-on-womens-reproductive-health

Zhou, L. (2018, December 27). Trump has gotten 66 judges confirmed this year. In his second year, Obama had gotten 49. *Vox*. Retrieved from https://www.vox.com/2018/12/27/18136294/trump-mitch-mconnell-republican-judges

Less Safe in the Ivory Tower: Campus Sexual Assault Policy in the Trump Administration

Leah C. Butler, Heejin Lee, and Bonnie S. Fisher

ABSTRACT

Since the late 20th century, the federal government has regulated colleges' and universities' handling of campus sexual and gender-based violence (CSGBV). Although the arc of history has bent toward establishing greater protections for victims of such violence, new proposed regulation by the U.S. Department of Education under the Trump administration focuses more heavily on ensuring due process rights for students accused of CSGBV. Most recently, in November 2018, U.S. Secretary of Education, Betsy DeVos submitted a proposed rule change to the regulation of *Title IX of the Education Amendments of 1972*. This article provides the historical context for this most recent proposed federal regulation of CSGBV and discusses the criticism of this proposal that, if it is implemented, students would become less safe in the ivory tower.

Under President Barack Obama's administration, the federal government cast light on the dark side of the ivory tower – the prevalence of campus sexual and gender-based violence (CSGBV[1]) – with an unprecedented degree of attention (Butler, Kulig, Fisher, & Wilcox, 2019). During the course of the Obama era, the federal government provided new policy directives and legislation on how colleges and universities address, investigate, and adjudicate disclosures and complaints in CSGBV cases, especially under Title IX of the Education Amendments of 1972 (herein, Title IX). Their activities include the publication of the 2011 Dear Colleague Letter (U.S. Department of Education, Office for Civil Rights [OCR], 2011), the passage of the 2013 Campus Sexual Violence Elimination Act (SaVE Act), and, in 2014, the establishment of the White House Task Force to Protect Students from Sexual Assault and launch of the "It's on Us" social media campaign (Butler et al., 2019; It's on Us, n.d.). Collectively, these initiatives aimed to raise awareness of CSGBV, to implement evidence-informed preventative measures, and to expand services and protections for CSGBV victims (Butler et al., 2019; Kaukinen, Miller, & Powers, 2017).

Federal legislation, regulation, and guidance on CSGBV not only shapes how colleges and universities that receive federal funding respond to this problem, but also is itself a response to the claims of key stakeholders, including grassroots student-focused activists (e.g., Clery Center, End Rape on Campus, Take Back the Night), and of violence scholars and their four decades of research (e.g., Banyard, Plante, & Moynihan, 2005; Fisher, Cullen, & Turner, 2000; Koss & Oros, 1982; Krebs et al., 2011). Thus, governance, activism, and research contribute to the social construction of the problem of CSGBV and the resulting responses to the problem. The seeds of the efforts of government officials, activists, and researchers emerged in the 1970s and continue strong today.

Under President Donald Trump's administration, the attention on CSGBV remains, but the goals of the federal response have diverged from the victim-centered goals of the Obama administration. Specifically, Trump's Secretary of Education, Betsy DeVos, has rescinded the 2011 Dear Colleague Letter on Sexual Violence (herein, 2011 Letter; OCR, 2011), issued new federal guidance on CSGBV, and proposed a rule change to the application of Title IX to CSGBV. Each of DeVos's actions shifts the attention on CSGBV to focus less heavily on prevention efforts and protections for these victims and more on requirements for the protection of due process rights for students who are accused of committing an act of sexual misconduct[2] (OCR, 2017b; Saul & Goldstein, 2017).

The first of these actions, rescinding the 2011 Letter, effectively eliminated the Obama-era guidance that defined the acts that are considered sexual assault, and "supplement[ed] the [2001 Revised Sexual Harassment Guidance] by providing additional guidance and practical examples" regarding how campuses are required to handle sexual assault under Title IX (OCR, 2011, p. 2). In the 2017 Dear Colleague Letter (herein, 2017 Letter) announcing that the 2011 Letter had been rescinded, the OCR argued that the 2011 Letter guidance required standards that were more stringent than those many schools already had in place, "led to the deprivation of rights for many students," and "imposed regulatory burdens without affording notice and the opportunity for public comment" (OCR, 2017a, p. 2). In the same 2017 Letter, the OCR announced the publication of *Q&A on Campus Sexual Misconduct* (herein, 2017 Q&A; OCR, 2017b). The 2017 Q&A provided new interim guidance that was later integrated into a proposed change to the regulation of Title IX that DeVos submitted to the Federal Register in November 2018 (Nondiscrimination on the Basis of Sex, 2018). This regulatory change would alter how schools that receive federal funding are required to respond to CSGBV cases, with several aspects of this change intended to expand protections to the due process rights of students accused of CSGBV (Nondiscrimination on the Basis of Sex, 2018).

In this article, we describe the changes and proposed changes that DeVos has made to federal CSGBV policy and guidance. We begin with an overview of how federal legislation, regulation, and guidance has shaped the collegiate response to CSGBV since the passage of Title IX in 1972 through the end of Obama's presidency in 2017. We also describe the social context in which such governance during this period unfolded. We then describe the efforts under the Trump administration to rollback this prior legislation and administrative guidance, in particular those issued during the Obama era. Finally, we discuss some of the responses from key stakeholders who claim college students will be less safe in the ivory tower should DeVos's proposed regulatory changes be implemented.

Historical developments in federal regulation of the collegiate response to CSGBV

Although the prevalence of CSGBV has been documented since the late 1950s (Kirkpatrick & Kanin, 1957; Koss, Gidycz, & Wisniewski, 1987; Koss & Oros, 1982), the federal government has not always been involved in shaping how campus administrators respond to this violence (Sloan & Fisher, 2011). In the 1960s and 1970s as part of the broader feminist movement, women founded grassroots organizations, such as Take Back the Night ("the first worldwide effort to combat sexual violence and violence against women," which began in the 1970s in the United States; Take Back the Night Foundation, n.d., para. 1), and the National Women's Law Center (founded 1972; National Women's Law Center, n.d.).

Shortly following the emergence of these grassroots advocacy organizations, legislation was passed in the late 20th century that provided the groundwork upon which federal policy on CSGBV is built today. This next section traces the history of federal regulation of the collegiate response to sexual assault, beginning with the passage of Title IX of the Education Amendments of 1972 and Title II of the Student Right-to-Know and Campus Security Act of 1990, then moves to a discussion of federal responses under the Bush and Obama administrations in the early 2000s, and finally describes the most recent actions and proposed actions by the Trump administration. Figure 1 presents key events along this timeline. We argue that the Trump administration's response to CSGBV is rooted in the federal government's decades-long struggle to address the issues concerning the reporting of and response to sexual and gender-based violence against college students.

Federal regulation of the collegiate response to CSGBV in the 20th century

Prior to the start of the Obama presidency in January 2009, the major pieces of federal legislation that governed colleges' and universities' responses to CSGBV were Title IX and Title II of the Student Right-to-Know and Campus Security Act (1990) – renamed the Jeanne Clery Disclosure of Campus Security Policy and Campus Crime Statistics Act in

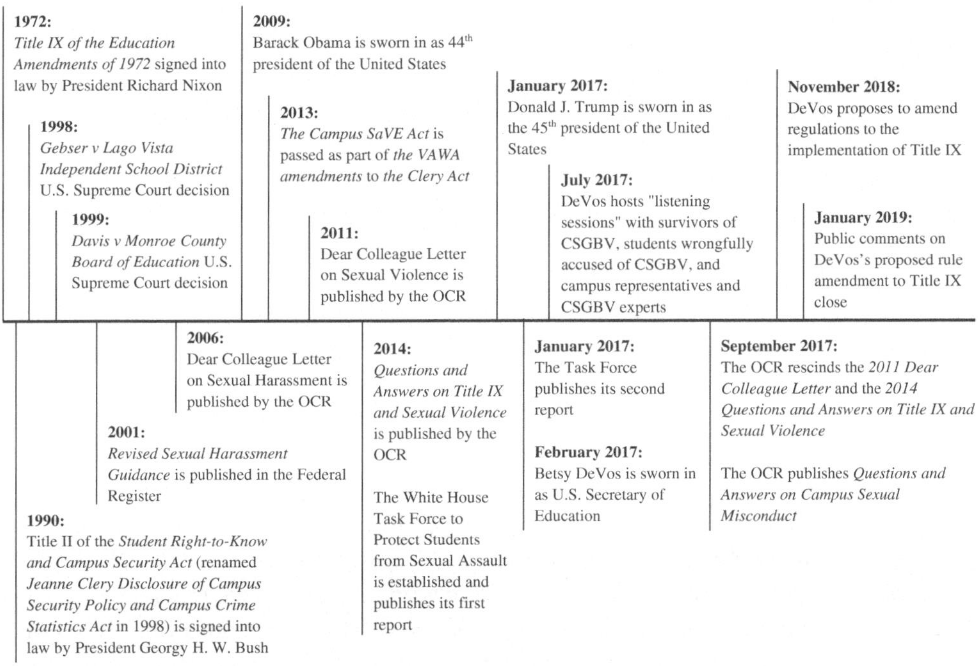

Figure 1. Milestones in federal policy on campus sexual assault and harassment.

1998 (herein, Clery Act; Jeanne Clery Disclosure of Campus Security Policy and Campus Crime Statistics Act of 1998; McCallion, 2014). Although the DeVos administration has not yet proposed to Congress changes to the regulation of latter, the Clery Act is an important avenue through which federal policy on campus sexual assault may be affected.

Jeanne Clery was raped and murdered in her dorm room on the Lehigh University campus in April 1986 (Sloan & Fisher, 2011). After her death, Jeanne's parents, Connie and Howard Clery founded the Clery Center (formerly Security on Campus, Inc.), a grassroots organization that advocated for improving student safety and awareness of crime on college campuses (Sloan & Fisher, 2011). The Clerys and the Clery Center lobbied in Congress and were successful in 1990 when George H. W. Bush signed the bill into law. The Clery Act requires all institutions of higher education that participate in Higher Education Act Title IV financial assistance programs to annually report campus crime statistics and campus security policies (Clery Center, 2019; McCallion, 2014). These annual reports not only contribute to public awareness of campus crime and security issues but can also serve as the fact basis for federal guidance and regulation (see e.g., Nondiscrimination on the Basis of Sex, 2018; OCR, 2011). Additionally, the Clery Act definition of sexual assault, "an offense that meets the definition of rape, fondling, incest, or statutory rape as used in the FBI's UCR program," is used in the other federal guidance, regulation, and policy discussed in this article. Thus, any changes to the Clery Act itself or to its regulation could impact the collection of crime data that serves as the fact basis for other legislation, regulation, and guidance on campus sexual assault. It is unknown whether DeVos will propose changes to the Clery Act before the 2020 election, but any such changes to the law itself (as opposed to changes to the administrative regulation of the law) would require Congressional approval (USAGov, 2019).

More central to our review of federal guidance, regulation, and policy on campus sexual assault is Title IX. Title IX states that "no person in the United States shall, on the basis of sex, be excluded from participation in, be denied the benefits of, or be subjected to discrimination under any education program or activity receiving federal financial assistance" (Education Amendments of 1972, p. 995). Congress's motivation for the passage of Title IX in 1972 was to address broad sex discrimination by educational institutions, including women's "limited access to educational programs" and exclusion "from 'male' programs, such as medicine" (U.S. Department of Justice, 2012, p. 2). However, in the late 1990s, two Supreme Court decisions drew attention to the application of Title IX to sexual harassment.

First, in *Gebser v. Lago Vista Independent School District* (herein, *Gebser*; 1998) the Supreme Court ruled that "a school can be liable for monetary damages if a teacher sexually harasses a student, an official who has authority to address the harassment has actual knowledge of the harassment, and that official is deliberately indifferent in responding to the harassment" (Revised Sexual Harassment Guidance, 2000, p. 66092). Then, in *Davis v. Monroe County Board of Education* (herein, *Davis;* 1999), the Court held that schools could be held liable for monetary damages in cases of student-on-student sexual harassment that meet the *Gebser* criteria (Revised Sexual Harassment Guidance, 2000). These Supreme Court decisions are referenced throughout the major federal guidance and regulations issued throughout the 2000s (see e.g., Nondiscrimination on the Basis of Sex, 2018; OCR, 2001, 2011, 2017b). It is to the federal regulatory activity during the first decade of the new millennium that we now turn.

Federal regulation of the collegiate response to CSGBV: 2000-2010

Early federal guidance and landmark research

A key piece of guidance from the federal government was issued by the OCR during George W. Bush's presidency in response to the *Gebser* and *Davis* decisions. In 2001, the OCR issued the *Revised Sexual Harassment Guidance* (herein, 2001 Revised Guidance). The 2001 Revised Guidance largely reaffirmed principles of the 1997 *Sexual Harassment Guidance* (herein, 1997 Guidance) but also issued new clarification of the 1997 Guidance in light of the *Gebser* and *Davis* decisions. The 2001 Revised Guidance also defined sexual harassment as "unwelcome sexual advances, requests for sexual favors, and other verbal, nonverbal, or physical conduct of a sexual nature" and clarified that "sexual harassment of a student can deny or limit, on the basis of sex, the student's ability to participate in or receive benefits, services, or opportunities in the school's program" (OCR, 2001, p. 2). Another key clarification was that "if the alleged harassment is sufficiently serious to create a hostile environment and it is the school's failure to comply with the procedural requirements of the Title IX regulations that hampers early notification and intervention and permits sexual harassment," the school would be responsible to "take corrective action, including stopping the harassment, preventing its recurrence, and remedying the effects of the harassment on the victim" (OCR, 2001, p. 14).

In addition to the 2001 Revised Guidance, the first few years of the new millennium were also marked by the publication of landmark research findings from studies funded by the National Institute of Justice (NIJ) and Bureau of Justice Statistics (BJS) in the U.S. Department of Justice (for an extensive review, see Butler et al., 2019; Kaukinen et al., 2017). Building from Koss's seminal work during the 1980s (Koss et al., 1987; Koss & Oros, 1982), Fisher et al. (2000) published *The Sexual Victimization of College Women*, which reported their findings from a "telephone survey of a randomly selected, national sample of 4,446 women who were attending a 2- or 4-year college or university during fall 1996" (p. 3). The study showed that 2.8% of female college students "had experienced either a completed … or attempted rape incident" which translates to "27.7 rapes per 1,000 female students" (Fisher et al., 2000, p. 10). Though these were not the first national-level estimates of the sexual victimization of college women, these estimates of the victimization rates of college women provided further empirical evidence to support the claims of activists that campus sexual assault was indeed a widespread social problem (Sloan & Fisher, 2011). Then, in 2000, Karjane, Fisher, and Cullen were funded by the NIJ to execute a nationwide study to examine, among other issues, Title IV's school's compliance with the Clery Act. Published in 2002, their results revealed nationwide inconsistencies in the reporting of campus crime statistics, the existence of campus sexual assault policies, the training of school officials and students on responding to sexual assault, and the implementation of sexual assault awareness education by colleges and universities (Karjane, Fisher, & Cullen, 2002). These findings showed that although campus sexual assault had been recognized as a social problem, the campuses' efforts to address the problem were lacking, at best, and absent, at worst.

In the years following the publication of these landmark studies, the federal government reaffirmed its concern about campus sexual assault when Congress funded three additional large-scale studies of campus sexual assault: (1) the Campus Sexual Assault study (Krebs, Lindquist, Warner, Fisher, & Martin, 2007); (2) Drug-Facilitated, Incapacitated, and Forcible Rape: A National Study (Kilpatrick, Resnick, Ruggiero, Conoscenti, & McCauley, 2007); and (3) the Historically Black Colleges and Universities

Campus Sexual Assault Study (Krebs et al., 2011). The federal government also reaffirmed its interest in campus sexual assault when the OCR issued a Dear Colleague Letter in January 2006, which reiterated the 2001 Revised Guidance and announced that the OCR planned to "conduct compliance reviews related to sexual harassment in schools" (OCR, 2006, para. 6).

The 2011 Dear Colleague Letter

The government's response to CSGBV reached unprecedented heights when the Obama-era OCR amended the 2001 Revised Guidance (OCR, 2001) with the issuance of the 2011 Letter (OCR, 2011). The 2011 Letter stated that Title IX prohibition of sexual harassment also prohibits a broader range of acts which constitute sexual violence, defined as "physical sexual acts perpetrated against a person's will or where a person is incapable of giving consent due to the victim's use of drugs or alcohol … [or] due to the victim's intellectual or other disability" (OCR, 2011, p. 1). This definition expanded the purview of Title IX beyond cases that meet the aforementioned definition of sexual harassment provided by the 2001 Revised Guidance by including cases in which the victim was incapable of giving consent. The OCR argued that these changes to federal guidance were made in the interest of victims of all forms of sexual violence, to ensure "that all students feel safe in their school, so that they have the opportunity to benefit fully from the school's programs and activities" (OCR, 2011, p. 2). However, critics of the 2011 Letter have expressed that there are a range of issues with the 2011 Letter's guidance.

First, the 2011 Letter explains that schools are required to publish nondiscrimination policies and recommends that these policies specifically state that sexual harassment and sexual violence are prohibited. The OCR also explains that schools must have grievance procedures in place by which students can report sexual harassment or sexual violence, that these procedures must be published publicly, and that Title IX coordinators and school law enforcement officers must be trained to understand these procedures. Although these points largely reaffirm the 2001 Revised Guidance, perhaps the most controversial new provision of the 2011 Letter is its statement that "in order for a school's grievance procedures to be consistent with Title IX standards, the school must use a preponderance of the evidence standard (i.e., it is more likely than not that sexual harassment or violence occurred)" (OCR, 2011, p. 11). Whereas prior to the 2011 Letter the OCR had no set requirement for the standard of evidence in grievance procedures, the 2011 requirement meant that schools using the clear and convincing standard of evidence ("i.e., it is highly probable or reasonably certain that the sexual harassment or violence occurred") or higher standards would be required to use the lower standard (OCR, 2011, p. 11).

The OCR (2011) justified this change by explaining that the Supreme Court "has applied a preponderance of the evidence standard in civil litigation involving discrimination under Title VII of the Civil Rights Act" and that the OCR itself uses this evidence standard "when resolving allegations of discrimination under all the statutes enforced by OCR, including Title IX" (pp. 10–11). On one hand, proponents of the change argued that the preponderance of the evidence standard is "the only standard that reflects the integrity of equitable student conduct processes which treat all students with respect and fundamental fairness" (Loschiavo & Waller, 2017). On the other hand, critics argued that the change was inappropriate because "Congress had already rejected legislation that lowered the standard" (i.e., an early version of the Campus SaVE Act) and because it can have "negative effects, such as the stripping away of the accused student's presumption of innocence" (Rice, 2018, pp. 774, 776). These arguments will be echoed in our discussion of the DeVos administration's criticism of the 2011 Letter.

Second, the 2011 Letter describes "steps to prevent sexual harassment and sexual violence and correct its discriminatory effects on the complainant and others" that it recommends schools to implement (OCR, 2011, p. 14). These include education and prevention programs such as "orientation programs for new students, faculty, staff, and employees" as well as additional training for other students, including residence assistants and athletes (p. 14). The Letter goes on to describe "remedies for the complainant" when they become aware of an incident of sexual harassment or violence, such as counseling and medical services, tutoring, or arranging to limit contact between the complainant and the alleged perpetrator (p. 16). Critics argue that the 2011 Letter's guidance that schools ensure their remedies "minimize the burden on the complainant" can place a burden on the alleged perpetrator (Rice, 2018, p. 775).

Third, critics argue that guidance from the 2011 Letter infringes upon the due process rights of students accused of sexual harassment or sexual violence (Rice, 2018). The 2001 Revised Guidance included a section that described the due process rights of those accused of sexual harassment and the 2011 Letter reiterates this section, stating that "public and state-supported schools must provide due process to the alleged perpetrator. However, schools should ensure that steps taken to accord due process rights to the alleged perpetrator do not restrict or unnecessarily delay the Title IX protections for the complainant" (OCR, 2011, p. 12). Although this statement is repeated almost verbatim from the 2001 Revised Guidance, Rice (2018) criticizes the 2011 Letter because it does not include a specific section on due process rights of the accused, because only two sentences in the 2011 Letter discuss due process.

However, this criticism should be considered in light of the facts that a Dear Colleague Letter is a distinct document from a final rule submitted to the Federal Register (as is the 2001 Revised Guidance), that the 2011 Letter includes a footnote directing readers to the explanation of due process in the 2001 Revised Guidance, and that the section devoted to due process in the 2001 Revised Guidance is only six sentences longer than the two-sentence explanation included by the 2011 Letter. Perhaps the strongest counterpoint to this criticism is that the 2011 Letter did not *add* to or *change* any guidance on due process rights of the accused provided in the 2001 Revised Guidance. Despite these criticisms, the Obama administration and activists continued to work toward greater protections for victims of CSGBV throughout the remainder of Obama's tenure as President, and social scientists continued to probe the question of how to best prevent CSGBV by conducting empirical research.

Federal regulation of the collegiate response to CSGBV: 2012-2017

The 2013 Campus SaVE Act was part of the 2013 Violence Against Women Reauthorization Act (VAWA, 2013) amendments (Sec. 304 of S. 47) to the Clery Act. One notable characteristic of the SaVE Act is that, in light of research that showed bystander intervention training programs had promising effects on increasing students' use of intervention strategies and decreasing students' support for rape myths (e.g., Banyard et al., 2005; Coker et al., 2011), it requires schools to provide "primary prevention and awareness programs for all incoming students and new employees" and "safe and positive options for bystander intervention" (Campus Sexual Violence Elimination Act, 2013, p. 90). Thus, the Campus SaVE Act represents a data-driven approach by the federal government to prevent CSGBV.

In the same year, college students founded the activist organizations Know Your IX and End Rape on Campus (End Rape on Campus, n.d.; Know Your IX, n.d.-b). Know Your IX "is a survivor- and youth-led project ... that aims to empower students to end sexual and dating violence in their schools" (Know Your IX, n.d.-a, para. 1). One of their activities is to educate students about "their legal rights to safe educations free from gender-based harms" afforded to them under Title IX (Know Your IX, n.d.-a, para. 3). End Rape on Campus "works to end campus sexual violence through direct support for survivors and their communities; prevention through education; and policy reform at the campus, local, state, and federal level" (End Rape on Campus, n.d., para. 1). These dedicated activist efforts, among others, have been instrumental in amplifying the voices of survivors of CSGBV and in advocating for "federal accountability for Title IX ... and Clery Act enforcement" (End Rape on Campus, n.d., para. 5).

Also influential have been the contributions of researchers from a range of disciplines who research the measurement, predictors, consequences, and prevention of CSGBV. Over this time period, researchers developed and administered campus climate surveys that would update and improve upon the validity of the prevalence and incidence estimates of CSGBV. Their efforts include the Administrator Researcher Campus Climate Collaborative (ARC3), the Campus Climate Survey Validation Study (CCSVS; Krebs, Lindquist, Berzofsky, Shook-Sa, & Peterson, 2016), and the Association of American Universities Climate Survey on Sexual Assault and Sexual Misconduct (Cantor et al., 2017). The results of these surveys have shown that a substantial number of college students experience CSGBV during their college tenure, with many being recurring victims (Kaasa, Fisher, Cantor, & Townsend, 2016) and have extended prior knowledge by showing that non-cisgender students are at a higher risk for sexual assault, stalking, and intimate partner violence than are cisgender students (Cantor et al., 2017).

To further clarify the guidance provided by the 2011 Letter, the OCR (2014) published *Questions and Answers on Title IX and Sexual Violence* (herein, 2014 Q&A). The 2014 Q&A also suggested "proactive efforts schools can take to prevent sexual violence" (p. ii) and responded to some of the contentious issues related to sexual violence complaints, such as the potential for retaliation against complainants. The 2014 Q&A also clarifies that "Title IX protects all students at recipient institutions from sex discrimination, including sexual violence" including "elementary to professional school students; male and female students; straight, gay, lesbian, and transgender students; part-time and full-time students; students with and without disabilities; and students of different races and national origins" (OCR, 2014, p. 5).

On January 22, 2014, the Obama administration established the White House Task Force to Protect Students from Sexual Assault (herein, Task Force). In response to research that showed as many as one-in-five of the college women surveyed "reported experiencing attempted or completed sexual assault since entering college" (Krebs et al., 2007, p. 53), the Task Force was established "with a mandate to strengthen federal enforcement efforts and provide schools with additional tools to combat sexual assault on their campuses" (White House Task Force to Protect Students from Sexual Assault, 2014, p. 6). In April 2014, the Task Force published *Not Alone: The First Report from the*

White House Task Force to Protect Students from Sexual Assault. This report recommended the expansion of campus climate surveys to collect information on the prevalence and incidence of CSGBV, further implementation of sustained prevention programs such as bystander intervention training, and the establishment of campus sexual misconduct policies that protect survivors' confidentiality when reporting victimization (White House Task Force to Protect Students from Sexual Assault, 2014).

In *The Second Report of the White House Task Force to Protect Students from Sexual Assault,* published in January 2017, the Task Force identified "six primary elements that should be considered when a school is developing their comprehensive plan to address sexual assault" including "1. Coordinated campus and community response; 2. Prevention and education; 3. Policy development and implementation; 4. Reporting options, advocacy, and support services; 5. Climate surveys, performance measurement, and evaluation; and 6. Transparency" (White Task Force to Protect Students from Sexual Assault, 2017, p. 7). This Task Force report describes at length how schools can implement each of these elements.

As of the writing of this article, there is no information on the White House website about the Task Force (aside from the archived 2014 and 2017 reports), thus the Task Force may have been disbanded when Obama left office. However, as alluded to throughout our discussion, the Trump administration has not abandoned interest in CSGBV. The next section details the changes and proposed changes to federal guidance, regulation, and legislation on campus sexual assault over the course of the Trump presidency thus far.

Federal CSGBV policy under the Trump administration

On February 7, 2017 – hours after Vice President Mike Pence cast the tie-breaking vote in the U.S. Senate to confirm Betsy DeVos's appointment to the position – she was sworn in as U.S. Secretary of Education (Boyer, 2017). The current administration's stated goals for the Department of Education (DOEd) focus primarily on making changes to federal policy on educational choice at the K-12 level and on reducing the "federal footprint in education" (DeVos, 2018, para. 3; see also, DeVos, 2017). However, DeVos's actions beginning in July 2017 suggest that the Trump administration views CSGBV as a problem from which the federal government cannot simply step away. The current section describes the actions DeVos has taken in her two-and-a-half-year tenure as Secretary of Education that are related to the issue of CSGBV (i.e., the listening sessions on the impact of Title IX sexual assault guidance, 2017 Dear Colleague Letter, and the 2018 proposed amendment to the regulation of the implementation of Title IX) and the OCR's stated reasoning and goals underlying these actions.

Listening sessions on the Department of Education's Title IX sexual assault guidance

In July 2017, DeVos's first move related to CSGBV as Secretary of Education was to hold three "listening sessions" to "discuss the impact of the Department's Title IX sexual assault guidance on students, families and institutions" (U.S. Department of Education, 2017, para. 1). The first session included nine students who were sexual assault survivors, represented by eight different organizations (U.S. Department of Education, 2017).[3] The second session focused on "students who have been falsely accused and disciplined under Title IX" and included seven student and two parent participants represented by three different organizations (U.S. Department of Education, 2017, para. 6).[4] The third session included 19 "representatives of educational institutions and subject matter experts" (U.S. Department of Education, 2017, para. 8).

As with the response to previous efforts by the federal government to address CSGBV, the reactions to DeVos's listening sessions were bifurcated. On one hand, proponents of the listening sessions expressed satisfaction that DeVos listened to students who had been wrongfully accused of committing CSGBV (Young, 2017). For example, one student who participated in the listening sessions and said he was falsely accused of sexual assault referred to the listening session as "uplifting" and stated that "it was a moment where you felt like you were finally being seen" (Reilly, 2017, para. 4). On the other hand, critics bemoaned that DeVos did not give equal attention to victims of CSGBV as she did to wrongfully accused students, who were represented by men's rights groups that have been marked as misogynistic and even hostile (Reilly, 2017).

After these listening sessions, DeVos referred to the day as "emotionally draining," (Guild, 2017, para. 4) and stated to reporters, "There are some things that are working. There are many things that are not working well … We need to get this right" (Kreighbaum, 2017, para. 3). She also said that there are "substantive legal questions [regarding Title IX] to be addressed, including the evidentiary standard, due process, and lack of public input" (Guild, 2017, para. 8). These three points would become the focus of the 2017 Dear Colleague Letter that marked DeVos's first change to federal guidance on CSGBV.

The 2017 Dear Colleague Letter

Following these listening sessions, on September 22, 2017, the OCR announced in a new Dear Colleague Letter (herein, 2017 Letter; OCR, 2017a) that it had rescinded the 2011 Letter and the 2014 Q&A. At the same time, the OCR announced the publication of *Q&A on Campus Sexual Misconduct* (herein, 2017 Q&A; OCR, 2017b). This document described schools' legal obligations to respond to sexual misconduct, and provided guidelines for the adjudication, decision-making, and appeals of sexual misconduct cases (OCR, 2017b).

The 2017 Q&A largely reverted guidance back to the 2001 Revised Guidance. However, the Q&A also provided specific guidance on the three problems DeVos claimed the 2011 Letter created. First, with regard to the evidentiary standard, the 2017 Q&A states that schools should use "either a preponderance of the evidence standard or a clear and convincing evidence standard" (OCR, 2017b, p. 5) but, in a footnote, goes on to explain that schools should use the same standard of evidence in sexual misconduct cases that they use in all other misconduct cases. The OCR (2017b) argues that "when a school applies special procedures in sexual misconduct cases," such as using a lower standard of evidence, "it suggests a discriminatory purpose and should be avoided" (p. 5). The 2017 Q&A also notes that schools are required to disclose the standard of evidence used in sexual misconduct cases in their annual Clery Act security reports.

The 2017 Q&A only discusses due process in a footnote, but notably, mentions that the "OCR has previously informed schools that it is permissible to allow an appeal only for the responding [(i.e., accused)] party" (OCR, 2017b, p. 7). This is a departure from the 2014 Q&A guidance, which stated that "if the school provides for an appeal, it must do so equally for both parties" (OCR, 2014, p. 26).

Finally, demonstrating its contrasting approach to the Obama administration's issuance of guidance outside of the rulemaking and public comment process, the 2017 Q&A states that "the Department intends to engage in rulemaking on the topic" at hand and "will solicit input from stakeholders and the public during that rulemaking process" (OCR, 2017b, p. 1). The OCR followed through on this promise with their proposal to amend the regulation of Title IX.

The 2018 proposed amendment to regulation of the implementation of Title IX

On November 29, 2018, DeVos submitted to the Federal Register a proposal to amend the regulations on the implementation of Title IX (herein referred to as the proposed rule; Nondiscrimination on the Basis of Sex, 2018). In the summary of the proposed rule, the OCR states that modifications and clarifications are made "pertaining to the availability of remedies for violations, the effect of Constitutional protections, the designation of a coordinator to address sex discrimination issues, the dissemination of a nondiscrimination policy, the adoption of grievance procedures, and the processes to claim a religious exemption" (Nondiscrimination on the Basis of Sex, 2018, p. 61462). Ultimately, the OCR claims that these amendments are "intended to promote the purpose of Title IX by requiring recipients to address sexual harassment, assisting and protecting victims of sexual harassment and *ensuring that due process protections are in place for individuals accused of sexual harassment*" (Nondiscrimination on the Basis of Sex, 2018, p. 61462, emphasis added).

This third stated goal is distinct from prior Title IX guidance and regulation not in that due process protections have been ignored previously (they have been included in prior OCR guidance), but in that due process rights of the accused have not been at the forefront of prior guidance and regulation. Thus, a major highlight of the proposed rule is its heightened attention to the due process rights of accused students. Confirming due process rights of the accused as a key goal of the proposed rule, DeVos stated that "every survivor of sexual violence must be taken seriously; and every student accused of sexual misconduct must know that guilt is not predetermined" (U.S. Department of Education, 2018, para. 2).

In a press release on the day the rule was proposed, the DOEd highlighted key provisions of the proposed rule and announced the 60-day period during which the proposal would be open for public comments to be submitted to the Federal Register (U.S. Department of Education, 2018). The public comment period closed on January 28, 2019, with many comments that infer from published research that the proposed Title IX rule change would negatively impact the safety of students on college and university campuses (Kreighbaum, 2019). The following section identifies the main rule changes to Title IX regulation that the DeVos administration has proposed and discusses concerns with these changes that have been voiced by two organizations made up of key stakeholders in the issue of CSGBV.

Less safe in the ivory tower: key stakeholders' responses to the proposed rule changes under the Trump administration

As of July 14, 2019, a total of 124,152 comments on DeVos's proposed rule were submitted to the Federal Register over the course of the 60-day comment period. To date, no comprehensive summary of all of the comments has been published. Although we are unable to provide a comprehensive discussion of the public comments, we have identified two extensive response letters that were submitted to the Federal Register by the Division of Women and Crime (DWC) of the American Criminological Society and by the Campus Advocacy & Prevention Professionals Association (CAPPA). The concerns of these letters are largely overlapping and can be summarized by three main points: (1) Title IX regulation under the proposed amendment would be a significant departure from prior regulation of Title IX and from data-driven policies and practices regarding CSGBV; (2) The proposed amendment would limit the scope of a school's responsibility to respond to sexual harassment; and (3) The changes would create harms to victims of sexual harassment. These concerns are discussed in the following sections.

Departure from prior guidance, regulation, and research

The CAPPA (2019) and the DWC (2019) argue that the proposed rule is a significant departure from prior guidance and regulation of Title IX, including the 1997 Guidance, the 2001 Revised Guidance, the 2011 Letter, and the 2014 Q&A. These departures include the proposed rule that would limit schools' responsibility to respond to sexual harassment that "occurs outside of a recipient's program or activity" (CAPPA, 2019, p. 15), the allowance for schools to implement "unregulated 'mediation' processes in lieu of investigations" (DWC, 2019, p. 6), and the allowance for "schools to delay investigations of sexual harassment" while "concurrent law enforcement investigation is ongoing" (DWC, 2019, p. 14). Further, the DWC claims that these major shifts in regulation would harm complainants. In addition to moving away from prior regulation, the DWC and CAPPA argue that the proposed rule ignores or even directly contradicts the practices that are supported by empirical research for investigating and adjudicating CSGBV cases. This first issue, the proposed rule's departure from prior guidance and research, is an overarching concern that applies to the additional issues that the DWC and CAPPA identified.

Limiting the scope of schools' responsibility to respond to CSGBV

Several of the proposed rule changes would limit the scope of schools' responsibility to respond to reports of CSGBV. First, the proposed rule changes the definition of sexual harassment. Under the 2011 Letter's guidance, schools are responsible to address an act of "harassing conduct ... [that] is sufficiently serious that it interferes with or limits a student's ability to participate in or benefit from the school's program" (OCR, 2011, p. 3). Under the proposed rule, sexual harassment is defined more narrowly as "unwelcome sexual conduct; or unwelcome conduct on the basis of sex that is so severe, pervasive, and objectively offensive that it effectively denies a person equal access to the recipient's education program or activity" (Nondiscrimination on the Basis of Sex, 2018, p. 61466). The definition of sexual harassment is also limited in the proposed rule, as it must occur within an institution's "education program or activity" and, for this reason, schools could avoid liability for responding to "a significant amount of sexual harassment such as incidents that occur in off-campus housing, online, or among students studying abroad" (DWC, 2019, p. 11). Again, this rule change would ignore research that shows a small minority of students who are sexually assaulted are victimized while at school or on their commute to/from school (e.g., Fisher et al., 2000; Sinozich & Langton, 2014).

Second, under the proposed rule, schools would only be liable to respond to sexual harassment if a complaint is made to the school's Title IX coordinator. As CAPPA (2019) points out, this would exempt schools from their responsibility to address sexual harassment cases that are reported to other school officials (including those who are required by the Clery Act to report the incident to the institution) and would be impractical for large institutions in which an unreasonable number of cases would fall under the purview of a single person. Further, the proposed rule requires that, in grievance procedures, "any individual designated by a recipient as a coordinator, investigator, or decision-maker not have a conflict of interest or bias for or against complainants or respondents generally or an individual complainant or respondent" (Nondiscrimination on the Basis of Sex, 2018, p. 61497). This standard would be difficult to meet if Title IX coordinators who have a background in victim advocacy or other related fields could be considered as having a general bias (CAPPA, 2019).

Third, "the proposed guidance would allow schools to adopt a 'clear and convincing standard' for sexual harassment complainants" rather than the preponderance of the evidence standard set by the 2011 Letter (DWC, 2019, p. 8). As the DWC (2019) explains, "Universities are not criminal courts of law. Higher levels of proof are required in criminal court because of the possible sanctions" (p. 8). The CAPPA (2019) also criticizes the clear and convincing standard because schools, unlike law enforcement, do not have the investigative resources to gather evidence to meet the clear and convincing standard and because this "singles out victims of sexual harassment and abuse for uniquely less protection than victims of race- or disability-based discrimination" (p. 26).

Creating potential for harms to victims of CSGBV

The third overarching criticism of the responses from the CAPPA and the DWC is that the proposed rule would create potential harms to victims of CSGBV. For example, the proposed rule would allow individual respondents (i.e., accused students) to claim that the interim supportive measures provided to the complainant cause unreasonable burden on them (CAPPA, 2019). According to the DWC (2019), this would "make it impossible for complainants to request that respondents be moved out of their dorm or classes as an interim accommodation" and this measure ignores "demonstrated psychological harm of allowing respondents to remain in classes and dorms with complainants" as well as "significant physical safety risk regarding revictimization of the complainant" (p. 20).

These potential harms to victims extend to the disciplinary process. The proposed rule would "require schools to establish procedures for live cross-examination of complainants and respondents by a party's advisor of choice" (DWC, 2019, p. 17). Both the DWC and the CAPPA note that live cross-examination, especially by individuals who are not trained in legal cross-examination, could retraumatize victims and create an unfair advantage to students who are able to secure legal counsel and that the DOEd "exceeds its authority by attempting to apply principals of criminal law to both regulatory compliance and school disciplinary settings" (CAPPA, 2019, p. 19). The process of cross-examining victims can also discourage victims from reporting. The proposed rule would also allow for informal, "unregulated 'mediation' processes in lieu of investigations" (DWC, 2019, p. 6). The DWC and CAPPA oppose this option and suggest that informal processes based on the restorative justice model would be a better alternative.

Conclusion

Two key points must be acknowledged in considering the changes to federal guidance on and regulation of campus's treatment of CSGBV. First, the proposed regulatory change under the Trump administration is different from the Obama-era response to campus sexual assault because it would impose *legal requirements* to how campuses respond to sexual assault, rather than guidance that cannot be legally enforced (such as that issued in the 2011 Letter). In the 2017 Letter, the Acting Assistant Secretary for OCR, Candice Jackson, criticized the 2011 Letter for failing to clarify Title IX requirements and for not undergoing the public review and comment required when a regulatory change is proposed to the Federal Register (OCR, 2017a). The 2017 Letter states that "the Department intends to implement" a policy that "responds to the concerns of stakeholders and that aligns with the purpose of Title IX to achieve fair access to educational benefits … through a rulemaking process that responds to public comment" (OCR, 2017a, p. 2). The Department followed through on this plan when they submitted the proposed Title IX rule change to the Federal Register.

Whereas a Dear Colleague Letter can be overridden by another Dear Colleague Letter, a final regulatory rule can only be altered by undergoing the same rulemaking procedure, which allows for review by the President and typically requires a 30 to 60-day (or longer) public comment period after a proposed rule change has been submitted to the Federal Register (Federal Register, n.d.). In order to publish a final rule, the agency must summarize the problem the rule is intended to address and the "facts and data the agency relies on," respond to criticism of the rule made in the public comments, and "[explain] why the agency did not choose other alternatives" (Federal Register, n.d., p. 7). After the final rule is published, it may still be subject to review by Congress, the President, and the Courts. Put simply, altering regulation is a lengthier process that involves more oversight by the public and by each branch of the federal government than issuing guidance does.

Second, although we highlight some of the responses to the proposed rule change, we cannot provide a comprehensive review of the public comments. There are more than 124,000 public comments on the proposed rule change. By contrast, for the 2001 *Revised Sexual Harassment Guidance*, the "OCR received approximately 11 comments representing approximately 15 organizations and individuals" (OCR, 2001, p. iii). All of the comments to the 2018 proposed rule change are available online to the public.[5] To our knowledge, the OCR has not yet publicly responded to the comments on the proposed rule change. The Federal Register's (n.d.) *A Guide to the Rulemaking Process* states that "at the end of the process, the agency must base its reasoning and conclusions on the rulemaking record, consisting of the comments, scientific data, expert opinions, and facts accumulated during the pre-rule and proposed rule stages" (p. 6). Further, "to move forward with a final rule, the agency must conclude that its proposed solution will help accomplish the goals or solve the problems identified [in the public comments]" (Federal Register, n.d., p. 6). Upon reviewing these comments, the DOEd may change the rule to address the issues raised in the public comments or it may terminate the rulemaking process without issuing a final rule (Federal Register, n.d.).

Although we do not yet know what DeVos's final rule will be (or if a final rule will be issued), federal policymakers will likely continue to grapple with developing and implementing policies that meet the goals of preventing and reducing CSGBV, ensuring the safety and wellbeing of survivors of such violence, and protecting the due process rights of students accused of perpetrating such violence. We argue that regardless of how an administration prioritizes these three goals, continued data collection via campus climate surveys will be imperative to developing evidence-based policies that address CSGBV. Additionally, just as grassroots activist organizations that seek to promote these goals have existed since well before the start of the Trump administration, these organizations will most likely continue to advocate for policy change throughout the Trump administration and throughout those that succeed it. Without their steadfast efforts at the federal level, students could be less safe in the ivory tower – a deeply troubling outcome for the nearly 20 million college students in the United States (National Center for Education Statistics, n.d.),

Notes

1. We use the term "campus sexual and gender-based violence" (CSGBV) to generally refer to acts that are encompassed by the terms "sexual harassment," "sexual assault," "sexual misconduct," "intimate partner violence," "stalking" and the various other terms used in the sources we reference. Where appropriate, we use the term that is used in the documents we reference.
2. This is the term used for CSGBV in the 2017 Dear Colleague Letter and 2017 Q&A on Campus Sexual Misconduct. Sexual misconduct includes "dating violence, domestic violence, sexual assault, or stalking" (OCR, 2017b, p. 2).
3. The participating organizations include End Rape on Campus, National Women's Law Center, Girls Inc., Liberty Education Forum, National Center for Transgender Equality, Rape Abuse Incest National Network, SurvJustice, and Human Rights Campaign (U.S. Department of Education, 2017).
4. National Coalition for Men Carolinas, Families Advocating for Campus Equality, and Stop Abusive and Violent Environments (U.S. Department of Education (2017)).
5. https://regulations.gov/docketBrowser?rpp=50&so=DESC&sb=postedDate&po=0&dct=PS&D=ED-2018-OCR-0064.

Disclosure statement

No potential conflict of interest was reported by the authors.

References

Banyard, V. L., Plante, E. G., & Moynihan, M. M. (2005). *Rape prevention through bystander education: Bringing a broader community perspective to sexual violence prevention* (Document No. 208701). Washington, DC: U.S. Department of Justice.

Boyer, D. (2017, February 7). DeVos sworn in as education secretary by Pence. *The Washington Times*. Retrieved from https://www.washingtontimes.com/news/2017/feb/7/betsy-devos-sworn-education-secretary-pence/

Butler, L. C., Kulig, T. C., Fisher, B. S., & Wilcox, P. (2019). Victimization at schools and on college and university campuses: Historical developments and applications of the opportunity framework. In M. D. Krohn, G. Penly Hall, A. J. Lizotte, & N. Hendrix (Eds.), *Handbook on crime and deviance* (pp. 53–84). Basingstoke, UK: Springer Nature.

Campus Advocacy & Prevention Professionals Association. (2019). *CAPPA letter to the Department of Education regarding the November 29, 2018 notice of proposed rulemaking amending regulations implementing Title IX of the Education Amendments of 1972.* Retrieved from https://static1.squarespace.com/static/55c37d16e4b02ce3fcfffd6e/t/5c521061bba22335f31ca40e/1548882020332/CAPPA+Title+IX+NPRM+Comment+%28links%29.pdf

Campus Sexual Violence Elimination Act, H.R. 812, 113rd Cong. (2013).

Cantor, D., Fisher, B., Chibnall, S. H., Townsend, R., Lee, H., Thomas, G., & Bruce, C. (2017). *Report on the AAU Campus Climate Survey on sexual assault and sexual misconduct (revised October 20, 2017).* Rockville, MD: Westat. Retrieved from https://www.aau.edu/sites/default/files/AAU-Files/Key-Issues/Campus-Safety/AAU-Campus-Climate-Survey-FINAL-10-20-17.pdf

Clery Center. (2019). *Summary of the Jeanne Clery Act.* Retrieved from https://clerycenter.org/policy-resources/the-clery-act/

Coker, A. L., Cook-Craig, P. G., Williams, C. M., Fisher, B. S., Clear, E. R., Garcia, L. S., & Hegge, L. M. (2011). Evaluation of Green Dot: An active bystander intervention to reduce sexual violence on college campuses. *Violence Against Women, 17,* 777–796. doi:10.1177/1077801211410264

Davis v. Monroe County Board of Education, 526 U.S. 629 (1999).

DeVos, B. (2017, June 6). Statement by Betsy DeVos Secretary of Education on the U.S. Department of Education fiscal year 2018 budget request. *U.S. Senate Committee on Appropriations.* Retrieved from https://www.appropriations.senate.gov/imo/media/doc/060617-DeVos-Testimony.pdf

DeVos, B. (2018, March 20). Prepared remarks by U.S. Secretary of Education Betsy DeVos on FY19 Budget. *U.S. Department of Education.* Retrieved from https://www.ed.gov/news/speeches/prepared-remarks-us-secretary-education-betsy-devos-fy19-budget

Division on Women and Crime. (2019). *DWC comment on the proposed changes to Title IX of the Education Amendments of 1972.* Retrieved from http://ascdwc.com/wp-content/uploads/2019/01/DWC_TitleIX_Commentary.pdf

Education Amendments of 1972, 20 U.S.C. ch. 38 § 1681 et seq. (1972).

End Rape on Campus. (n.d.). *Mission & vision.* Retrieved from https://endrapeoncampus.org/our-team-1

Federal Register. (n.d.) *A guide to the rulemaking process.* Retrieved from https://www.federalregister.gov/uploads/2011/01/the_rulemaking_process.pdf

Fisher, B. S., Cullen, F. T., & Turner, M. G. (2000). *The sexual victimization of college women* (Report No. NCJ182369). Washington, DC: U.S. Department of Justice. Retrieved from https://www.ncjrs.gov/pdffiles1/nij/182369.pdf

Gebser v. Lago Vista Independent School District, 524 U.S. 274 (1998).

Guild, B. (2017, July 13). DeVos looks to "hear from all sides" on campus sexual assault. *CBS News.* Retrieved from https://www.cbsnews.com/news/devos-looks-to-hear-from-all-sides-on-campus-sexual-assault/

It's on Us. (n.d.). *Our story.* Retrieved from https://www.itsonus.org/our-story/

Jeanne Clery Disclosure of Campus Security Policy and Campus Crime Statistics Act of 1998, 20 U.S.C. ch. 28 § 1092(f). (1998).

Kaasa, S., Fisher, B. S., Cantor, D., & Townsend, R. (2016). *Recurring victimization in the AAU Climate Survey on sexual assault and sexual misconduct.* Rockville, MD: Westat. Retrieved from https://www.aau.edu/sites/default/files/@%20Files/Climate%20Survey/Recurring%20Victimization%20in%20the%20AAU%20Climate%20Survey%20on%20Sexual%20Assault%20and%20Sexual%20Misconduct.pdf

Karjane, H. M., Fisher, B. S., & Cullen, F. T. (2002). *Campus sexual assault: How America's institutions of higher education respond, final report.* Washington, DC: National Institute of Justice. Retrieved from https://www.ncjrs.gov/pdffiles1/nij/grants/196676.pdf

Kaukinen, C., Miller, M., & Powers, R. A. (Eds.). (2017). *Addressing violence against women on college campuses*. Philadelphia, PA: Temple University Press.

Kilpatrick, D. G., Resnick, H. S., Ruggiero, K. J., Conoscenti, L. M., & McCauley, J. (2007). *Drug-facilitated, incapacitated, and forcible rape: A national study* (Report No. NCJ 219181). Charleston, SC: National Crime Victims Research & Treatment Center.

Kirkpatrick, C., & Kanin, E. (1957). Male sex aggression on a university campus. *American Sociological Review*, *22*, 52–58. doi:10.2307/2088765

Know Your IX. (n.d.-a). *Learn about Know Your IX*. Retrieved from https://www.knowyourix.org/about/

Know Your IX. (n.d.-b). *Our team*. Retrieved from https://www.knowyourix.org/our-team/

Koss, M. P., Gidycz, C. A., & Wisniewski, N. (1987). The scope of rape: Incidence and prevalence of sexual aggression and victimization in a national sample of higher education students. *Journal of Consulting and Clinical Psychology*, *55*, 162–170. doi:10.1037//0022-006x.55.2.162

Koss, M. P., & Oros, C. J. (1982). Sexual experiences survey: A research instrument investigating sexual aggression and victimization. *Journal of Consulting and Clinical Psychology*, *50*, 455–457. doi:10.1037//0022-006x.50.3.455

Krebs, C., Lindquist, C., Berzofsky, M., Shook-Sa, B., & Peterson, K. (2016). *Campus Climate Survey Validation Study final technical report*. Washington, DC: Bureau of Justice Statistics.

Krebs, C. P., Barrick, K., Lindquist, C. H., Crosby, C. M., Boyd, C., & Bogan, Y. (2011). The sexual assault of undergraduate women at historically black colleges and universities (HBCUs). *Journal of Interpersonal Violence*, *26*, 3640–3666. doi:10.1177/0886260511403759

Krebs, C. P., Lindquist, C. H., Warner, T. D., Fisher, B. S., & Martin, S. L. (2007). *The Campus Sexual Assault (CSA) study* (Document No. 221153). Washington, DC: National Institute of Justice.

Kreighbaum, A. (2017, July 14). DeVos hints at changes in Title IX enforcement. *Inside Higher Ed*. Retrieved from https://www.insidehighered.com/news/2017/07/14/after-full-day-meetings-title-ix-devos-says-improvements-needed

Kreighbaum, A. (2019, January 31). College groups blast DeVos Title IX proposal. *Inside Higher Ed*. Retrieved from https://www.insidehighered.com/news/2019/01/31/higher-ed-groups-call-major-changes-devos-title-ix-rule

Loschiavo, C., & Waller, J. L. (2017). The preponderance of evidence standard: Use in higher education campus conduct processes. *Association for Student Conduct Administration*. Retrieved from https://www.theasca.org/files/The%20Preponderance%20of%20Evidence%20Standard.pdf

McCallion, G. (2014). *History of the Clery Act: Fact sheet* (Congressional Research Service Report No. R43759). Retrieved from https://crsreports.congress.gov/product/pdf/R/R43759

National Center for Education Statistics (n.d.) *Fast facts*. Retrieved from https://nces.ed.gov/fastfacts/display.asp?id=372

National Women's Law Center. (n.d.). *NWLC about*. Retrieved from https://nwlc.org/about/

Nondiscrimination on the Basis of Sex in Education Programs or Activities Receiving Federal Financial Assistance, 83 Fed. Reg. 61,462 (proposed Nov. 29, 2018) (to be codified at 34 C.F.R. pt. 106).

Reilly, K. (2017, July 11). Accused students found Betsy DeVos' meetings on campus sexual assault 'uplifting'. Victim's advocates did not. *Time*. Retrieved from https://time.com/4857377/betsy-devos-campus-sexual-assault-meeting/

Revised Sexual Harassment Guidance: Harassment of Students by School Employees, Other Students, or Third Parties, 65 Fed. Reg. 66,092 (proposed Nov. 2, 2000).

Rice, K. (2018). Understanding the implications of the 2011 Dear Colleague Letter: Why colleges should not adjudicate on-campus sexual assault claims. *DePaul Law Review*, *67*, 763–792.

Saul, S., & Goldstein, D. (2017, September 7). Betsy DeVos says she will rewrite rules on campus sex assault. *The New York Times*. Retrieved from https://www.nytimes.com/2017/09/07/us/devos-campus-rape.html

Sinozich, S., & Langton, L. P. (2014). *Rape and sexual assault among college-age females, 1995–2013*. Retrieved from http://www.bjs.gov/content/pub/pdf/rsavcaf9513.pdf

Sloan, J. J., III, & Fisher, B. S. (2011). *The dark side of the ivory tower: Campus crime as a social problem*. New York, NY: Cambridge University Press.

Student Right-to-Know and Campus Security Act, S. 580, 101st Cong. (1990).

Take Back the Night Foundation. (n.d.). *TBTN history*. Retrieved from https://takebackthenight.org/history/

U.S Department of Education. (2017). *Secretary DeVos to host Title IX listening sessions*. Retrieved from https://www.ed.gov/news/press-releases/secretary-devos-host-title-ix-listening-sessions

U.S. Department of Education. (2018). *Secretary DeVos: Proposed Title IX rule provides clarity for schools, support for survivors, and due process rights for all*. Retrieved from https://www.ed.gov/news/press-releases/secretary-devos-proposed-title-ix-rule-provides-clarity-schools-support-survivors-and-due-process-rights-all

U.S. Department of Education Office for Civil Rights. (2001). *Revised sexual harassment guidance: Harassment of students by school employees, other students, or third parties*. Retrieved from https://www2.ed.gov/about/offices/list/ocr/docs/shguide.pdf

U.S. Department of Education Office for Civil Rights. (2006). *Dear colleague letter*. Retrieved from https://www2.ed.gov/about/offices/list/ocr/letters/sexhar-2006.html

U.S. Department of Education Office for Civil Rights. (2011). *Dear colleague letter*. Retrieved from https://www2.ed.gov/about/offices/list/ocr/letters/colleague-201104.html

U.S. Department of Education Office for Civil Rights. (2014). *Questions and answers on campus sexual misconduct*. Retrieved from https://www2.ed.gov/about/offices/list/ocr/docs/qa-201404-title-ix.pdf

U.S. Department of Education Office for Civil Rights. (2017a). *Dear colleague letter*. Retrieved from https://www2.ed.gov/about/offices/list/ocr/letters/colleague-title-ix-201709.pdf

U.S. Department of Education Office for Civil Rights. (2017b). *Questions and answers on campus sexual misconduct*. Retrieved from https://www2.ed.gov/about/offices/list/ocr/docs/qa-title-ix-201709.pdf

U.S. Department of Justice. (2012). *Equal access to education: Forty years of Title IX*. Retrieved from https://www.justice.gov/sites/default/files/crt/legacy/2012/06/20/titleixreport.pdf

USAGov. (2019). *How laws are made and how to research them*. Retrieved from https://www.usa.gov/how-laws-are-made

Violence Against Women Reauthorization Act of 2013, Pub. L. No. 113-4, 127 Stat. 54 (2013).

White House Task Force to Protect Students from Sexual Assault. (2014). *Not alone: The first report of the White House Task Force to Protect Students from Sexual Assault*. Retrieved from https://www.justice.gov/archives/ovw/page/file/905942/download

White House Task Force to Protect Students from Sexual Assault. (2017). *The second report of the White House Task Force to protect students from sexual assault*. Retrieved from https://www.whitehouse.gov/sites/whitehouse.gov/files/images/Documents/1.4.17.VAW%20Event.TF%20Report.PDF

Young, C. (2017, July 21). Betsy DeVos is right: Sexual assault policy is broken. *The New York Times*. Retrieved from https://www.nytimes.com/2017/07/21/opinion/betsy-devos-college-sexual-assault.html?searchResultPosition=18

Part II

Borders and Beyond

America First? Trump, Crime, and Justice Internationally

Ronen Ziv, Amanda Graham, and Liqun Cao

ABSTRACT

"America First," as presented by President Trump, argues for an international strategy that persistently places America's interests above those of anyone or anything else. Consequently, Trump has reshaped the international perceptions of the United States and has created more difficulties for the U.S. in coordinating of global leaders in resolving complex issues in the world. This essay reflects on how Trump and the United States are viewed internationally, the impacts of Trump's anti-immigrant and pro-White nationalist rhetoric, Trump's responses to humanitarian crises around the globe, and the potential impact of Trump's stance on global climate change. Given these considerations, it is questionable whether "America First" policy has made "America Great Again" in the eyes of the world.

Even from before the founding of America, it was believed that its land and people were provided an opportunity to be exceptional – to stand apart from other countries, such as England, and avoid the mistakes these countries had made. In 1630, in route to the Massachusetts Bay Colony, Puritan John Winthrop preached this vision to his fellow Puritan passengers:

> For we must consider that we shall be as a city upon a hill. The eyes of all people are upon us. So that if we shall deal falsely with our God in this work we have undertaken, and so cause Him to withdraw His present help from us, we shall be made a story and a by-word through the world. (Winthrop, 1630)

Evident from this message is the implicit belief that these people were on a divine mission to create a society that would be held in high regard around the world.

Just over 200 years later, on his first visit to America, Frenchman Alexis de Tocqueville more explicitly described these beliefs as "American Exceptionalism" (Martin, 2007). Unlike nationality from a shared history or ethnicity like Europeans, de Tocqueville describes American nationality as a set of common beliefs that include being "relatively distrustful of public authority, self-reliant, inclusive, egalitarian, classless, and democratic" and that Americans "could somehow make their lives better economically, religiously, or politically if they only worked hard enough" (Martin, 2007, p. 113). It is these values of democracy, liberty, equality, and social mobility that were uniquely American, thus providing the basis of "American Exceptionalism."

In a more contemporary sense, American exceptionalism has been described as "the idea of the United States as uniquely democratic and destined to exercise benevolent power in the world" (Shohat & Stam, 2007, p. 23). Ronald Reagan echoed these views of American exceptionalism in his 1989 farewell address when describing his vision of America as the "shining city on a hill."

> [I]n my mind it was a tall proud city built on rocks stronger than oceans, windswept, God blessed, and teeming with people of all kinds living in harmony and peace – a city with free ports that hummed with commerce and creativity, and if there had to be city walls, the walls had doors and the doors were open to anyone with the will and the heart to get here. (Reagan, 1989)

Only recently, this persistent view of American exceptionalism been challenged, and in particular, by one political figure – Donald J. Trump. Campaigning on the slogan "Make America Great Again," Trump proclaimed that "the American Dream is dead" (*Time, 2015*) and, in his view, was exceptional in the past but needs to be brought back to this level of exceptionalism through his political wisdom (Tumulty, 2017). At the core of his creed is the buzz phrase "America First," which Trump has used to encompass his international policy positions (The White House, 2018). Although idealistic sounding, many have not ignored this phrase's similarity to the name of the 1940s America First Committee, which often used anti-Semitic and pro-fascist rhetoric in its vision to pressure against American intervention in World War II (Bennett, 2017). Thus, in the making of Donald Trump's "city on a hill," his call for building a wall on the southern border to keep immigrants out and meeting with internationally known dictators resonate with the views held by many in the America First Committee.

However, as U.S. president, the influence of Trump's view of American exceptionalism are felt well beyond the United States. As the leader of the "free world," his comments and policy positions reflect the ideals and values of an entire Nation – regardless of if they are truly reflective of its residents – for social, economic, and political issues. In this essay, we will specifically touch on four key areas of international impact. First, we review the affinity, or lack thereof, for Trump and the United States under a Trump presidency. Second, we reflect on the international effects of Trump's stance on immigration and White nationalism. Third, we discuss Trump's responses, or lack thereof, to human rights violations around the world. And fourth, we consider the implications of Trump's inaction in combating climate change.

The Ugly American: disliking Trump and the international polls

Described as "arrogant, loud, ignorant and totally self-absorbed" (quoted in Clark, 2006), the pejorative "The Ugly American" is derived from the namesake book by Lederer and Burdick (1958), but appears to capture much of the international perceptions of Donald Trump and thus currently of America. Globally, approval of Trump's leadership is substantively lower than that of previous U.S. leaders, such as Obama, Bush, and Clinton. Trump's leadership approval ratings around the world fell by 10 or more percentage points from Obama-era levels in almost half (48.5%) of the countries surveyed in 2017 – many of them U.S. partners and allies (Gallup, 2018). These ratings have remained low in 2018 ratings of Trump's leadership (Gallup, 2019).

More specifically, the vast majority (70%) of international respondents surveyed by the Pew Research Center (Wike et al., 2018) had no confidence that Trump would "do the right thing regarding world affairs." This rating of no confidence at the world stage was worse than other world leaders, such as Angela Merkel, Emmanuel Macron, Xi Jinping, and even Putin. When examined by country, ratings of no confidence were highest in Western Europe and Mexico. Additionally, in a conservative comparison[1] to his predecessor, most respondents hold lower confidence in Trump as a leader of the United States (e.g., Germany: 71% Obama, 10% Trump; Mexicans: 38% Obama, 6% Trump; Canadians: 76% Obama, 25% Trump).

But these declining approval ratings are not necessarily universal. In fact, views of "U.S. leadership" improved in 29 countries and regions between 2016 (Obama) and 2017 (Trump) – In Iraq, this increase in approval led to a record-high approval rating of U.S. leadership (Gallup, 2018). Other countries with increases in approval of U.S. leadership include Liberia (+17%), Israel (+14%), and Russia (+6%). In terms of world affairs, 27% of international respondents felt confident in Trump with highest support coming from Israel (69%) and the Philippines (78%) (Wike et al., 2018). Additionally, in Israel, compared to Obama, whose levels of confidence varied between 49% and 71% during his presidency, confidence in Trump has remained relatively high (69%) (Wike et al., 2018). Furthermore, 52% of Israeli's surveyed believed that Trump understood Israel's real interests "to a great extent" and another 42% "to a small extent" (The Guttman Center, 2017c). Likewise, roughly three in four (76%) Israeli respondents believed that Trump views Israel's interests as "very important" or "moderately important" (The Guttman Center, 2018).

Apart from Trump as U.S. president, his key policies are also largely unsupported by the international community. For example, Fetterolf (2017) reports that Trump's wall between the United States and Mexico as well as his withdrawal from major trade agreements are near-universally disapproved of on the international stage. Likewise, the majority disapprove of his plan to withdraw from global climate change and Iran nuclear agreements. Additionally, over several surveys, Israeli's have felt Trump's plan for Israeli-Palestinian peace has a low chance of success (59%–72%; The Guttman Center, 2017a, 2017b, 2018, 2019a, 2019b). Although still disapproved of by a majority, Trump's most supported policy internationally involves the restriction of travel from some majority-Muslim countries, with the most ardent support coming from Russia.

As the leader of the "free world," Trump's policies, beliefs, and statements not only reflect his values but also those of the United States as a whole. Therefore, his actions and inactions have attributed to declining sentiments toward the United States on the world stage. For example, only 30% of Germans, 32% of Mexicans, and 39% of Canadians held favorable views of the United States during Trump's presidency, compared to the conservative values of 50%, 52%, and 64%, respectively, during the Obama presidency (Wike et al., 2018). In addition, 55% of Russians, 66% of Canadians, 66% of Mexicans, and 80% of Germans felt that relations between their country and the United States had become worse since 2017 (the previous year) (Wike et al., 2018). Furthermore, the majority of international respondents (70%) felt that the United States considered the concerns of countries like theirs "not too much/not at all." when making decisions (Wike et al., 2018). This aligns with the 37% of respondents who felt that the America was doing less, compared to a few years ago, to "help address major global problems" – another 34% felt the nation was doing about the same (Wike et al., 2018). In particular, the majority of

Canadians (63%), Germans (75%), Swedes (75%), Dutch (62%), and UK respondents (55%) believed that United States was doing less to address major global problems.

But much like views of Trump, views about the United States are not unanimously negative. For example, in Israel, largely favorable views of the nation (83%) were retained in the Trump presidency, compared to the favorable views held during the Obama presidency (varied between 71% and 84% throughout presidency) and even the Bush presidency (78% favorable) (Wike et al., 2018). Furthermore, 79% of respondents from Israel and 48% from Nigeria feel that relations between their country and the United States have become better over the last year (2017–2018). Overall, 48% of international respondents reported feeling no change in relations between their country and the United States (Wike et al., 2018). Furthermore, when examining views about addressing global problems, Israeli and Nigerian respondents believed the United States was doing more compared to a few years ago (Wike et al., 2018). This aligns with the majority of respondents (86%) in Israel who believe that America takes into account counties like theirs "a great deal/fair amount" when making decisions (Wike et al., 2018).

As a whole, "opinions of the United States vary greatly around the world, with enthusiastic ratings among people in Israel, the Philippines, and South Korea and unenthusiastic ratings in Germany, Russia and Mexico" (Wike et al., 2018). Nonetheless, the United States is still viewed as a world-leading economic power, compared to China, the European Union, and Japan, and furthermore, most (63%) still prefer the United States as world leader compared to China (Wike et al., 2018). But why do such diverse and tumultuous views exist about the United States and Trump? The following three sections attempt to address some of the key reasons, starting with Trump's bullying of immigrants and implicit, if not explicit, support of White nationalism around the world, followed by his approach to human right's violations, and addressing climate change.

Global bullying: attacking immigrants and encouraging White nationalism

Trump's disdain for "others" (e.g., immigrants, racial/ethnic minorities) is no state secret. Upon announcing his candidacy, he defined his presidency as one that would address immigration, in part, via a border wall – to keep out the "bad hombres" (Trump, 2019c) – and promising to ban Muslim immigrants – terrorists – from entering America (Giorgis, 2019; Shear & Davis, 2017) despite the evidence that immigrants are not more crime-prone than those born stateside (Sampson, 2006; Stowell, Messner, McGeever, & Raffalovich, 2009; Wadsworth, 2010). In addition, Trump has sought to criminalize the many refugees who come to the southern border seeking asylum from dangers in their country of origin claiming – without evidence – that these groups harbor terrorists and criminals (Brest, 2019; Gilsinan, 2018). Furthermore, he argues that the mistreatment of these refugees (e.g., separation of parents and children, overcrowding, poor conditions) should serve as a deterrent to those wanting to come here (Entralgo, 2019; Kanno-Youngs, 2019; Marcelo, 2019). Likewise, on several occasions, Trump has argued that immigrants, and even those who look like immigrants, within this country should "go back to where they came from" (i.e., four female Democratic members of the U.S. Congress known as the Squad) (Dwyer & Limbong, 2019), would never go "back to their huts" after seeing America (i.e., Haitians) (Saletan, 2019), or belong to "s–thole countries" (i.e., El Salvador, Haiti, African nations) (Gambino, 2018). All of these examples, and many more, provide evidence that Trump does not seek inclusionary policies for people desiring to come to America – let alone those already here, – which arguably contribute to the physical and emotional harm of those with legitimate claims of citizenship, residency, or asylum.

Although Trump has made his views about immigration to America well-known, he has also expressed support for other world leaders who have, or wished to, restrict immigration. On immigration in Europe, Trump noted, "Allowing the immigration to take place in Europe is a shame … So I think allowing millions and millions of people to come into Europe is very, very sad … I think you are losing your culture" (Dunn, 2018). Likewise, Trump has praised Israel's use of its border wall to stop illegal immigration arguing a Southern border wall in the U.S. would achieve the same results (Booth, 2017). In a further rejection of asylum seekers, Trump praised Australia's highly controversial anti-asylum posters (Withers, 2019), which provided slogans such as "No Way: You will not make Australia home" and "If you come here by boat without a visa you won't be settled in Australia" (Trump, 2019d).

Trump's concerns about international immigration are also closely tied to his support for isolationism, authoritarianism, and White nationalist values. These isolationist values, as noted above, have been seen in Trump's perspective on immigration. As will be discussed, Trump has expressed his share of support for authoritarian leaders (e.g., Duterte of the Philippines, Kim Jong Un of North Korea, Putin of Russia, Xi of China). Furthermore, in his tweets, Trump promotes isolationism and White nationalist views about the U.S. election and Brexit, expressing that "people want their country back" (Trump, 2016b). Likewise, he has promoted French nationalism, in a largely white country, noting that "there is no country more Nationalist than France, very proud people-and rightfully so!" (Trump, 2018e).

Beyond his refusal to denounce White supremacist groups within the U.S. (e.g., Charlottesville attack) (Marcos, 2017), Trump has also promoted the conspiracy theory of "white genocide" that is alleged to be occurring to White farmers in South Africa by asking his administration to investigate these alleged attacks (Mosbergen, 2019). In these examples and more, Trump exports his ideals of isolationism, authoritarianism, and White nationalism to other countries. Although not necessarily overtly dangerous, "When populist-right parties make breakthroughs, they signal to other white conservatives that it's more acceptable to vote this way," which can "generate a positive feedback loop in which higher votes facilitate even higher votes" (Kaufmann, 2019, p. 23). Thus, the rise of Trump in America promotes and encourages his isolationist, authoritarian, and White nationalist views not only in America but also throughout the world.

Human rights: it is an internal matter

Unlike his laser focus on racial and ethnic minority immigrants, Trump has often taken a laissez-faire approach to human rights violations internationally. However, he has also legitimated leaders committing these offenses as well as promoted these violations in certain circumstances.

In line with his "America First" approach, Trump has chosen to ignore many of the human rights violations occurring around the world – unless otherwise pressured – opting for these countries to handle the issues internally. For example, prior to his presidency, Trump's position on U.S. intervention in Bashar al-Assad of Syria's use of chemical and sarin gas on his own citizens was that of nonintervention (Trump, 2013a, 2013b, 2013c).

However, 63 hours after another chemical attack by Assad in Syria, President Trump employed military action after encouragement by his daughter – even then, some American and international leaders felt his actions were inappropriate (Dwyer, 2017; Haberman, 2017; Johnson, 2017; Prokop, 2017).

In another example, Trump's response to the murder and dismemberment of *Washington Post* journalist Jamal Khashoggi, at the hands of Saudi Arabia's Crown Prince Mohammed bin Salman was, and remains, nonexistent (Ryan, 2019). Although "extremely angry and very unhappy" (Quoted in Malloy, 2019), Trump continues to support Salman and his claims of innocence (Lander, 2018; Trump, 2018a, 2018b), despite a UN report naming Salman as responsible (Robertson & McGee, 2019). Furthermore, in the "extrajudicial killings" of his own people under the guise of a "war on drugs," Trump's response to the Philippines' President Rodrigo Duterte has been warm and supportive, while also ignoring such atrocities (Davis, 2017; Kaiman, 2017; Sanger & Haberman, 2017). Moreover, Trump has ignored the human rights violations of Palestinians at the hands of the Israeli government (e.g., restriction of movement of people and goods into and out of the Gaza strip, excessive lethal force) as well as those committed by Palestinian authorities in the West Bank and Gaza (e.g., torture, arbitrary arrest, trial without due process) (Human Rights Watch, 2019c).

Beyond ignoring such heinous acts, Trump has also acted to legitimize known human-rights-violating leaders, such as North Korea's Kim Jong Un and Russia's Vladimir Putin. Despite being known for the curtailment of "all basic liberties, including freedom of expression, religion, and conscience, assembly, and association … prohibit[ing] political opposition, independent media, civil society, or trade unions" (Human Rights Watch, 2019a), Trump's meetings with and adoration for the North Korean Dictator Kim Jong Un has provided legitimacy to this leader's regime on the world stage (Heydarian, 2018; Simon, 2018). In addition, Trump's warm relationship, both before and after the 2016 U.S. election, with Russia's Vladimir Putin denies the current and former human rights violations at the hands of Putin and his administration, such as the "tightened control over free expression, assembly, and speech, … fabrication of criminal cases, attacks on property and threats of retaliation against family members" (Human Rights Watch, 2019b; Trump, 2013d, 2016a, 2018c, 2018d, 2019a, 2019b).

Of even greater concern to human rights is Trump's outright support for such violations by the United States. For example, on multiple occasions, he has supported torture and waterboarding for accused terrorists (Trump, 2011a, 2013e, 2013f, 2013g, 2014), despite this being a clear violation of human rights per the United Nations Convention against Torture (United Nations Human Rights, 2019). Furthermore, Trump has promoted and approved the use of Guantanamo Bay detention camp, which has previously been used to indefinitely hold "unlawful combatants" who experienced torture, threats of death, and other ill-treatment at the hand of the U.S. military despite this treatment being a violation of international human rights laws (Human Rights Watch, 2011, 2018). In addition to keeping this facility open, Trump has expressed an intention to "load it up with some bad dudes" (Quoted in Welna, 2016). Furthermore, on multiple occasions, Trump has communicated his desire to kill terrorists' families (Beauchamp, 2016; Gass, 2015; Kranz, 2018), despite this being a violation of the Geneva convention's "Protection of Civilian Person in Time of War" (International Committee of the Red Cross, n.d.). By ignoring, legitimizing, and outright supporting human rights violations and those who engage in this misconduct, Trump's views have demonstrated a dramatic shift in U.S. values in terms of human rights.

Climate change: a future of crime and disruption

Although a global responsibility, Trump's responses to global climate change as a representative of the United States – the shining city upon a hill – have drawn ire. Even before his election, Trump has denied the existence of climate change claiming the concept "was created by and for the Chinese in order to make the U.S. manufacturing non-competitive" (Trump, 2011b). Within the U.S. government, Trump has rendered the Environmental Protection Agency (EPA) impotent through budget cuts, the repeal of regulation, and the installation of a former anti-EPA lobbyist to run the agency (Gibbens, 2019; Jacobson, 2018; King, 2019; PEER, 2019). These actions have implicitly signaled to the rest of the world that such "a pivotal issue of our time" (Netanyahu, 2015) is not a pressing priority for this administration, despite previous administrations' efforts (Grumke, 2019; Levin, 2019; Yudelevich, 2019).

In a much more explicit manner, Trump's failure to sign the Trans-Pacific Partnership deal, which included a comprehensive trade agreement and one of the "most robust enforceable environment commitments of any trade agreement in history" (USTR, n.d.), demonstrate a lack of interest from Trump and America in protecting the world from the results of climate change and preserving the environment. Likewise, his retreat from the Paris climate accord, which sought to reduce greenhouse gas emissions and provide aid to countries combating climate change, expresses a dramatic shift in American policy and priorities (Rafferty, n.d.; United Nations, 2019). Furthermore, his distinct absence from both the 2018 and 2019 G7 conference sessions on climate has left a literal empty seat at the table for attempting to solve this global crisis (Associated Press, 2019; Samuels, 2019). As such, some have argued that these absences, disinterests, and withdrawals from global matters may serve as a source of resentment internationally (Wike et al., 2018).

However, Trump's resistance to addressing climate change may have implications well beyond his presidential term and the United States. In addition to the melting ice in both the Antarctic and Greenland, rising waters, endangering and loss of certain species, and volatile weather (IPCC, 2018), it is estimated that the effects of climate change will create difficulty for humans around the world. For example, in response to a changing climate, an estimated 200 million people by 2050 will be forced to migrate due to extreme climate conditions, such as drought, famine, sea-level rise, water shortage, and monsoons (Myers, 2005; Oliver-Smith, 2012). As a result of this migration, population density in urban areas is likely to rise, along with related urban problems, such as the spread of disease, and inadequate health and education services (Brown, 2008). Furthermore, psychologists argue that climate change will adversely impact the mental health of all affected either directly (e.g., trauma of experiencing extreme weather events or displacement) or indirectly (e.g., worry or anxiety, depression, grief, vicarious trauma) (Doherty & Clayton, 2011). Moreover, these effects will disproportionately impact developing countries, who are "the least responsible for emissions of greenhouse gases" (Brown, 2008, p. 31).

Additionally, an increase in violence is expected to accompany climate change. For example, competition for increasingly scarce resources is anticipated to create violence and even war when previously separated groups move into closer proximity (Brown, 2008; Guterres, 2009). At an individual level, hot temperatures are expected to increase aggression and hostility and thus violent crime (Anderson, 2001). Furthermore, increased strain and beliefs that are favorable to crime, reduced social control and support, and increased opportunities for crime are believed to foster higher levels of individual, group, corporate, and state crime as a result of climate change (Agnew, 2011). In fact, one estimate claims that, "climate change will cause an additional 22,000 murders, 180,000 cases of rape, 1.2 million aggravated assaults, 2.3 million simple assaults, 260,000 robberies, 1.3 million burglaries, 2.2 million cases of larceny, and 580,000 cases of vehicle theft in the United States" alone between 2010 and 2099 (Ranson, 2014). Thus, ignoring the global implications of climate change as a world leader has larger ramifications than the U.S. 2020 election.

America First?

In placing "America First," Trump has made himself and the United States unpopular in many places around the globe. He attacked immigrants and promoted White nationalism, ignored serious human rights violations, and set a tone of deafness to the impacts of climate change. Trump's America does not reflect the "city on a hill" as envisioned by Winthrop or Reagan. Instead of a country "teeming with people of all kinds living in harmony and peace," Trump seeks to homogenize the population to promote White nationalism. And, instead of "if there had to be city walls, the walls had doors and the doors were open to anyone with the will and the heart to be here," Trump has espoused views of rejecting immigrants and building walls to keep "others" out. However, as noted by Winthrop, "the eyes of all people are upon us" – this remains true. Unlike Winthrop and Reagan's views of the city on a hill, it seems Trump's vision is more akin to Trump tower on a hill. The world has taken notice of this version of American Exceptionalism and has begun to respond accordingly. We urge our readers to decide for themselves, from an international perspective, is American Great Again?

Note

1. The phrase "conservative" estimate here and further in this discussion refers to the use of the lowest values observed during the course of Obama's presidency.

Disclosure statement

No potential conflict of interest was reported by the authors.

References

Agnew, R. (2011). Dire forecast: A theoretical model of the impact of climate change on crime. *Theoretical Criminology*, *16*, 21–42. doi:10.1177/1362480611416843

Anderson, C. A. (2001). Heat and violence. *Current Directions in Psychological Science*, *10*, 33–38. doi:10.1111/1467-8721.00109

Associated Press. (2019, August 26). Trump skips climate discussion at G-7 summit. *NBC News*. Retrieved from https://www.nbcnews.com/politics/donald-trump/trump-skips-climate-discussion-g-7-summit-n1046536

Beauchamp, Z. (2016, January 25). Donald Trump said he'd kill terrorists' families at a rally. His crowd went wild. *Vox*. Retrieved from https://www.vox.com/2016/1/25/10828770/trump-terrorist-family-appeal

Bennett, B. (2017, January 20). 'America First,' a phrase with a loaded anti-Semetic and isolationist history. *Los Angeles Times*. Retrieved from https://www.latimes.com/politics/la-na-pol-trump-america-first-20170120-story.html

Booth, W. (2017, January 29). Israel's Netanyahu applauds Trump's plan for wall; Mexico not pleased. *The Washington Post*. Retrieved from https://www.washingtonpost.com/news/world views/wp/2017/01/29/israels-netanyahu-applauds-trumps-plan-for-wall-mexico-not-pleased/

Brest, M. (2019, July 16). Trump claims Honduras and Guatemala are sending 'hardened criminals' in caravans. *The Washington Examiner*. Retrieved from https://www.washingtonexaminer.com/news/trump-claims-honduras-and-guatemala-are-sending-hardened-criminals-in-caravans

Brown, O. (2008). *Migration and climate change*. Geneva, Switzerland: International Organization for Migration.

Clark, H. (2006, May 19). Are you an Ugly American. *Forbes*. Retrieved from https://www.forbes.com/2006/05/19/keith-reinhard-diplomatic-action-cx_hc_0519reinhard.html#2eedb3062ee7

Davis, J. H. (2017, November 13). Trump lauds 'great relationship' with Duterte in Manila. *The New York Times*. Retrieved from https://www.nytimes.com/2017/11/13/world/asia/trump-duterte-philippines.html

Doherty, T. J., & Clayton, S. (2011). The psychological impacts of global climate change. *American Psychologist*, *66*, 265–276. doi:10.1037/a0023141

Dunn, T. N. (2018, July 13). Trump's Brexit blast: Donald Trump told Thersa May how to do Brexit 'but she wrecked it'- and says the US trade deal is off. *The Sun*. Retrieved from https://www.thesun.co.uk/news/6766531/trump-may-brexit-us-deal-off/

Dwyer, C. (2017, April 7). How is the rest of the world reacting to the U.S. strike on Syria? *National Public Radio*. Retrieved from https://www.npr.org/sections/thetwo-way/2017/04/07/523001065/how-is-the-rest-of-the-world-reacting-to-the-u-s-strike-on-syria

Dwyer, C., & Limbong, A. (2019, July 15). 'Go back to where you came from' The long rhetorical roots of Trump's racist tweets. *National Public Radio*. Retrieved from https://www.npr.org/2019/07/15/741827580/go-back-where-you-came-from-the-long-rhetorical-roots-of-trump-s-racist-tweets

Entralgo, R. (2019, July 1). Homeland Security admits it's using abhorrent conditions at detention centers to deter migration. *Thinkprogress*. Retrieved from https://thinkprogress.org/dhs-oig-homeland-security-report-el-paso-detention-center-conditions-used-to-deter-migration-9b0420b7e70b/

Fetterolf, J. (2017, July 28). *Border wall is Trump's least popular policy internationally*. Pew Research Center. Retrieved from https://www.pewresearch.org/fact-tank/2017/07/28/border-wall-is-trumps-least-popular-policy-internationally/

Gallup. (2018). *Rating world leaders: 2018: The U.S. vs. Germany, China and Russia*. Washington, DC: Author.

Gallup. (2019). *Rating world leaders: 2019: The U.S. vs. Germany, China and Russia*. Washington, DC: Author.

Gambino, L. (2018, January 11). Trump pans immigration proposals as bring people from 'shithole countries'. *The Guardian*. Retrieved from https://www.theguardian.com/us-news/2018/jan/11/trump-pans-immigration-proposal-as-bringing-people-from-shithole-countries

Gass, N. (2015, December 2). Trump: We have to take out ISIL members' families. *Politico*. Retrieved from https://www.politico.com/story/2015/12/trump-kill-isil-families-216343

Gibbens, S. (2019, February 1). 15 ways the Trump administration has changed environmental policies, *National Geographic*. Retrieved from https://www.nationalgeographic.com/environment/2019/02/15-ways-trump-administration-impacted-environment/

Gilsinan, K. (2018, December 11). Trump keeps invoking terrorism to get his border wall. *The Atlantic*. Retrieved from https://www.theatlantic.com/international/archive/2018/12/trump-incorrectly-links-immigration-terrorism/576358/

Giorgis, H. (2019, January 13). The faulty logic in Trump's Travel ban. *The Atlantic*. Retrieved from https://www.theatlantic.com/politics/archive/2019/01/trumps-travel-ban-logic-flaw/579631/

Grumke, K. (2019, July 8). How Trump's environmental record compares to his claims. *PBS*. Retrieved from https://www.pbs.org/newshour/politics/how-trumps-environmental-record-compares-to-his-claims

Guterres, A. (2009). Climate change, natural disasters and human displacement: A UNHCR perspective. *UNHCR*. Retrieved from https://www.unhcr.org/cgi-bin/texis/vtx/home/opendocPDFViewer.html?docid=4901e81a4&query=displacement%20scenarios

Haberman, M. (2017, April 7). 63 hours: From chemical attack to Trump's strike in Syria. *The New York Times*. Retrieved from https://www.nytimes.com/2017/04/07/us/politics/syria-strike-trump-timeline.html?smid=tw-nytimes&smtyp=cur

Heydarian, R. J. (2018, June 16). In the end, all the Trump-Kim summit did was legitimize a notorious dictator. *Business Insider*. Retrieved from https://www.businessinsider.com/trump-kim-summit-legitimized-notorious-dictator-2018-6

Human Rights Watch. (2011, January 24). *US: Prolonged indefinite detention violates international law*. Retrieved from https://www.hrw.org/news/2011/01/24/us-prolonged-indefinite-detention-violates-international-law

Human Rights Watch. (2018, June 27). *Q&A:Guantanamo Bay, US detentions, and the Trump administration*. Retrieved from https://www.hrw.org/news/2018/06/27/qa-guantanamo-bay-us-detentions-and-trump-administration

Human Rights Watch. (2019a). *North Korea*. Retrieved from https://www.hrw.org/asia/north-korea

Human Rights Watch. (2019b). *Russia*. Retrieved from https://www.hrw.org/europe/central-asia/russia

Human Rights Watch. (2019c). *Israel and Palestine: Events of 2018*. Retrieved from https://www.hrw.org/world-report/2019/country-chapters/israel/palestine

International committee of the Red Cross. (n.d.). *Geneva Conventions of 1949 and additional protocols, and heir commentaries*. Retrieved from https://ihl-databases.icrc.org/applic/ihl/ihl.nsf/vwTreaties1949.xsp

IPCC. (2018). *Special report: Global warming of 1.5°C*. Geneva, Switzerland: Intergovernmental Panel on Climate Change. Retrieved from https://www.ipcc.ch/sr15/

Jacobson, J. (2018, April 26). How much have Republicans cut EPA budget, staff in two years? *Politifact*. Retrieved from https://www.politifact.com/truth-o-meter/statements/2018/apr/26/evan-jenkins/how-much-have-republicans-cut-epa-budget-staff-two/

Johnson, S. (2017, April 11). Ivanka Trump influenced my father to launch Syria strikes, reveals brother Eric. *The Telegraph*. Retrieved from https://www.telegraph.co.uk/news/2017/04/10/ivanka-trump-influenced-father-launch-air-strikes-against-assad/

Kaiman, J. (2017, November 10). When Trump meets the Philippines' Duterte 'drug war' killings will be the elephant in the room. Trump will probably ignore it. *Los Angeles Times*. Retrieved from https://www.latimes.com/world/asia/la-fg-trump-duterte-20171110-story.html

Kanno-Youngs, Z. (2019, July 3). Trump says migrants are 'living far better' in overcrowded border facilities. *The New York Times*. Retrieved from https://www.nytimes.com/2019/07/03/us/politics/trump-border-patrol.html

Kaufmann, E. (2019). *Whiteshift*. New York, NY: Abrams Press.

King, L. (2019, March 8). Andrew Wheeler, who's been leading trump deregulatory charge, confirmed by Senate as EPA chief. *USA Today*. Retrieved from https://www.usatoday.com/story/news/politics/2019/02/28/trumps-new-epa-chief-andrew-wheeler-who-replaced-scott-pruitt/3014406002/

Kranz, M. (2018, April 6). 'Why did you wait?': Trumpreportedly asked the CIA why it paused for target to walk away from his family before striking. *Business Insider*. Retrieved from https://www.businessinsider.com/trump-cia-drone-strike-terrorist-families-2018-4

Lander, M. (2018, November 20). In extraordinary statement, Trump stands with Saudis despite Khashoggi Killing. *The New York Times*. Retrieved from https://www.nytimes.com/2018/11/20/world/middleeast/trump-saudi-khashoggi.html

Lederer, W. J., & Burdick, E. (1958). *The ugly American*. New York, NY: W. W. Norton & Company.

Levin, B. (2019, April 8). Trump's 2020 pitch: No one cares more about the environment than me. *Vanity Fair*. Retrieved from https://www.vanityfair.com/news/2019/04/trumps-2020-no-one-cares-more-about-the-environment-than-me

Malloy, A. (2019, June 30). Trump says he is 'extremely angry' about Khashoggi murder, but defends mbs relationship. *CNN*. Retrieved from https://edition.cnn.com/2019/06/29/politics/trump-khashoggi-bin-salman/index.html

Marcelo, P. (2019, August 26). Administration ends protection for migrant medical care. *Associated Press News*. Retrieved from https://www.apnews.com/e27485eced6e480ca10a6a4c1c043f0c

Marcos, C. (2017, August 16). House Dems push to censure Trump over Charlottesville response. *The Hill*. Retrieved from https://thehill.com/blogs/floor-action/house/346814-house-dems-call-for-censuring-trump-over-charlottesville-response

Martin, D. (2007). *Rebuilding brand America: What we must do to restore our reputation and safeguard the future of American business abroad*. New York, NY: Amacom Books.

Mosbergen, D. (2019, June 4). Fox news host Tucker Carlson just promoted a White nationalist conspiracy theory. *Huffpost*. Retrieved from https://www.huffpost.com/entry/tucker-carlson-south-african-farmers_n_5cf5e368e4b0a1997b6fce80

Myers, N. (2005, May). *Environmental Refugees: An emergent security issue*. Presented at the 13th Economic Forum, Prague, Czech Republic.

Netanyahu, B. (2015, November 30). *Prime Minister Benjamin Netanyahu's remarks at the Climate Conference in Paris*. Retrieved from https://www.gov.il/en/search?searchofficeID=e744bba9-d17e-429f-abc3-50f7a8a55667&query=climate

Oliver-Smith, A. (2012). Debating environmental migration: Society, nature and population displacement in climate change. *Journal of International Development*, *24*, 1058–1070. doi:10.1002/jid.2887

PEER. (2019, January 15). *Criminal enforcement collapse at EPA*. Retrieved from https://www.peer.org/news/press-releases/criminal-enforcement-collapse-at-epa.html

Prokop, A. (2017, April 6). Syria strike reactions: What top republicans and democrats in congress are saying. *Vox*. Retrieved from https://www.vox.com/2017/4/6/15214844/trump-syria-airstrike-reactions

Rafferty, J. P. (n.d.). U.S. exits Paris climate agreement. *Britannica*. Retrieved from https://www.britannica.com/story/us-exits-paris-climate-agreement

Ranson, M. (2014). Crime, weather, and climate change. *Journal of Environmental Economics and Management*, *67*, 274–302. doi:10.1016/j.jeem.2013.11.008

Reagan, R. (1989, January 12). Transcript of Reagan's farewell address to American people. *The New York Times*. Retrieved from https://www.nytimes.com/1989/01/12/news/transcript-of-reagan-s-farewell-address-to-american-people.html

Robertson, N., & McGee, L. (2019, June 20). *10 key findings from the report into Jamal Khashoggi's killing*. Retrieved from https://www.cnn.com/2019/06/19/middleeast/khashoggi-saudi-arabia-un-report-findings-intl/index.html

Ryan, F. (2019, April 1). It's been six months since Jamal Khashoggi's murder, and Trump has done nothing. *The Washington Post*. Retrieved from https://www.washingtonpost.com/opinions/global-opinions/its-been-six-months-since-jamal-khashoggis-murder-and-trump-has-done-nothing/2019/04/01/38bbded0-5251-11e9-88a1-ed346f0ec94f_story.html

Saletan, W. (2019, July 17). Trump's "go back" spears are a dangerous escalation of his bigotry. *Slate*. Retrieved from https://slate.com/news-and-politics/2019/07/trump-go-back-racist-tweets-squad-immigration.html

Sampson, R. J. (2006, March 11). Open doors don't invite criminals: Is increased immigration behind the drop in crime? *The New York Times*. Retrieved from https://www.nytimes.com/2006/03/11/opinion/open-doors-dont-invite-criminals.html?mtrref=www.google.com&gwh=40362E86777306B0D0D91DC4FC4933BD&gwt=pay&assetType=REGIWALL

Samuels, B. (2019, August 26). Trump absent from G-7 session on climate. *The Hill*. Retrieved from https://thehill.com/homenews/administration/458785-trump-absent-from-g-7-session-on-climate

Sanger, D. E., & Haberman, M. (2017, May 23). Trump praises Duterte for Philippine drug crackdown in call transcript. *The New York Times*. Retrieved from https://www.nytimes.com/2017/05/23/us/politics/trump-duterte-phone-transcript-philippine-drug-crackdown.html

Shear, M. D., & Davis, J. H. (2017, December 23). Stoking fears, Trump defied bureaucracy to advance immigration agenda. *The New York Times*. Retrieved from https://www.nytimes.com/2017/12/23/us/politics/trump-immigration.html

Shohat, E., & Stam, R. (2007). *Flagging patriotism: Crises of narcissism and anti-Americanism*. New York, NY: Routledge.

Simon, S. (2018, October 6). Donald Trump 'fell in love' with Kim Jong Un. *National Public Radio*. https://www.npr.org/2018/10/06/654857533/opinion-donald-trump-fell-in-love-with-kim-jong-un

Stowell, J. I., Messner, S. F., McGeever, K. F., & Raffalovich, L. E. (2009). Immigration and the recent violent crime drop in the United States: A pooled, cross-sectional time-sectional time-series analysis of metropolitan areas. *Criminology*, *47*, 889–928. doi:10.1111/j.1745-9125.2009.00162.x

The Guttman Center for Public Opinion and Policy Research. (2017a, June). *The peace index, June 2017*. Retrieved from http://dataisrael.idi.org.il

The Guttman Center for Public Opinion and Policy Research. (2017b, May). *The peace index, May 2017*. Retrieved from http://dataisrael.idi.org.il

The Guttman Center for Public Opinion and Policy Research. (2017c, December). *The peace index, December 2017*. Retrieved from http://dataisrael.idi.org.il

The Guttman Center for Public Opinion and Policy Research. (2018, June). *The peace index, June 2018*. Retrieved from http://dataisrael.idi.org.il

The Guttman Center for Public Opinion and Policy Research. (2019a, June). *The peace index, June 2019*. Retrieved from http://dataisrael.idi.org.il

The Guttman Center for Public Opinion and Policy Research. (2019b, February). *The peace index, February 2019*. Retrieved from http://dataisrael.idi.org.il

The White House. (2018, January 30). *President Donald J. Trump's foreign policy puts America First* [press release]. Retrieved from https://www.whitehouse.gov/briefings-statements/president-donald-j-trumps-foreign-policy-puts-america-first/

TIME staff. (2015, June 16). Here's Donald Trump's presidential announcement speech. *Time*. Retrieved from https://time.com/3923128/donald-trump-announcement-speech/

Trump, D. J. (2011a, November 15). *Real Donald Trump Twitter account*. Retrieved from https://twitter.com/realdonaldtrump/status/136555844597841921

Trump, D. J. (2011b, November 6). *Real Donald Trump Twitter account*. Retrieved from https://twitter.com/realdonaldtrump/status/265895292191248385?lang=en

Trump, D. J. (2013a, September 3). *Real Donald Trump Twitter account*. Retrieved from https://twitter.com/realDonaldTrump/status/375075774644363264

Trump, D. J. (2013b, September 5). *Real Donald Trump Twitter account*. Retrieved from https://twitter.com/realDonaldTrump/status/375609403376144384

Trump, D. J. (2013c, September 9). *Real Donald Trump Twitter account*. Retrieved from https://twitter.com/realDonaldTrump/status/377038618407493632

Trump, D. J. (2013d, June 18). *Real Donald Trump Twitter account*. Retrieved from https://twitter.com/realdonaldtrump/status/347191326112112640

Trump, D. J. (2013e, October 31). Real Donald Trump twitter account. Retrieved from https://twitter.com/realdonaldtrump/status/396012884397805568

Trump, D. J. (2013f, April 21). *Real Donald Trump Twitter account*. Retrieved from https://twitter.com/realdonaldtrump/status/326089541641445377

Trump, D. J. (2013g, February 7). *Real Donald Trump Twitter account*. Retrieved from https://twitter.com/realdonaldtrump/status/299530494457020417

Trump, D. J. (2014, December 12). *Real Donald Trump Twitter account*. Retrieved from https://twitter.com/realdonaldtrump/status/543310458946850818

Trump, D. J. (2016a, July 25). *Real Donald Trump Twitter account*. Retrieved from https://twitter.com/realdonaldtrump/status/757538729170964481

Trump, D. J. (2016b, June 24). *Real Donald Trump Twitter account*. Retrieved from https://twitter.com/realdonaldtrump/status/746458701565988864

Trump, D. J. (2018a, October 15). *Real Donald Trump Twitter account*. Retrieved from https://twitter.com/realdonaldtrump/status/1051814214212485120

Trump, D. J. (2018b, October 16). *Real Donald Trump Twitter account.* Retrieved from https://twitter.com/realdonaldtrump/status/1052268011900555265

Trump, D. J. (2018c, July 17). *Real Donald Trump Twitter account.* Retrieved from https://twitter.com/realdonaldtrump/status/1019225830298456066

Trump, D. J. (2018d, March 21). *Real Donald Trump Twitter account.* Retrieved from https://twitter.com/realdonaldtrump/status/976532956557737984

Trump, D. J. (2018e, November 13). *Real Donald Trump Twitter account.* Retrieved from https://twitter.com/realdonaldtrump/status/1062333534214520832

Trump, D. J. (2019a, May 4). *Real Donald Trump Twitter account.* Retrieved from https://twitter.com/realdonaldtrump/status/1124672389416144905

Trump, D. J. (2019b, May 3). *Real Donald Trump Twitter account.* Retrieved from https://twitter.com/realdonaldtrump/status/1124359594418032640

Trump, D. J. (2019c, May 17). *Real Donald Trump Twitter account.* Retrieved from https://twitter.com/realDonaldTrump/status/1129336982319050752

Trump, D. J. (2019d, June 26). *Real Donald Trump Twitter account.* Retrieved from https://twitter.com/realDonaldTrump/status/1144033134129758208

Tumulty, K. (2017, January 18). How Donald Trump came up with 'Make America Great Again'. *The Washington Post.* Retrieved from https://www.washingtonpost.com/politics/how-donald-trump-came-up-with-make-america-great-again/2017/01/17/fb6acf5e-dbf7-11e6-ad42-f3375f271c9c_story.html

United Nations. (2019). *d Paris agreement.* United Nations Treaty Collection. Retrieved from https://treaties.un.org/pages/ViewDetails.aspx?src=TREATY&mtdsg_no=XXVII-7-d&chapter=27&clang=_en

United Nations Human Rights. (2019). *Convention against Torture and other cruel, inhuman or degrading treatment or punishment.* Retrieved from https://www.ohchr.org/EN/ProfessionalInterest/Pages/CAT.aspx

USTR. (n.d.). *The Trans-Pacific Partnership.* Washington, DC: Office of the United States Trade Representative. Retrieved from https://ustr.gov/tpp/

Wadsworth, T. (2010). Is immigration responsible for the crime drop? An assessment of the influence of immigration on changes in violent crime between 1990 and 2000. *Social Science Quarterly, 91*, 531–553. doi:10.1111/(ISSN)1540-6237

Welna, D. (2016, November 14). Trump has vowed to fill Guantanamo with 'some bad dudes'-but who? *National Public Radio.* Retrieved from https://www.npr.org/sections/parallels/2016/11/14/502007304/trump-has-vowed-to-fill-guantanamo-with-some-bad-dudes-but-who

Wike, R., Stokes, B., Poushter, J., Silver, L., Fetterolf, J., & Delvin, K. (2018, October 1). *Trump's international ratings remain low, especially among key allies.* Washington, DC: Pew Research Center.

Winthrop, J. (1630). *A model of christian charity.* Retrieved from https://www.winthropsociety.com/doc_charity.php

Withers, R. (2019, July 3). Trump is right that "Much can be learned" from Australia's immigration policies. *Slate.* Retrieved from https://slate.com/news-and-politics/2019/07/trump-morrison-australia-immigration-manus-nauru.html

Yudelevich, E. (2019, January 21). Climate change in opportunity for Israel-U.S. cooperation. *The Jerusalem Post.* Retrieved from https://m.jpost.com/Opinion/Climate-change-an-opportunity-for-Israel-US-cooperation-578189/amp

"Murderers, Rapists, and Bad Hombres": Deconstructing the Immigration-Crime Myths

Cecilia Chouhy and Arelys Madero-Hernandez

ABSTRACT
Immigration control is at the center of the political debate and it is an important component of the Trump administration agenda. Restrictive immigration policies have expanded under the current administration justified in rhetoric that portrays immigrants as criminals and threats to public safety. This article presents the different mythologies surrounding the immigration and crime link and critically appraise the empirical evidence investigating the relationship between immigration and crime. The review provides ample evidence contradicting the commonly held belief that immigration increases crime. At the macro-level, research shows that immigrant communities have no higher crime rates than non-immigrant communities and that sanctuary cities do not foster crime. At the micro-level, research shows that neither immigrants in general nor undocumented immigrants, in particular, engage in more criminal behavior than non-immigrants. In fact, evidence seems to suggest the opposite. Despite researchers largely agreeing that the portrait of immigrants as a threat is not founded in empirical reality, the consequences of the immigrant threat narrative and the policies they promote are all too real.

Anti-immigration messages have dominated public discourse in the United States for decades. A common thread among such messages is the idea that immigration is inextricably linked with a host of social issues, most notably violence. Enforcement of immigration laws has been a priority tied to public safety for years, as reflected in the growth in the number of deportations since 2003, which reached a record high of 435,000 in 2013 (United States Office of Immigration Statistics, 2017). Other anti-immigration efforts have been implemented via state legislation such as the controversial provisions in SB 1070 in Arizona that originally required police officers to verify the documentation of individuals suspected to be in the country without authorization.

In 2016, comments by President Donald Trump, then-Republican-candidate for president, specifically singled out Mexican immigrants as criminals. Once elected, President Trump enacted an executive order that tied immigration with public safety and set the tone for the administration's focal efforts on enforcement (Executive Order No. 13768, 2017), including policies such as the expansion of the range of deportable offenses (Kopan, 2018), the increase in removals of immigrants through interior and administrative arrests (United States Immigration and Customs Enforcement, 2018), and, most recently, the controversial policy of family separation at the border (Karaim, 2018). The threat of crime and the attribution of criminality to immigrants are now constitutive parts of the immigration debate both implicitly and explicitly, and are often used to justify restrictive immigration and asylum policies and human rights abuses at the border (Amnesty international, 2018).

In this anti-immigration era, the notion that immigration does not have the purported connection with crime and may even have crime protective effects could seem counter-intuitive, yet it is borne out of extensive research to date. Studies have revealed interesting and paradoxical findings that indicate a very different effect of immigration on communities. On the one hand, assuming that immigrants were disproportionately likely to commit crimes, one would expect to see higher crime rates after the arrivals of high numbers of immigrants. Yet, crime rates in the United States dropped exponentially in the late 1990s – the very period of most growth in recent immigration (Ramey, 2013; Stowell, Messner, McGeever, & Raffalovich, 2009; Wadsworth, 2010). Between 1994 and 2007, the nation's violent crime declined by a third, while the number of immigrants in the population rose from 9 to about 13% (Rumbaut & Ewing, 2007). On the other hand, the purported immigration-crime link would forecast a scenario where cities with high concentrations of immigrants were ranked as the top most violent in the country, but crime statistics indicate quite the opposite – places such as New York City, Chicago, and Los Angeles, well known for being immigrant hubs, all experienced drastic reductions in violent crime during the 1990s (MacDonald & Sampson, 2012). Simply put, "cities of concentrated immigration are some of the safest places around" (Sampson, 2008, p. 30).

The immigration-crime view also assumes that cities and towns with more immigrants in the population would have higher rates of crime simply because of a compositional effect – as immigrants presumably perpetrate crime in greater proportion than nonimmigrants. This is the core idea behind President Trump's "bad hombres" thesis, which has been reiterated in several of his speeches, both in presidential and campaigning capacities. In particular, in his now-famous campaign announcement speech, then Candidate Trump argued the following:

> When Mexico sends its people, they're not sending their best. They're not sending you. They're not sending you. They're sending people that have lots of problems, and they're bringing those problems with us. They're bringing drugs. They're bringing crime. They're rapists. And some, I assume, are good people … But I speak to border guards and they tell us what we're getting … They're sending us not the right people.

To conflate the idea of immigration and crime more broadly, he then added that he was not referring specifically to Mexicans:

> It's coming from more than Mexico. It's coming from all over South and Latin America, and it's coming probably – probably – from the Middle East. But we don't know … And it's got to stop and it's got to stop fast. (Trump, 2015 cited in Schwartz, 2015).

Of course, whether this vision generalizes to all immigrants is subject to debate. Not only political pundits but also a wide range of scholars have denounced the racism embedded in Trump's anti-immigrant rhetoric (see, e.g., Brown, 2016; Hayduk & García-Castañon, 2018; Kim, Sagás, & Cespedes, 2018; Romero, 2018; Waldinger, 2018). This racialized portrait of immigrants did not start with President Trump. Rather, it has been a long-standing component of immigration debates (see, e.g., Farris & Silber Mohamed, 2018; Valdez, 2016; Waldinger, 2018). Setting aside the racist undertones underlying the construction of immigrant as threats, there is little doubt that this type of rhetoric is prevalent in the political and social debate on immigration. A narrower iteration of the immigrant threat focuses on undocumented persons or "criminal aliens." Immigrants who cross the border illegally or overstay their visas become "deportable aliens" and are automatically attributed criminal intent (more on this later). In this manner, the rhetoric divides immigrants into two groups: documented and undocumented; the latter are deemed as the "bad immigrants" and attributed with greater negative propensities and higher involvement in criminality.

These assumptions have been refuted by empirical studies showing that foreign-born individuals have less of an involvement in criminal activity and far lower rates of incarceration than the native-born (Bersani, 2014a; Bersani, Loughran, & Piquero, 2014; Butcher & Piehl, 2007; Morenoff & Astor, 2006). Immigrants' lower involvement in crime despite their concentration in areas of high economic disadvantage has been described as an "immigrant paradox" (Sampson, 2008). Furthermore, empirical studies focusing on undocumented immigrants also challenge this portrayal (Ewing, Martínez, & Rumbaut, 2015; Hickman & Suttorp, 2008; Landgrave & Nowrasteh, 2017a, 2017b, 2019; Nowrasteh, 2018a).

In this article, we draw from the above-discussed ideas to identify four different myths about immigration and crime. Myths #1 and #2 refer to the relationship between immigration and crime at the macro level. Myth #1 states that ecological units with higher levels of immigrants will have higher crime rates, while myth #2 assumes that sanctuary cities foster crime. The remaining two myths relate to the immigration-crime nexus at the individual level. Myth #3 posits that immigrants will be more involved in crime than non-immigrants, while myth #4 states that undocumented immigrants will show more involvement in crime than non-immigrants. In addition to discussing these myths, we critically appraise the empirical evidence on the immigration and crime nexus to either support or refute them.

The article is organized into four sections. We first discuss public views about immigration in recent decades and the Trump era, showing a polarized scenario in how the public views immigrants. Second, we focus on the macro-level myths regarding immigration and crime (Myths #1 and #2). Third, we assess the relationship between immigration and crime at the individual level (Myths #3 and #4). Finally, we discuss the very real consequences of these widely held myths, showing how they have contributed to the criminalization of immigration and the enactment of restrictive immigration policies. We also discuss some studies that evaluate the effects of such restrictive policies on immigrant families and some racialized communities (especially Latino communities).

Public opinion about immigration and crime in the Trump era

The United States is internationally known as a multicultural, immigrant nation. In 2017, there were 44.4 million immigrants residing in the U.S., nearly 14% of the population. Yet, public attitudes toward immigrants and immigration have been mixed. Data from the Gallup organization, which has periodically polled immigration attitudes in the United States since the 2000s, show that in 2019, 76% of respondents believed that immigration was a "good thing" versus 19% who indicated it to be a "bad thing" (Gallup, 2019). This relatively positive assessment of immigration broadly contrasts with perceptions immigration as linked with crime. In one study, "crime or criminals" emerged as the most frequent characterization of immigrants in a comprehensive content analysis of over 4,000 news stories from newspapers in Southern U.S. states (Brown, Jones, & Becker, 2018). Data from the General Social Survey (GSS), a nationally representative sample of adults in U.S households, allows for examining trends in the perceived crime threat of immigration over time. The survey includes a question that measures agreement with the statement "immigrants increase crime rates." In 2014, 45% of respondents agreed or strongly agreed with that statement (Pryce, 2018). Similarly, in 2019, 42% of respondents stated that immigration was making the crime situation worse (Gallup, 2019). Thus, despite a majority of pro-immigrant attitudes broadly, the country remains divided on the effects of immigration on crime.

This divide was illustrated by the 2019 partial shutdown of the federal government over disagreements between Congress and the Trump administration regarding the financing of border security (Van Sant, 2019). Considered a focal priority of the administration's efforts to protect public safety in the homeland, the construction of a physical barrier across the southern border with Mexico has been a controversial proposal. In 2018, 41% of Americans expressed support for the expansion of the wall, whereas 57% opposed or strongly opposed it (Gallup, 2019). The statistics are almost identical to those reported in 2006 – 42% support vs. 56% opposition. Interestingly, the lowest levels of support for the wall construction are reported among Hispanics and Blacks, and the highest levels among Whites.

Why are perceptions about immigration so varied? What shapes these perceptions? Research to date has unveiled a number of factors that predict public attitudes on immigration, from community-level variables such as population composition and the economy, to individual-level variables including sex, education, and political ideology. Studies generally find that women, political liberals, college-educated, and more patriotic individuals are significantly more likely than their counterparts to hold pro-immigrant views (Berg, 2009a; Chandler & Tsai, 2001; Pryce, 2018). In contrast, persons who score higher on xenophobic scales, were previously victims of crime, or had a pessimistic view of the economy are more likely to support anti-immigrant messages (Chandler & Tsai, 2001; Pryce, 2018). The evidence is less conclusive as to the role of race, income, and religion (Ceobanu & Escandell, 2010).

With respect to contextual determinants, there is support for group threat theories that suggest that as the size of ethnic/racial minorities increases, the dominant group perceives them to be a threat to their political, economic, and social power, which in turn leads to a greater prevalence of prejudiced views of these ethno-racial groups. Perceived cultural threats, measured as a preference for the exclusive use of English as the official language, have been associated with greater anti-immigrant opinions (Chandler & Tsai, 2001). Wang (2012) found that the perceived size of the undocumented immigrant population is a strong predictor of perceptions of undocumented immigrants as a criminal threat, regardless of the actual size of the immigrant population. Others have reported an unexpected positive correlation between the size of the immigrant population and pro-immigration views, perhaps explained by greater inter-group contact and more interactions with immigrants (Berg, 2009a; Ceobanu & Escandell, 2010). Another macro-level predictor is the area economy – studies find that anti-immigration attitudes vary inversely with economic prosperity. In areas with higher unemployment rates, the competition for jobs (particularly in low-skilled occupations traditionally taken by immigrants) is greater, which in turn affects how immigrants are perceived (Ceobanu & Escandell, 2010; Wang, 2012).

In summary, the public opinion on the immigration-crime link in the Trump era can be best characterized as divided. This polarization features two accounts of the net benefits from welcoming immigrants into the country: one that perceives them as a public safety threat and the other that views immigration as a vital force that injects human capital. Which one of these two accounts best fits the empirical data? Are public perceptions of immigration aligned with the reality, or are they discrepant? To answer these critical questions, in the next section, we synthesize and critically appraise the existing evidence from research studies on the connection between immigration and crime, both at the macro and individual levels.

Immigration and crime at the macro level

It is apparent that the "bad hombres" discourse is now embedded in American politics. Coupled with mixed public opinions and the enactment of more restrictive public policies on immigration matters, the status quo reinforces the widespread view that immigration is detrimental to American cities, particularly because of its assumed inextricable connection with high crime. In the next two sections, we investigate the validity of these claims, particularly with respect to two myths that pertain to macro-level units of analysis.

Myth #1: immigrant communities are criminogenic

Theoretical foundations

The idea that immigration and community crime are linked is hardly new. Starting with the Chicago School of Criminology, early urban ecology studies portrayed immigrant communities as areas of differential cultural values, weakened bonds, and social disorganization. Shaw and McKay's (1942) social disorganization theory postulates that three community-level factors: low socioeconomic status, ethnic heterogeneity, and residential mobility, lead to the disruption of social controls, which in turn increases crime. Scholars have interpreted the theory to suggest a positive relationship between immigration and crime (Lee & Martinez, 2002; Olson, Laurikkala, Huff-Corzine, & Corzine, 2009), as communities with high immigrant concentrations often have high ethnic heterogeneity and residential instability – two of the three variables that Shaw and McKay saw as criminogenic. Interestingly, empirical studies stemming from this theoretical tradition have failed to find the expected crime-inducing effects of high immigration (see Martinez & Lee, 2000), and an alternative perspective called immigrant revitalization has been proposed (Lee, Martinez, & Rosenfeld, 2001; Morenoff & Astor, 2006; Portes & Rumbaut, 2001; Portes & Stepick, 1993; Vélez, 2009).

The immigrant revitalization perspective proposes that an influx of immigrants can have positive effects on a community's social fabric by strengthening social networks, boosting local economic growth, and reinvigorating community ties with local institutions such as churches, schools, and nonprofit or government agencies (Lee et al., 2001; Vélez, 2009). Immigration not only strengthens social ties and institutions but also plays a role in diluting existing cultural values compatible with violence (MacDonald & Sampson, 2012; Sampson, 2008). These changes, in turn, can result in a reduction of crime. Ethnic enclaves illustrate three transformative processes described in the immigrant revitalization perspective: (1) labor and economy dynamics; (2) strong social ties and networks; and (3) cultural attenuation.

Like other ethnic minorities, immigrants tend to reside in areas of concentrated disadvantage, but these ethnic enclaves have strong ties to the labor market, albeit in the form of low-wage jobs in unskilled or informal labor industries (Portes & Rumbaut, 2014). The phrase "Latinos are poor but working" captures the observation that Latinos' consistent attachment to work mitigates the deleterious effects of poverty (Martinez & Lee, 2000). Labor attachment also presents new job prospects, especially in a context of tight-knit immigrant communities, as illustrated by ethnographic research of Mexican communities in Los Angeles (Massey, Alarcón, Durand, & González, 1990). The authors described how memberships in soccer clubs facilitated the exchange of news and information on employment opportunities among migrants, mostly through their habitual Sunday soccer games. With respect to the local economy, ethnic enclaves are filled with small businesses owned by immigrants to serve their growing populations of co-ethnics – restaurants, grocery stores, and street vendors (Vélez, 2009). These businesses not only employ residents and bring financial capital to the community; they also serve as role models that instill in local youth the values of working hard and participating in the formal economy (Stansfield, 2013). The economic revitalization thesis is captured in Portes and Jensen's work, where the authors portray ethnic enclaves as "a network of small enterprises that offer employment comparable to those of the mainstream economy to recent immigrants who speak little English. This network creates new entrepreneurial opportunities for newcomers – opportunities that are absent elsewhere" (Portes & Jensen, 1992, p. 420).

Strong social ties are another characteristic of ethnic enclaves, most notably, ties among family and kinship networks (Portes & Rumbaut, 2014). Latino immigrants are particularly known for their attachment to family and feelings of loyalty, respect, reciprocity, and solidarity toward family members, or "familism" (Sabogal, Marin, Otero-Sabogal, Marin, & Perez-Stable, 1987). Studies depict immigrant families as composed of nuclear and extended family members that provide emotional support during the assimilation process (Keefe, Padilla, & Carlos, 1979). Kinship ties develop among co-ethnics settling in the same neighborhood, although it is not uncommon for these ties to exist even before migrants left their homeland (Massey et al., 1990). Family and kinship ties are further reinforced by chain immigration and by the shared language, ethnic identity, and cultural traditions present in ethnic enclaves (Alba & Nee, 2003; Feldmeyer, 2009). Social ties serve to enhance informal social control, as they are the conduit whereby residents can realize and reinforce shared values. As Portes (1996) notes, the immigrant enclave provides valuable tools for exercising social control to the extent that parents call on co-ethnics to set rules and supervise youth. From an instrumental stance, residents of ethnic enclaves draw from these ties and networks for childcare, transportation, employment, housing, and health needs (Portes & Rumbaut, 2014). These support systems for families play a key role in reducing violence (Feldmeyer, 2009). Thus, immigrant communities have a kind of social capital that is unique and helps mitigate criminogenic conditions. As Massey and colleagues note, immigrants "may be poor in financial resources, but they are wealthy in social capital, which they can readily convert into jobs and earnings in the United States." (1990, p. 170).

A transformation in cultural values is a third trait of ethnic enclaves. With each wave of immigrants, new morals and values are introduced to the community. Unlike social disorganization theory, where a mix of cultural values was associated with the inability of residents to realize common values and exercise social control, in this perspective of "cultural attenuation," the cultural mix brings crime-protective effects. Sampson (2008) argues that immigration helps dilute oppositional cultural values existing in American society, as first-generation immigrants' values emphasize an appreciation for working hard and a desire to stay out of trouble. In other words, "Selective immigration in the current era may be leading to the greater visibility of competing non-violent mores that affect not just immigrant communities but diffuse and concatenate through social interactions to tamp down violent conflict in general" (2008, p. 33). Besides the attenuation of oppositional values, an influx of immigrants has the effect of reinvigorating certain cultural assets, most notably religion. In this vein, Harris and Feldmeyer (2015) suggest that Latino immigration acts as a "shot of morality." They describe how Latino communities have high levels of church participation and civic engagement, as well as uniformity in religious values. They hypothesize that these characteristics are negatively associated with violence, and mediate the link between immigration and crime. The strengthening of religious institutions and churches in ethnic enclaves is believed to lead to an increase in social control and a decrease in crime, via processes of increased solidarity, reinforcement of shared community values, and the emergence of community-based organizations (Shihadeh & Winters, 2010).

In summary, scholarship to date suggests that an influx of immigrants can have powerful revitalization effects in a community, as opposed to the dislocating effects predicted by social disorganization theory. Immigration can engender a new kind of social organization where co-ethnics draw from social ties and engage in reciprocated exchanges that strengthen social control, ensure access to steady jobs, promote cultural attenuation, and facilitate upward assimilation in an urban environment that would otherwise be mostly criminogenic (Davies & Fagan, 2012; Lee & Martinez, 2002; MacDonald & Sampson, 2012; Portes & Rumbaut, 2014).

Empirical evidence

Having reviewed the theoretical arguments as to why one would expect areas with greater concentrations of foreign-born to have lower crime rates, we now turn our attention to the empirical evidence from macro-level studies. This evidence can either refute or confirm the widespread myth that immigration causes crime. Over the past two decades, the body of literature examining the immigration-crime connection at the macro level expanded rapidly. A recent meta-analysis of this literature found over 50 macro-level studies published in the period between 1994 and 2014 (Ousey & Kubrin, 2018). Research findings have been so consistent that scholars have reached a point of consensus: There is either an inverse relationship or no relationship between immigration and crime (Lee & Martinez, 2009; Martinez & Lee, 2000; Ousey & Kubrin, 2018). This pattern holds even after controlling for longstanding crime correlates such as neighborhood concentrated disadvantage, population, unemployment, and racial heterogeneity (Feldmeyer, 2009; Feldmeyer, Madero-Hernandez, Rojas-Gaona, & Sabon, 2019; Kubrin & Desmond, 2015; Kubrin, Hipp, & Kim, 2018; Lyons, Vélez, & Santoro, 2013; Martinez, Stowell, & Cancino, 2008; Ousey & Kubrin, 2014; Ramey, 2013; Stowell et al., 2009; Vélez, 2009; Xie & Baumer, 2018). These studies demystify the idea that immigration is criminogenic while also showing ways in which it protects against crime (Martinez, 2002, 2010; Rojas-Gaona & Madero-Hernandez, 2018).

Early research into this issue was conducted on three known immigrant U.S. cities: San Diego, Miami, and El Paso. Lee et al. (2001) examined Black and Latino homicide data in these cities from 1989 to 1995 and found that recent immigration generally does not increase homicides. Other studies have documented the absence of crime-inducing effects in high immigration cities like New York, Chicago, San Antonio, Orlando, and Houston (Davies & Fagan, 2012; Kubrin & Ishizawa, 2012; Lee & Martinez, 2006; Martinez, 2002, 2010; Martinez & Stowell, 2012; Olson et al., 2009), as well as in analyses of pooled data across metropolitan areas nationwide (Butcher & Piehl, 1998; Ousey & Kubrin, 2014; Reid, Weiss, & Adelman, 2005). Thus, net of the effects of socio-demographic and economic factors, rates of lethal violence are lower in places with more immigrants.

With immigration being a process that unfolds over time, longitudinal research is best to unravel any criminogenic effects. Only a handful of studies have examined the immigration-crime connection over time, although their findings have been consistent. Ousey and Kubrin (2009) used data from 159 U.S. cities to assess changes in violent crime rates between 1980 and 2000. Results from fixed-effect models showed that immigration lowers violence over time; a one-unit increase in immigration is associated with a decrease of 253 violent crimes per 100,000 persons. Stowell et al. (2009) similarly reported that relative surges in the Latino immigrant population were associated with decreases in violent crime, robbery, and assault rates over a period of ten years. Other studies have replicated these findings in smaller geographical areas, such as neighborhoods. Martinez, Stowell, and Lee (2010) analyzed pooled homicide data (1980–2000) in San Diego census tracts and found that increases in foreign-born populations lead to decreases in lethal violence over time, particularly for Latinos and Whites. MacDonald, Hipp, and Gill (2013) reported that a 19% increase in immigrant concentration in Los Angeles tracts was associated with a reduction of 36% in total crime, and 41% in violent crime between 2000 and 2005. In sum, the crime-reducing effects of immigration do not appear to be an artifact of cross-sectional data (see also Ousey & Kubrin, 2014; Ramey, 2013; Wadsworth, 2010).

With compelling evidence that immigration does not increase crime and could even suppress it, researchers have begun to examine the circumstances under which immigration brings crime-protective effects (versus null effects). Emergent research has probed into the particularities of the immigration-crime link in three areas: (1) race-specific immigration effects; (2) conditioning effects by context of reception; and (3) causal mechanisms at work. Below we describe these three research areas.

Whereas most of the immigration-crime research studies to date have examined crime rates for the total population, a few studies have disaggregated crime by race (Davies & Fagan, 2012; Harris, Gruenewald, & Painter-Davis, 2015; Martinez & Stowell, 2012; Nielsen, Lee, & Martinez Ramiro, 2005; Shihadeh & Barranco, 2010a; Xie & Baumer, 2018). These studies test the racial invariance hypothesis – the idea that an influx in foreign-born populations is expected to impact Black, Latino, and White crime equally. Racial variance is also likely, as researchers suggest, for example, that surges in Latino immigration can be criminogenic for racial minorities, but not Whites, due to high competition between marginalized racial groups in the low-wage unskilled labor market (Harris et al., 2015; Shihadeh & Barranco, 2010a). Research findings in this area have been mixed. Lee et al. (2001) found that percent of new immigrants is associated with reduced homicides of Latinos in El Paso and Blacks in Miami, but with increased homicides of Blacks in San Diego. Analogous results emerged in subsequent analyses of the same dataset, as reported by Nielsen et al. (2005). Shihadeh and Barranco (2010a) reported that the positive relationship between Latino immigration and Black homicide disappears when controlling for Black unemployment. Thus, immigration may be criminogenic when it shifts the racial composition of job markets, reducing the economic prospects of Blacks.

The effects of immigration could also vary by the ecological context of reception, particularly between "traditional" versus "new" immigrant destinations. *Traditional destinations* are locations with long histories of immigrant settlement (e.g., New York City, Chicago, Los Angeles). Having experienced successive waves of immigration, they have well-established labor/housing markets and support systems in place for newcomers, which facilitates the incorporation process (Ferraro, 2016). *New destinations* are places with recent growth in immigration, not known as old immigrant gateways (e.g., Arizona, New Mexico, South Carolina, North Carolina, Georgia). From a theoretical stance, it is hypothesized that lacking support systems for immigrants in these new destinations could lead to blocked labor opportunities, marginalization, and social disorganization, which in turn could increase crime (Ferraro, 2016; Shihadeh & Winters, 2010). However, the handful of studies on this issue have reported mixed results. Shihadeh and Barranco (2010b) found that linguistic isolation, a measure of immigration, is inversely related to Latino homicides in traditional immigration areas, but positively related to Latino homicides in new destinations. Shihadeh and Winters (2010) reported that Latino immigration significantly reduces Latino homicide, but only in traditional immigration areas. In Harris and Feldmeyer's (2013) analysis of census tracts in California, New York, and Texas, the authors reported that recent immigration decreases Latino violence in traditional destinations, though it has no effects on either Black or White violence. In new destinations, immigration increases Latino and Black violence, while not significantly affecting White violence. Unlike these studies, Ferraro's (2016) analysis revealed that that recent immigration in new destinations is associated with significant declines in both property and violent crime over time, declines that are greater than observed in any other locations (see also Painter-Davis, 2016; Ramey, 2013).

Finally, emerging research has started to investigate the mediating and moderating effects that may underlie the immigration and crime relationship. Social capital is one of the factors believed to mediate the effects of immigration on crime, although studies to date reveal divergent patterns. Burchfield and Silver (2012) reported that neighborhoods of high immigrant concentration have higher robbery rates, and this association is mediated by lower levels of collective efficacy. In contrast, Feldmeyer et al. (2019) reported opposite and offsetting pathways connecting immigration and violence: while immigrant concentration is associated with lower collective efficacy, which increases violence, it is also linked with more friendship and kinship ties, thereby resulting in less violence. Religion is another factor hypothesized to mediate the effects of immigration on crime, although the research in this area is limited. Two studies published to date suggest that Latino concentration is associated with higher levels of Catholicism, civically engaged religious adherence, and religious homogeneity, which in turn are inversely linked with violent crime (Harris & Feldmeyer, 2015; Shihadeh & Winters, 2010).

The last two variables believed to mediate the immigration-crime relationship are political opportunities and local economies. Political opportunities for immigrants are reflected in a city's support for pro-immigration legislation, more elected ethnic minorities in office, and wider networks of social support for immigrants. Lyons et al. (2013) report that these conditions enhance the crime-reducing effects of immigration; in fact, the inverse association between immigrant concentration and homicide rates is strongest in cities with greater political incorporation of Asians and Latinos. As to the role of local economies, Stansfield (2013) argues that the economic growth brought about by recent immigration buffers the effects of concentrated disadvantage and thereby reduces crime. The author found support for this idea, as seen in a negative association between immigration and property crime rates in U.S. cities, a relationship that is reduced to non-significance after controlling for Latino-owned businesses.

In conclusion, there is no shortage of macro-level research into the question as to whether immigration causes crime. Our recent history highlights anti-immigration rhetoric that often depicts immigrants as a destabilizing force to communities. Two theories, social disorganization and immigrant revitalization, offer alternative and opposite predictions as to the criminogenic effects of immigration, or lack thereof. Drawing from a large body of literature to date, we can objectively assess the argument that immigrants are "harmful to American society." The current evidence demystifies the idea that immigration causes crime to rise. In some cases, immigration actually reduces crime rates (Lee & Martinez, 2009; MacDonald & Sampson, 2012; Martinez, 2010; Ousey & Kubrin, 2018; Rojas-Gaona & Madero-Hernandez, 2018). Yet, more research is needed to better understand the causal mechanisms underlying the immigration-crime link.

Myth #2: sanctuary cities foster crime

In the wake of the anti-immigration rhetoric that unfolded over the last decades, local jurisdictions across the United States took steps to ensure a more welcoming atmosphere for immigrant populations through the enactment of ordinances and laws that restrict the participation of local police in the enforcement of immigration violations. These jurisdictions, popularly known as "sanctuary cities," grew in number recently. In 2018, it was estimated that 114 counties had provisions that banned the use of local resources for the enforcement of immigration violations (Avila, Bello, Graber, & Marquez, 2018), up from the 53 estimated to have such bans two years earlier (Graber & Marquez, 2016). Others indicate that the number of sanctuary jurisdictions across the country exceeds 300, including counties, cities, and townships (Karaim, 2018). Despite their recent growth, sanctuary cities date back to the so-called "sanctuary movement" of the 1980s (Martinez, Martinez-Schuldt, & Cantor, 2018). San Francisco, California, enacted its "City and County of Refuge" ordinance in 1989 to prevent local police from assisting with deportations of refugees fleeing violence in Central America. Amended in 2016, the ordinance prohibits the use of city funds to enforce federal immigration laws, except for violent or serious felony crimes (San Francisco Administrative Code, 2016).

Although there is no universal definition for sanctuary cities, the term generally denotes "jurisdictions that willfully refuse to comply with 8 U.S.C. 1373" (Executive Order No. 13768, 2017), which refers to a federal statute prohibiting government entities from withholding information from the U.S. Citizenship and Immigration Services regarding the immigration status or citizenship of a person. Alternative definitions, like the one used by the U.S. Department of Justice, allude broadly to policies that limit the enforcement of immigration laws by local authorities, thus including things like refusal to share information and lack of cooperation in honoring of detainers (i.e., holds issued by the U.S. Immigration and Customs Enforcement or ICE). These detainers prolong the confinement of suspected undocumented persons in local jails past the point when they have been cleared by local authorities, until ICE takes over custody, typically 48 hours. Yet, a third way to define sanctuary cities is by their lack of participation in any of the programs that authorize local police to perform immigration functions, including the 287(g) program, the Secure Communities program, and the Criminal Alien Program (Graber & Marquez, 2016).

Sanctuary cities have sparked much controversy in light of the Trump administration's position on it. The administration states that sanctuary provisions "willfully violate Federal law in an attempt to shield aliens from removal from the United States" and "caused immeasurable harm to the American people and to the very fabric of our Republic." (Executive Order No. 13768, 2017). Efforts to crackdown included a campaign to have the Attorney General or the Secretary withhold federal grants from sanctuary jurisdictions, an action blocked by the Ninth Circuit Court of Appeals (Egelko, 2018). Later, President Trump took to Twitter to threaten the release of migrants detained at the border in sanctuary cities, a policy that the White House did not confirm (Sullivan, 2019).

There are mixed opinions on the effects that sanctuary policies have on crime. On the one hand, critics embrace the rhetoric that sanctuary cities have more crime. This position suggests a positive correlation between sanctuary status and crime rates, likely due to two mechanisms. One is a behavioral change whereby immigrants established in the city begin perpetrating more crimes due to decreased deterrence, as summarized by former Attorney General Jeff Sessions: "When cities like Philadelphia, Boston, or San Francisco advertise that they have [sanctuary] policies, the criminals take notice." (Sessions, 2017). Another mechanism is a shift in the composition of the immigrant population attracted to the city, from lower to higher criminal propensities (Treyger, Chalfin, & Loeffler, 2014).

On the other hand, proponents claim that sanctuary policies facilitate citizen-police relations that help police solve crimes, thereby making cities safer. For instance, Lyons et al. (2013) argue that cities that adopt pro-immigrant legislation can boost social control processes by engendering trust in civic institutions such as the police. Others cite arguments from the community policing and procedural justice framework that the looming prospect of deportation presents a barrier that prevents victims and witnesses from reporting crimes and collaborating with prosecutors. This, in turn, results in greater proportions of immigrants at risk of victimization, and more perpetrators not being apprehended (Kirk, Papachristos, Fagan, & Tyler, 2012; Skogan & Steiner, 2004). Simply put, "without assurances that they will not be subject to an immigration investigation and possible deportation, many immigrants with critical information would not come forward" (Tramonte, 2011, p. 6).

In light of this controversy, scholars have started to investigate what, if any, are the effects of sanctuary policies on crime. The studies published to date are new and few in number, therefore, their conclusions are limited in scope. However, their findings have begun to inform our understanding of the crime dynamics in sanctuary cities. These studies move us beyond accounts based on anecdotal evidence or high-profile cases of crimes perpetrated by undocumented immigrants, such as was the case of Kathryn Steinle in San Francisco, touted by political pundits as proof that immigrants are dangerous (Kulig & Cullen, 2019; Martinez et al., 2018).

A first study was conducted by Wong (2017) and published in a report by the National Immigration Law Center. Wong found that crime is significantly lower in sanctuary counties; on average, there are 35.5 fewer crimes committed per 10,000 people in such counties. An important limitation of this study was the bivariate nature of the results reported, as important differences between sanctuary and non-sanctuary cities may exist that are not accounted for (e.g., poverty rates, population, unemployment). In a separate study, Gonzalez,

Collingwood, and El-Khatib (2019) evaluated differences in crime in sanctuary cities, using data for over 100 U.S. cities between 2000 and 2014. The authors matched sanctuary cities with non-sanctuary cities of comparable sociodemographic profile, thereby providing a strong research design for drawing causal inferences. They reported no discernible differences on violent crime, property crime, and rape between sanctuary and non-sanctuary cities; whereas some cities experienced increases in crime following the enactment of sanctuary protections, others had no change or even reported reductions in crime over time. Gonzalez et al. concluded that "sanctuary cities have essentially no impact one way or the other" (2019, p. 31). Martinez-Schuldt and Martinez (2017) similarly found that the adoption of sanctuary policies is associated with decreases in robbery. The authors also reported that increases in the unauthorized Mexican immigrant population are linked with reductions in homicides, though only in sanctuary cities.

In closing, there is no significant evidence that sanctuary cities have more crime than non-sanctuary cities. This conclusion is limited to a handful of studies, and more research is needed in order to replicate or refute their findings (see Martinez, Martinez-Schuldt, & Cantor, 2017). Yet, the overall picture that emerges from this research is consistent with other studies that find that programs that authorize local enforcement of immigration, such as Secure Communities, have little to no impact on crime (Ciancio, 2017; Cox & Miles, 2015; Treyger et al., 2014).

Immigration and crime at the individual level

As noted in the previous section, there is ample evidence showing that the influx of immigrants has a neutral or even crime reducing effect in different ecological units and that immigrant communities tend to have lower crime rates than non-immigrant communities with similar levels of disadvantage. In this section, we discuss evidence tackling other core myths regarding immigration: the idea that immigrants commit more crimes than non-immigrant U.S. citizens and that undocumented immigrants pose a special threat to U.S. security.

Myth #3: immigrants commit more crimes than non-immigrants

Most research on immigration and crime has been done at the macro and meso levels of analysis. However, an important part of the mythology of immigration rests on the idea that immigrants are themselves "bad" people and, specifically, more criminal than the native U.S. population. Here, the myth is not that the influx of immigrants increases crime in a community or geographical unit by a series of complex social processes (e.g., labor market changes, social disorganization), it is precisely the belief that immigrants are criminals (or crime-prone) themselves. In other words, according to this notion, immigrants are the ones who commit more crimes than their U.S.-born counterparts.

Theoretical perspectives on immigration and crime

Scholars have elaborated potential explanations for why immigrants would be expected to commit more crimes than non-immigrants (see, Butcher & Piehl, 2007; Mears, 2002). To understand these potential theoretical links between immigrants and crime, it is important to take notice of the demographic characteristics of U.S. immigrants throughout its history. While the first wave of immigrants comprised predominantly White low-skilled workers from rural areas from Europe, more recent immigrants (post-1965) are way more heterogeneous in their composition (Portes & Rumbaut, 2001; Portes & Zhou, 1993). These new immigrants belong to minoritized racial and ethnic groups (coming largely from Latin America and Asia) and differ sharply in terms of their education, capital, skills, and in their legal status (Portes & Rumbaut, 2014). The context of reception they encounter at their arrival is also sharply different. Immigrants not only differ in terms of their documented status but also face different levels of discrimination at their destination and are also differentially supported by their co-ethnic communities. Some immigrants are thus welcome by strong and resourceful co-ethnic communities while in other cases, immigrants rely on impoverished and marginalized communities. In some destinations, co-ethnic communities do not even exist.

The criminogenic pressures that immigrants face seem straightforward. As social disorganization theory would point out, first-wave immigrants moving to rapidly growing urban areas tended to settle into the socially disorganized zones in transition (Burgess, 1925). There, they experienced strain and were exposed to different criminal and non-criminal subcultures. The breakdown of social controls produced by the social disorganization of the areas and their poor structural conditions also impacted the socialization and supervision of children, all of which exerted criminogenic pressures on the population residing in those areas. Thus, the macro-level conditions that recently arrived immigrants were exposed to were deemed to increase their exposure to micro-level criminogenic pressures and thus, theoretically, to engage in more crime (Chouhy, 2018; Ousey & Kubrin, 2009; Shaw & McKay, 1942).

Nevertheless, in an era of rapid industrialization and economic growth, these criminogenic pressures were not supposed to last long. Older immigrants would achieve upward mobility and move out of the zones in transition, while new immigrants would take their place. In their seminal study, Shaw and McKay (1942) show that, as immigrants moved out of these zones, the criminogenic pressures that they faced faded and their criminal engagement decreased. As previously discussed, this finding gave origin to the racial invariance thesis that posited that high crime areas were the result of the structural and organizational features of such areas – and the criminogenic pressures they created for individuals – and not the product of the cultural characteristics of the communities that inhabited them. Socially disorganized communities remained socially disorganized, despite changing in terms of their ethnic composition. Even though Shaw and McKay did not compare the criminality of immigrants versus non-immigrants, social disorganization theory suggested that recent immigrants would engage in more crime than the native population – given their exposure to more criminogenic environments. Consistent with straight-line assimilation perspectives, social disorganization theory posited that, as immigrants progressively assimilated into the U.S. society and seized the upward mobility ladders offered to them and moved out from criminogenic areas, their criminality would decrease. The path of assimilation offered opportunities to thrive (Alba & Nee, 2003; Feldmeyer, 2018; Portes & Rumbaut, 2001).

The prospects have been bleaker for more recent immigrants. Unlike their predecessors, second-wave immigrants face the reality of deindustrialization, a fragmented labor market with meager opportunities for low-skilled workers, and highly segregated cities, all of which block their opportunities to achieve the American Dream

(Portes & Zhou, 1993). Many immigrants – especially low-skilled immigrants from Latin America and some parts of Asia – also face an increasingly hostile context of reception. Because of the different racial and ethnic makeup of the second wave of immigrants, they are often racialized and face rampant discrimination that further blocks their opportunities. Changes in immigration policies have also made it more challenging for large portions of the immigrant population to obtain authorization to live and work in the United States, which sharply constraints their opportunities.

This worsening scenario for large portions of the immigrant population (especially marginalized unskilled and undocumented workers) could be deemed to increase the criminogenic pressures and lead to increased engagement in crime. Paradoxically, the opposite seems to be the case: A wide array of studies has documented that immigrants tend to engage less in crime than the native U.S. population (Butcher & Piehl, 2007; Rumbaut & Ewing, 2007; Salas-Wright, Vaughn, Schwartz, & Córdova, 2016; Vaughn, Salas-Wright, DeLisi, & Maynard, 2014). This common finding – which extends to other areas such as academic achievement and health – has been referred to as the "immigrant paradox" (Marks, Ejesi, & García Coll, 2014; Sampson, 2008; Suárez-Orozco, Rhodes, & Milburn, 2009).

Empirical studies about immigration and crime

The findings of this negative relationship between immigrant status and crime have been remarkably robust across studies focusing on either national or local samples, youth or adult subjects, and assessing different types of behaviors – ranging from externalizing and antisocial behaviors to violent offending. For example, analyzing a nationally representative sample, Vaughn et al. (2014) examined the differences in self-reported involvement in a wide range of violent and nonviolent antisocial behaviors between immigrants and native-born adults. In their study, immigrants reported lower rates of engagement in all the types of behaviors studied. This difference achieved statistical significance for all but a few types of behaviors. These results held when the researchers controlled for relevant covariates such as gender, race/ethnicity, income, region, and other potential confounding individual and family characteristics. Additionally, they found that this lower involvement in antisocial behavior for immigrants was observed regardless of the immigrants' region of origin considered (Africa, Asia, Europe, or Latin America).

A similar finding was reported by Butcher and Piehl (1998) when, analyzing a national-level sample of youth, they compared immigrants and the native-born population's self-reported crimes. Remarkably, their study is aligned with Vaughn et al.'s (2014) findings. The analysis shows that raw levels of involvement in crime are lower for immigrants even though immigrants tend to have lower levels of education, income, and reside in cities – all factors correlated with higher involvement in crime. When those factors are accounted for in the analysis, the differentials in crime involvement between immigrants and non-immigrants become even larger.

Several survey studies have yielded similar results. Thus, Salas-Wright et al. (2016) found lower levels of involvement in externalizing behaviors in a nationally representative sample of youth, whereas Hernandez, Denton, Macartney, and Blanchard (2012) found significant differences between immigrants and non-immigrants Whites' delinquent involvement, before and after controlling for socioeconomic status. Harris (1999) also found lower levels of involvement in risky behaviors (including delinquency) between immigrants and native-born youths. Again, in her study, this lower level of involvement in risky behavior held when the sample was disaggregated by ethnic group. Sampson, Morenoff, and Raudenbush (2005) and Burrington (2015) reported a negative effect of being an immigrant in different measures of self-reported violent offending for a sample of Chicago youths.

This relationship seems to hold for samples of juveniles and adults involved with the criminal justice system. In this regard, Bersani et al. (2014) analyzed a sample of youth adjudicated for a serious offense in Arizona and Pennsylvania and found that immigrants reported lower levels of serious offending. Furthermore, their study shows that immigrants are less likely to be persistent offenders and tend to desist from crime sooner than their non-immigrant counterparts. Ibañez et al. (2017) investigated a convenience sample of Latino community corrections clients in Miami, including their lifetime and recent reports of criminal activity for both violent and nonviolent offenses. Their findings also reveal lower levels of criminal involvement for foreign-born when compared with U.S.-born Latinos.

A different set of studies has examined the relationship between immigration and crime using measures of involvement with the justice system, thus comparing rates of arrest, convictions, and incarcerations of immigrants and non-immigrants. These studies have also reached a similar conclusion than those based on self-reports of criminal and problematic behavior. Ewing et al. (2015) analyzed data from the 2010 American Community Survey and found that the incarceration rate for immigrant males aged between 18 and 39 years old was 1.6%, while the rate for native-born males in the same age range was 3.3%. Butcher and Piehl (2007) also analyzed institutionalization rates using publicly available micro-samples of the U.S. census and showed a similar gap in these rates between immigrants and the native-born from males in this same age range in 1980, 1990, and 2000.

Moehling and Piehl (2009) further investigate this issue from a historical perspective analyzing the gap in prison commitment rates for serious crimes between foreign-born and White males for different age ranges. While in 1904 the commitment rate for serious offenses was higher for immigrant youths aged 18 and 19 years old, compared to their native-born counterparts, all other age groups exhibited similar incarceration rates. This trend is reversed by 1930 when foreign-born of all ages start to exhibit lower rates of prison commitments for serious crimes than the native-born. Thus, the authors show that the gap increases over time due to the incarceration rate of immigrants remaining stable and that of the native-born sharply increasing. The authors acknowledge that the rates of commitments for minor offenses (such as vagrancy or drunkenness) are higher for immigrants than non-immigrants. Still, they argue that those commitment rates likely reflect differential criminal justice processing of immigrants and not true differential engagement in the behavior being considered.

In a similar vein, Hagan and Palloni (2012) used data from the Survey of State Prisons to calculate ratios of immigrant-to-citizens incarceration rates for male immigrants of different nationalities. The raw ratios show higher imprisonment rates for most immigrant groups. However, in an innovative analysis, the authors use data from El Paso and San Diego felony cases to estimate the differential probabilities of pre-trial detention, conviction, and sentencing faced by immigrants and non-immigrants. Their analysis of El Paso and San Diego cases clearly shows that, upon arrest, immigrants are disproportionately more likely to be sent to pre-trial detention, convicted, and sentenced to prison. Thus, when they use those coefficients to adjust the ratios (on top of an adjustment for age), they show that all immigrant groups exhibit lower imprisonment ratios than their U.S. citizen counterparts. According to the authors, these adjusted ratios more truly represent differences in involvement in criminal behavior between immigrants and non-immigrants and show that, for all groups, immigrants tend to be considerably less likely to engage in criminal behavior than U.S. citizens. In fact, the ratios range from 0.57 for Cubans to 0.11 for Salvadorians, showing a substantially lower involvement in crime for immigrants.

Making sense of the immigrant paradox

The empirical evidence is somewhat clear in showing that immigrants tend to engage in lower levels of criminal and problem behaviors than their non-immigrants counterparts. Less understood are, however, the reasons why this is the case. Emerging research on this matter is less conclusive and scattered across studies.

An important line of research that provides some keys to understanding this apparent paradox is that focused on comparing different generations of immigrants in terms of a variety of outcomes. Thus, many studies focused on immigration and crime have examined the differential criminal or delinquent involvement of first-, second-, and sometimes third-generation immigrants, instead of directly comparing immigrants versus non-immigrants. This literature is also robust in showing that first-generation immigrants tend to exhibit lower levels of criminal and problem behaviors than second and third generations (Bersani, 2014b; Burrington, 2015; Haller, Portes, & Lynch, 2011; Morenoff & Astor, 2006; Portes, Fernández-Kelly, & Haller, 2005). An important note in this regard comes from Bersani and Piquero (2017), who use official and self-reported data on delinquent involvement on a sample of adjudicated youth to show that the differential in self-reported delinquency often observed in non-immigrants does not come from systematic underreporting. In fact, according to their study, there are no differences in reporting bias across different generations of immigrants and youth from non-immigrant families.

Borrowing from segmented assimilation theory, these studies point out the problematic role of acculturation, especially for those immigrants assimilating into the lowest strata of U.S. society, which exhibit higher differences between first and further generations of immigrants (Rumbaut & Ewing, 2007; Salas-Wright et al., 2016; Vaughn et al., 2014). This effect of acculturation is also observed when comparing first-generation immigrants according to their time in the United States. These studies also show that the longer the immigrants have been in the United States, the higher their involvement in different types of problem behaviors. Other studies provide different measures of acculturation and enculturation (such as adoption of English, use of own language, ethnic identity, and strength of co-ethnic community) to show that immigrant families who maintain their ethnic customs and language and/or receive support from their co-ethnics do better than those that rapidly acculturate (Alvarez-Rivera, Nobles, & Lersch, 2014; Desmond & Kubrin, 2009; Morenoff & Astor, 2006; Nagasawa, Qian, Wong, & Wong, 2001; Xie & Greenman, 2005). This negative effect seems to be contingent upon the strata immigrants are assimilating into, impacting more severely low-skilled immigrants from minoritized groups.

Importantly, as Bersani (2014a) points out, the finding that the children of immigrants fare worse than their predecessors in a wide range of outcomes does not mean that they are at higher risk of involvement in criminal behavior than the children of the native-born. Rather, studies show that successive immigrant generations "catch up" on their counterparts and progressively resemble the larger U.S. population, thus exhibiting similarly high levels of problem behaviors than children from families with longer trajectories in the United States (Bersani, 2014a; Rumbaut & Ewing, 2007)

Besides acculturation, other studies have explored different potential explanations of the immigrant paradox, further examining potential differences between immigrants and either their children or the non-immigrant population that may explain their differential involvement in criminal and problem behaviors. Piquero, Bersani, Loughran, and Fagan (2016) examined differences in legal socialization between first generation, second generation, and everyone else in a sample of adjudicated youth. Their study found that first-generation immigrants consistently show a more positive view of the law and lower levels of legal cynicism than other groups. Immigrant youth also reported higher social costs associated with breaking the law. In their analysis of incarceration records in 1980, 1990, and 2000, Butcher and Piehl (2007) evaluated different potential explanations for the lower incarceration rates consistently observed for immigrants. Their data suggests that the deportation faced by immigrants who commit crime does not drive these differences. Rather, by observing lower rates of institutionalization for those natives who live outside the state they were born in, the authors posit that the lower rates are the result of the self-selection process of migration, which results in lower propensities to engage in crime and, among other things, higher susceptibilities to deterrence. A similar argument is made by Bersani (2014a) when she compares second-immigration immigrants with youth from non-immigrant families. Her findings of children of immigrants catching up with the rest of the population suggest a regression to the mean. The characteristics upon which immigrants self-select fade across generations, resulting in successive generations of immigrants progressively resembling the rest of the population. This explanation seems to directly contradict President Trump's claim that "Mexico is not sending us their best" and to suggest that the opposite may indeed be the case.

Myth #4: undocumented immigrants commit more crime than the general population

A common variation of the myth of immigrant criminality focuses not on the immigrant population overall but on a specific subgroups of immigrants: those who are undocumented (Berg, 2009b; Hickman & Suttorp, 2008; Rumbaut & Ewing, 2007; Stupi, Chiricos, & Gertz, 2016). Although less extensive, the extant research on this topic seems to contradict this commonly held assumption. Thus, similar to what is found for the general population of immigrants, studies examining the criminality of undocumented immigrants show that they do not engage in more crime than the native-born population. Rather, some studies seem to indicate quite the opposite.

Research aiming at measuring criminal involvement of undocumented immigrants faces the specific challenge of identifying the number of undocumented immigrants in official data, which generally lacks information about documented status in the United States. For that reason, researchers have relied on different computation methods to estimate this population. Ewing et al. (2015) compared rates of native-born, Mexican, and Guatemalan/Salvadoran men aged 18–39 who did not have a high-school diploma. They found a sharp difference in the incarceration rate of the native-born group when compared with Mexican and Guatemalan/Salvadorans. In fact, while the incarceration rate for the native-born in 2010 was 10.7%, that of Mexicans was 2.8% while being 1.7% for Guatemalan/Salvadorans. Even more stark differences were found in 2000.

Using a different method to estimate the likely unauthorized immigrants, researchers from the CATO Institute (a libertarian think tank) analyzed data from the American Community Survey to compare rates of incarceration of native-born, authorized, and unauthorized immigrants (Landgrave & Nowrasteh, 2017a, 2019). Their analyses using data from 2014 revealed that incarceration rates of the undocumented immigrants are higher than those of documented immigrants (0.85% vs. 0.47%) but still substantially lower than those of the native-born (1.53%). Incarceration rates of undocumented immigrants of every region of birth were lower than the native-born rate. The undocumented immigrants' incarceration rate remained below that of the native-born when disaggregated by race and ethnicity (Landgrave & Nowrasteh, 2017a.). In a more updated and detailed analysis based on 2017 data, they corroborated these findings. Their estimations reveal that documented immigrants have the lowest incarceration rates across the three groups considered, followed by undocumented immigrants. Native-born individuals, on the contrary, exhibit the highest incarceration rates. This finding remains the same across age, education, and race and ethnicity groups (Landgrave & Nowrasteh, 2019). Overall, these studies challenge findings based on federal prison data, which show higher rates of undocumented immigrants in federal prisons. Even though neither Ewing et al. (2015) nor Nowrasteh (2018b) contest these figures, they question their reliability. Immigrant offenses are considered federal crimes. This fact inflates the share of undocumented immigrants serving time and makes the proportion of immigrants serving time at federal prisons an unreliable measure of immigrant criminality, especially when being used to compare immigrant and non-immigrant criminality. Further, they note that federal inmates only account for roughly 10% of the U.S. incarcerated population.

Using a similar methodology, Landgrave and Nowrasteh (2017b) also estimate the incarceration rates of Deferred Action for Childhood Arrivals (DACA) recipients, a program that grants temporary authorization to live and work in the U.S. to certain formerly undocumented immigrants who arrived in the United States as children. Their results show that DACA recipients have a very similar but slightly lower incarceration rate than their U.S.-born counterparts with the same demographic characteristics (0.98 percent vs. 1.12), albeit considerably higher than documented immigrants (0.24%). With only a few exceptions, these findings also hold when disaggregating by education, race/ethnicity, and gender.

Two other studies offer important insights into this issue. First, using data from Texas, Nowrasteh (2018a) estimated the arrest and conviction rates for different crimes for documented and undocumented immigrants and U.S.-born citizens. Given that Texas is the only state that registers the immigrant status of arrestees and convicted individuals, these data allow us to more reliably estimate the differential rates across groups. The findings are aligned with that from previous studies and show those undocumented immigrants have lower rates of arrest (for homicides, sex crimes, and larceny) than their U.S.-born counterparts – and higher than documented immigrants. The same is observed for conviction rates for all the offenses considered. Second, Hickman and Suttorp (2008) examined recidivism rates of immigrants released from the Los Angeles County Jail. They classified individuals based on whether they were considered deportable or not. Deportable individuals were those that had entered the United States without authorization and those who were authorized to enter into the U.S. but no longer eligible to stay (due to visa overstays or to convictions for felony or misdemeanor crimes). Their analysis shows no difference in recidivism between deportable and non-deportable individuals, suggesting that "deportable aliens" do not pose a special threat to public safety.

The real consequences of immigration policy

In the previous sections, we provided evidence showing the general consensus that has been reached in academia debunking commonly held myths that immigration does not increase (and may even decrease) crime and that immigrants are not more likely (if not less likely) to be involved in crime than non-immigrants. The fact that these myths are not supported by empirical evidence does not preclude them from having very real consequences for immigrants and their families in particular, and more broadly, for the whole U.S. population. In this section, we briefly discuss some of the consequences of policies derived from these widely held mythologies that feed the notion of the immigrant threat.

Crimmigration: the criminalization of immigration enforcement

The criminalization of immigration law and enforcement is hardly a new phenomenon. Scholars have acknowledged a progressive move toward a criminal approach to immigration that started way before Trump's presidency and has been taking place not only in the United States but across the industrialized world (Bourbeau, 2019; Bowling & Westenra, 2018; Ewing et al., 2015; Menjívar & Alvord, 2018; Stumpf, 2006). They termed this convergence of immigration and criminal law "crimmigration." According to Stumpf, "The 'crimmigration' merger has taken place on three fronts: (1) the substance of immigration law and criminal law increasingly overlaps; (2) immigration enforcement has come to resemble criminal law enforcement; and (3) the procedural aspects of prosecuting immigration violations have taken on many of the earmarks of criminal procedure" (2006, p. 14).

The crimmigration expansion was part of the punitive turn that began in the 1970s and led to the era of mass incarceration. Scholars trace the parallels between the growth of the carceral state and the social sensibilities and public discourses that enabled it and the "governing immigration through crime" imperative (Golash-Boza, 2016; Inda & Dowling, 2013). Similar to the "super-predator" narrative, the new immigration enforcement paradigm relied on a symbology of immigrants as threats of public safety, which led to the construction of the "criminal alien" problem. The construction of the immigration problem as a problem of social security allows the mobilization of an enforcement apparatus closely entrenched with that of the criminal justice system and results in the convergence of different law enforcement agencies over-policing immigrant communities and larger portions of the population – not necessarily only those that fit the definition of "criminal aliens" – and larger amounts of people being under control of immigrant officials, held at immigration detention facilities, and deported (Armenta, 2017; Inda & Dowling, 2013; Menjívar & Alvord, 2018). In this manner, the crimmigration movement can be understood as a system of racialized social control analogous to the mass incarceration movement that suppressed native-born African American and Latinos in the past decades, as described in *The New Jim Crow* by Michelle Alexander (2012).

Despite the fact that the (over)criminalization (Chacón, 2012) of immigration control has a longer history, many researchers affirm that this idea of immigrants as threats that need to be controlled was magnified by 9/11 (Inda & Dowling, 2013; Stumpf, 2006). Crimmigration scholars are not shy in pointing out how the criminalization of immigration control was also a salient component of the Barack Obama administration (Golash-Boza, 2016; Vázquez, 2017). In fact, Vázquez (2017) discusses this omission, given that immigration reform was absent from the criminal reform discussion during the Obama era. In her view, the "smart on crime" movement has failed to recognize the role that crimmigration has had on the expansion of the criminal justice system. As such, it has overlooked the stark similarities of the effects of this expanded immigration control machine on poor immigrant and Latino communities with the effects that mass incarceration has had on impoverished Black communities. In fact, the immigration apparatus was a vital component of the carceral state and an instrument for the expansion of social control and targeting of minorities that reinforced their precarious status and increased their subordination (Armenta, 2016; Golash-Boza, 2016; Golash-Boza & Hondagneu-Sotelob, 2013). According to Vázquez (2017) any attempt at prison and criminal reform that does not simultaneously seek to curb the crimmigration complex will fall short on its goal, not only of scaling back the deleterious consequences of mass incarceration on the more vulnerable populations – the moral cost – but also on cutting its exorbitant and ineffective expenditure – the fiscal cost (see Fan, 2014).

Even if there is room to debate whether the United States is turning the page on its mass incarceration project (Petersilia & Cullen, 2015), there is little doubt that the crimmigration complex is sharply expanding under Trump's administration and reaching unprecedented levels (Kalhan, 2017; Rosenbloom, 2018). To carry out its restrictive immigration agenda, Trump's administration has built upon preexisting institutions and regulations that have given the executive branch far-reaching powers that allowed them to go far beyond just criminalizing immigration and enabled the restriction of immigration and immigrants' access to benefits, negated them due process, and made them easy targets of local law enforcement (Kalhan, 2017).

Again, an important driver of this increasing severity in immigration policy was the "minority threat" notion that links immigration and crime and thus offers a criminal solution to the immigration problem (Chiricos, Stupi, Georgia, Stults, & Gertz, 2014; Stupi et al., 2016). Thus, the "construction of immigrants as symbolic assailants" (Jiang & Erez, 2018, p. 6) was constitutive of this immigration control expansion. Importantly, crimmigration scholars emphasize the symbolic role of immigration policies (and criminal justice policies in general) in signaling those undeserving of rights and benefits (Stumpf, 2006). Aligned with the social construction of the undeserving poor that gave basis to the rise of the carceral state as posited by Wacquant (2010), Inda and Dowling (2013, pp. 5–6) argue that:

> It has been common for both individuals and groups to cast undocumented migrants – typically racialized as Mexican – as anti-citizens who threaten the overall well-being and security of the social body. The fundamental problem with the undocumented has been deemed to be their illegality. For many people, 'illegal' immigrants are inherently lawbreakers and necessarily criminals.

An important characteristic of the crimmigration expansion was that it targeted an ever-growing category of "criminal aliens," who were deemed to be a threat to social order. For many scholars, immigration enforcement is a heavily gendered and racialized process that targets mostly Latino men (Armenta, 2016; Golash-Boza & Hondagneu-Sotelob, 2013).

Perhaps paradoxically, the Trump administration seems to have blurred the line between deserving and undeserving immigrants and made the racialization of immigration enforcement more explicit. Thus, while immigration policies before Trump tended to be characterized by the interplay between increasing severity toward "criminal aliens" but also increasing discretion to give relief to "deserving aliens," current immigration policies seem to be qualitatively different and focused on targeting nonwhite immigrants all the same. Although these types of labels have been often racialized (see Mukherjee, Molina, & Adams, 2013), their coded racial messages are becoming increasingly explicit and encompass not only criminalized young men but also women and children who are also seen as threats.

> At the heart of the Trump Administration's approach to immigration lies an across-the-board restrictionism and an overtly racialized nativism that have not found mainstream acceptance in the United States since the early twentieth century: the notion that all forms of immigration should be drastically limited, and that all non-white immigrants are potentially suspect. Starkly absent is the particular variety of line drawing that has constituted such a central element of U.S. immigration policy in previous years: the distinction between "good" immigrants and "bad" immigrants. (Rosenbloom, 2018, p. 664)

The far-reaching deleterious consequences of crimmigration

The expansion of the immigration control complex has important consequences for large groups of the U.S. population and are not circumscribed solely to deportable immigrants. A growing line of research has aimed at examining the many life domains that are affected by changing immigration policies. Other studies explore how the risk of deportation – or deportation and detention itself – affects families of mixed documented status.

Zayas and Bradlee (2014) discuss the effects of deportation and detention on citizen children of undocumented immigrants, while Yoshikawa and Kalil (2011) focus on the impact of parents' undocumented status on the developmental context of children. Drawing from prior research, both studies identify critical consequences of immigration enforcement on children's well-being, from lower access to social services and welfare programs, lower rates of pre-school enrollment, poorer housing, and parental precarious working conditions, to deteriorated parent-child relationships. These studies aim at expanding the understanding of the collateral effects of harsher immigration policies and include its deleterious consequences for children into the immigration debate (see also Suárez-Orozco, Yoshikawa, Teranishi, & Suárez-Orozco, 2011).

Philbin, Flake, Hatzenbuehler, and Hirsch (2018), reviewed research on the impact of state-level immigration policies on health disparities in the U.S. Their review shows that immigration policies can have serious consequences, not only for undocumented immigrants and their families but also have spillover effects on immigrants in general or even Latino citizens. For example, they posit that omnibus immigration enforcement laws in Arizona tend to target the Latino population as a whole and were shown to increase food insecurity in families of undocumented immigrants and lowered their access to food stamps. These policies also had negative mental health consequences for Latino youth, decreasing their psychological well-being and self-esteem. They also generate barriers for documented immigrants and refugees in accessing benefits that they are legally entitled to have. Policies restricting access to work, education, and health care have also been shown to have consequential impacts on physical and mental health outcomes through limiting opportunities, restricting access to health care, and increasing material deprivation. In this vein, Vargas (2016) shows that deportation risk is associated with lower levels of Medicaid use, while Van Hook and Balistreri's (2006) study reveals that enacting a regulation that made non-citizens ineligible for food stamps increased food insecurity for children of non-citizens.

Finally, research has also focused on how immigration status impacts family relations (see, Kerwin, Alulema, & Nicholson, 2018). Exploring how immigration enforcement impact family relationships and subjective identities, Abrego (2019) describes how U.S. citizen children living in mixed-status families navigate their privileged documented status within their family and deal with fear of deportation, family expectations, conceal their families' undocumented status, and assume prematurely an increased financial and logistic responsibility toward their families (see also, Menjívar & Lakhani, 2016).

Conclusion

In an era of increasingly harsh immigration policies and rhetoric that usually portrays immigrants as threats, this article aimed at shedding light into commonly held beliefs regarding the link between immigration and crime. We focused on four commonly held myths regarding this link. At the macro-level, we first discussed empirical evidence showing that immigrant communities do not tend to exhibit the higher rates of crime commonly attributed to them. We showed how a large amount of research has debunked this myth and is now focused on better understanding the nuanced link between immigration and crime. Second, we presented emerging research aiming at testing whether sanctuary cities foster crime. Our review of the literature also shows that this claim seems not to be supported by the extant empirical evidence.

At the micro-level, we described different studies that provide evidence to the "immigrant paradox," the robust finding that, contrary to beliefs, immigrants engage in less criminal acts (and other types of risky and problem behaviors) than the native-born population. We also described mounting evidence indicating that the same seems to be true for undocumented immigrants. In other words, the empirical evidence to date seems to suggest that undocumented immigrants engage in less crime than their U.S. born counterparts.

All in all, the evidence seems to be robust in showing that there is no support for a link between immigration and crime. However, the fact that this commonly held belief can be characterized as a myth does not preclude it from having real consequences. Indeed, we discussed how this view of immigrants as threats to public safety enables the progressive criminalization of immigration in what many scholars have depicted as the expansion of the crimmigration complex. The levels of criminalization of immigration reached during the Trump era have serious consequences for large portions of the U.S. population, including documented immigrants and U.S. citizens – consequences that should be taken seriously. Moreover, as scholars point out, the expansion of the crimmigration complex places serious challenges to criminal justice reforms. With a renewed focus on criminalizing immigration, it appears that the punitive rhetoric and the "get tough" movement are far from gone. Rather, they have found a different target.

Disclosure statement

No potential conflict of interest was reported by the authors.

References

Abrego, L. J. (2019). Relational legal consciousness of U.S. citizenship: Privilege, responsibility, guilt, and love in latino mixed-status families. *Law & Society Review*, *53*, 1–30.

Alba, R., & Nee, V. (2003). Rethinking assimilation theory for a new era of immigration. *International Migration Review*, *31*, 826–874. doi:10.1177/019791839703100403

Alexander, M. (2012). *The New Jim Crow: Mass incarceration in the age of colorblindness*. New York, NY: The New Press.

Alvarez-Rivera, L. L., Nobles, M. R., & Lersch, K. M. (2014). Latino immigrant acculturation and crime. *American Journal of Criminal Justice*, *39*, 315–330. doi:10.1007/s12103-013-9203-9

Amnesty international. (2018). *USA: 'You don't have any rights here.' Illegal pushbacks, arbitrary detention & ill-treatment of asylum-seekers in the United States*. London, UK: Author.

Armenta, A. (2016). Racializing crimmigration: Structural racism, colorblindness, and the institutional production of immigrant criminality. *Sociology of Race and Ethnicity*, *3*, 82–95. doi:10.1177/2332649216648714

Armenta, A. (2017). Policing immigrants or policing immigration? Understanding local law enforcement participation in immigration control. *Sociology Compass*, *11*, 1–10. doi:10.1111/soc4.12453

Avila, K., Bello, K., Graber, L., & Marquez, N. (2018). *The rise of sanctuary: Getting local officers out of the business of deportations in the Trump era*. Retrieved from https://www.ilrc.org/sites/default/files/resources/rise_of_sanctuary-lg-20180201.pdf

Berg, J. A. (2009a). Core networks and whites' attitudes toward immigrants and immigration policy. *Public Opinion Quarterly*, *73*, 7–31. doi:10.1093/poq/nfp011

Berg, J. A. (2009b). White public opinion toward undocumented immigrants: Threat and interpersonal environment. *Sociological Perspectives*, *52*, 39–58. doi:10.1525/sop.2009.52.1.39

Bersani, B. E. (2014a). A game of catch-up? The offending experience of second-generation immigrants. *Crime & Delinquency*, *60*, 60–84. doi:10.1177/0011128713502406

Bersani, B. E. (2014b). An examination of first and second generation immigrant offending trajectories. *Justice Quarterly*, *31*, 315–343. doi:10.1080/07418825.2012.659200

Bersani, B. E., Loughran, T. A., & Piquero, A. R. (2014). Comparing patterns and predictors of immigrant offending among a sample of adjudicated youth. *Journal of Youth and Adolescence*, *43*, 1914–1933. doi:10.1007/s10964-013-0045-z

Bersani, B. E., & Piquero, A. R. (2017). Examining systematic crime reporting bias across three immigrant generations: Prevalence, trends, and divergence in self-reported and official reported arrests. *Journal of Quantitative Criminology*, *33*, 835–857. doi:10.1007/s10940-016-9314-9

Bourbeau, P. (2019). Detention and immigration: Practices, crimmigration, and norms. *Migration Studies*, *7*, 83–99. doi:10.1093/migration/mnx069

Bowling, B., & Westenra, S. (2018). 'A really hostile environment': Adiaphorization, global policing and the crimmigration control system. *Theoretical Criminology*. Advance online publication. doi:10.1177/1362480618774034

Brown, H. E., Jones, J. A., & Becker, A. (2018). The racialization of Latino immigrants in new destinations: Criminality, ascription, and countermobilization. *The Russell Sage Foundation Journal of the Social Sciences*, *4*, 118–140. doi:10.7758/rsf.2018.4.5.06

Brown, J. A. (2016). Running on fear: Immigration, race and crime framings in contemporary GOP presidential debate discourse. *Critical Criminology*, *24*, 315–331. doi:10.1007/s10612-016-9317-8

Burchfield, K. B., & Silver, E. (2012). Collective efficacy and crime in Los Angeles neighborhoods: Implications for the Latino paradox. *Sociological Inquiry*, *83*, 154–176. doi:10.1111/j.1475-682X.2012.00429.x

Burgess, E. W. (1925). The growth of the city: An introduction to a research project. In R. E. Park & E. W. Burgess (Eds.), *The city* (pp. 47–62). Chicago, IL: University of Chicago Press.

Burrington, L. A. (2015). Neighborhood structure, immigrant status, and youth violence: Assessing the role of parental supervision. *Youth Violence and Juvenile Justice, 13*, 367–390. doi:10.1177/1541204014547723

Butcher, K. F., & Piehl, A. M. (1998). Cross-city evidence on the relationship between immigration and crime. *Journal of Policy Analysis and Management, 17*, 457–493. doi:10.1002/(ISSN)1520-6688

Butcher, K. F., & Piehl, A. M. (2007). *Why are immigrants' incarceration rates so low? Evidence on selective immigration, deterrence, and deportation* (Working Papers 13229). National Bureau of Economic Research.

Ceobanu, A. M., & Escandell, X. (2010). Comparative analyses of public attitudes toward immigrants and immigration using multinational survey data: A review of theories and research. *Annual Review of Sociology, 36*, 309–314. doi:10.1146/annurev.soc.012809.102651

Chacón, J. M. (2012). Overcriminalizing immigration. *Journal of Criminal Law and Criminology, 102*, 613–652.

Chandler, C. R., & Tsai, Y. (2001). Social factors influencing immigration attitudes: An analysis of data from the general social survey. *The Social Science Journal, 38*, 177–188. doi:10.1016/S0362-3319(01)00106-9

Chiricos, T., Stupi, E. K., Georgia, W., Stults, B. J., & Gertz, M. (2014). Undocumented immigrant threat and support for social controls. *Social Problems, 61*, 673–692. doi:10.1525/sp.2014.13137

Chouhy, C. (2018). Segmented assimilation and crime: Rethinking the relationship between assimilation and crime. In H. V. Miller & A. Peguero (Eds.), *Routledge handbook on immigration and crime* (pp. 35–48). New York, NY: Routledge.

Ciancio, A. (2017). *The impact of immigration policies on local enforcement, crime and policing efficiency* (Unpublished doctoral dissertation). University of Pennsylvania, Philadelphia.

Cox, A. B., & Miles, T. J. (2015). *Legitimacy and cooperation: Will immigrants cooperate with local police who enforce federal immigration law?* (University of Chicago Coase-Sandor Institute for Law & Economics Research Paper No. 734). 15–17. Retrieved from https://ssrn.com/abstract=2658265

Davies, G., & Fagan, J. (2012). Crime and enforcement in immigrant neighborhoods: Evidence from New York city. *The Annals of the American Academy of Political and Social Science, 641*, 99–124. doi:10.1177/0002716212438938

Desmond, S. A., & Kubrin, C. E. (2009). The power of place: Immigrant communities and adolescent violence. *Sociological Quarterly, 50*, 581–607. doi:10.1111/j.1533-8525.2009.01153.x

Egelko, B. (2018, April 12). Trump's "Sanctuary cities" policy receives chilly reception in court. *Tribune News Service*. Retrieved from https://www.governing.com/topics/public-justice-safety/tns-trump-sanctuary-city-court.html

Ewing, W. A., Martínez, D. E., & Rumbaut, R. G. (2015). *The criminalization of immigration in the United States*. Washington, DC: American Immigration Council.

Executive Order No. 13768, Vol. 82 *Federal Register*. 8799–8803 (January 25, 2017).

Fan, M. D. (2014). The case for crimmigration reform. *North Carolina Law Review, 92*, 75–148.

Farris, E. M., & Silber Mohamed, H. (2018). Picturing immigration: How the media criminalizes immigrants. *Politics, Groups, and Identities, 6*, 814–824. doi:10.1080/21565503.2018.1484375

Feldmeyer, B. (2009). Immigration and violence: The offsetting effects of immigrant concentration on Latino violence. *Social Science Research, 38*, 717–731. doi:10.1016/j.ssresearch.2009.03.003

Feldmeyer, B. (2018). The classical assimilation model. A controversial canon. In H. V. Miller & A. Peguero (Eds.), *Routledge handbook on immigration and crime* (pp. 35–48). New York, NY: Routledge.

Feldmeyer, B., Madero-Hernandez, A., Rojas-Gaona, C. E., & Sabon, L. (2019). Immigration, collective efficacy, social ties, and violence: Unpacking the mediating mechanisms in immigration effects on neighborhood-level violence. *Race and Justice, 9*, 123–150. doi:10.1177/2153368717690563

Ferraro, V. (2016). Immigration and crime in the new destinations, 2000–2007: A test of the disorganizing effect of migration. *Journal of Quantitative Criminology, 32*, 23–45. doi:10.1007/s10940-015-9252-y

Gallup. (2019). *Topics in depth: Immigration.* Retrieved from https://news.gallup.com/poll/1660/immigration.aspx

Golash-Boza, T. (2016). The parallels between mass incarceration and mass deportation: An intersectional analysis of state repression. *Journal of World-Systems Research, 22,* 484–509. doi:10.5195/JWSR.2016.616

Golash-Boza, T., & Hondagneu-Sotelob, P. (2013). Latino immigrant men and the deportation crisis: A gendered racial removal program. *Latino Studies, 11,* 271–292. doi:10.1057/lst.2013.14

Gonzalez, B., Collingwood, L., & El-Khatib, S. O. (2019). The politics of refuge: Sanctuary cities, crime, and undocumented immigration. *Urban Affairs Review, 55,* 3–40. doi:10.1177/1078087417704974

Graber, L., & Marquez, N. (2016). *Searching for sanctuary: An analysis of America's counties & their voluntary assistance with deportations.* Retrieved from https://www.ilrc.org/sites/default/files/resources/sanctuary_report_final_1-min.pdf

Hagan, J., & Palloni, A. (2012). Sociological criminology and the mythology of Hispanic immigration and crime. *Social Problems, 46,* 617–632. doi:10.2307/3097078

Haller, W., Portes, A., & Lynch, S. M. (2011). Dreams fulfilled, dreams shattered: Determinants of segmented assimilation in the second generation. *Social Forces, 89,* 733–762. doi:10.1353/sof.2011.0003

Harris, C. T., & Feldmeyer, B. (2013). Latino immigration and White, Black, and Latino violent crime: A comparison of traditional and non-traditional immigrant destinations. *Social Science Research, 42,* 202–216. doi:10.1016/j.ssresearch.2012.08.014

Harris, C. T., & Feldmeyer, B. (2015). A shot of morality? Hispanic immigration, religious contextual characteristics, and violence. *Sociological Spectrum, 35,* 229–253. doi:10.1080/02732173.2015.1021062

Harris, C. T., Gruenewald, J., & Painter-Davis, N. (2015). Hispanic immigration and black violence at the macro-level: Examining the conditioning effect of victim race/ethnicity. *Sociological Forum, 30,* 62–82. doi:10.1111/socf.2015.30.issue-1

Harris, K. M. (1999). The health status and risk behaviors of adolescents in immigrant families. In D. J. Hernandez (Ed.), *Children of immigrants: Health, adjustment, and public assistance* (pp. 286–347). Washington, DC: National Academies Press.

Hayduk, R., & García-Castañon, M. (2018). Xenophobia, belonging and agency: Citizenship in immigrant America. *New Political Science, 40,* 309–316. doi:10.1080/07393148.2018.1449936

Hernandez, D. J., Denton, N. A., Macartney, S., & Blanchard, V. L. (2012). Children in immigrant families: Demography, policy, and evidence for the immigrant paradox. In C. G. Coll & A. K. Marks (Eds.), *The immigrant paradox in children and adolescents: Is becoming American a developmental risk?* (pp. 17–36). Washington, DC: American Psychological Association.

Hickman, L. J., & Suttorp, M. J. (2008). Are deportable aliens a unique threat to public safety? Comparing the recidivism of deportable and nondeportable aliens. *Criminology & Public Policy, 7,* 59–82. doi:10.1111/cpp.2008.7.issue-1

Ibañez, G. E., Agudo, M., Martin, S. S., O'Connell, D. J., Auf, R., & Sheehan, D. (2017). Offending behavior, drug use, and mental health among foreign-born versus U.S. born Latino criminal justice clients. *Journal of Immigrant and Minority Health, 19,* 674–685. doi:10.1007/s10903-016-0497-9

Inda, J. X., & Dowling, J. A. (2013). Governing migrant illegality. In J. A. Dowling & J. X. Inda (Eds.), *Governing immigration through crime. A reader* (pp. 1–36). Stanford, CA: Stanford University Press.

Jiang, J., & Erez, E. (2018). Immigrants as symbolic assailants: Crimmigration and its discontents. *International Criminal Justice Review, 28,* 5–24. doi:10.1177/1057567717721299

Kalhan, A. (2017). Revisiting the 1996 experiment in comprehensive immigration severity in the age of Trump. *Drexel Law Review, 9,* 261–268.

Karaim, R. (2018, June 4). Will dreamers be protected from deportation? *CQ Researcher.* Retrieved from http://library.cqpress.com/cqresearcher/document.php?id=cqr_ht_immigration_2018

Keefe, S., Padilla, A., & Carlos, M. L. (1979). The Mexican-American extended family as an emotional support system. *Human Organization*, *38*, 144–152. doi:10.17730/humo.38.2.575482483n134553

Kerwin, D., Alulema, D., & Nicholson, M. (2018). Communities in crisis: Interior removals and their human consequences. *Journal on Migration and Human Security*, *6*, 226–242. doi:10.1177/2331502418820066

Kim, J. K., Sagás, E., & Cespedes, K. (2018). Genderacing immigrant subjects: 'Anchor babies' and the politics of birthright citizenship. *Social Identities*, *24*, 312–326. doi:10.1080/13504630.2017.1376281

Kirk, D. S., Papachristos, A. V., Fagan, J., & Tyler, T. R. (2012). The paradox of law enforcement in immigrant communities: Does tough immigration enforcement undermine public safety? *The Annals of the American Academy of Political and Social Science*, *641*, 79–98. doi:10.1177/0002716211431818

Kopan, T. (2018, March 2). How Trump changed the rules to arrest more non-criminal immigrants. *CNN*. Retrieved from https://www.cnn.com/2018/03/02/politics/ice-immigration-deportations/index.html

Kubrin, C. E., & Desmond, S. A. (2015). The power of place revisited: Why immigrant communities have lower levels of adolescent violence. *Youth Violence and Juvenile Justice*, *13*, 345–366. doi:10.1177/1541204014547590

Kubrin, C. E., Hipp, J. R., & Kim, Y.-A. (2018). Different than the sum of its parts: Examining the unique impacts of immigrant groups on neighborhood crime rates. *Journal of Quantitative Criminology*, *34*, 1–36. doi:10.1007/s10940-016-9320-y

Kubrin, C. E., & Ishizawa, H. (2012). Why some immigrant neighborhoods are safer than others: Divergent findings from Los Angeles and Chicago. *The Annals of the American Academy of Political and Social Science*, *641*, 148–173. doi:10.1177/0002716211431688

Kulig, T. C., & Cullen, F. T. (2019). Kate's Law: The social construction of crime in the Trump era. In D. L. Rothe & V. E. Collins (Eds.), *Explorations in critical criminology in honor of William J. Chambliss* (pp. 59–89). Leiden, The Netherlands: Brill.

Landgrave, M., & Nowrasteh, A. (2017a). *Criminal immigrants: Their numbers, demographics, and countries of origin* (Immigration Research and Policy Brief No. 1). Washington, DC: Cato Institute.

Landgrave, M., & Nowrasteh, A. (2017b). *The dreamer incarceration rate* (Immigration Research and Policy Brief No. 3). Washington, DC: Cato Institute.

Landgrave, M., & Nowrasteh, A. (2019). Criminal immigrants in 2017 their numbers, demographics, and countries of origin (Immigration Research and Policy Brief No. 11). Washington, DC: Cato Institute.

Lee, M. T., & Martinez, R. J. (2006). Immigration and Asian homicide patterns in urban and suburban San Diego. In R. J. Martinez (Ed.), *Immigration and crime: Race, ethnicity, and violence* (pp. 90–113). New York: New York University Press.

Lee, M. T., Martinez, R., Jr., & Rosenfeld, R. (2001). Does immigration increase homicide? Negative evidence from three border cities. *Sociological Quarterly*, *42*, 559. doi:10.1111/j.1533-8525.2001.tb01780.x

Lee, M. T., & Martinez, R. J. (2002). Social disorganization revisited: Mapping the recent immigration and black homicide relationship in Northern Miami. *Sociological Focus*, *35*, 363–380. doi:10.1080/00380237.2002.10570709

Lee, M. T., & Martinez, R. J. (2009). Immigration reduces crime: An emerging scholarly consensus. *Sociology of Crime, Law and Deviance*, *13*, 3–16.

Lyons, C. J., Vélez, M. B., & Santoro, W. A. (2013). Neighborhood immigration, violence, and city-level immigrant political opportunities. *American Sociological Review*, *78*, 604–632. doi:10.1177/0003122413491964

MacDonald, J., Hipp, J., & Gill, C. (2013). The effects of immigrant concentration on changes in neighborhood crime rates. *Journal of Quantitative Criminology*, *29*, 191–215. doi:10.1007/s10940-012-9176-8

MacDonald, J., & Sampson, R. J. (2012). The world in a city: Immigration and America's changing social fabric. *The Annals of the American Academy of Political and Social Science, 641*, 6–15. doi:10.1177/0002716212438939

Marks, A. K., Ejesi, K., & García Coll, C. (2014). Understanding the U.S. immigrant paradox in childhood and adolescence. *Child Development Perspectives, 8*, 59–64. doi:10.1111/cdep.2014.8.issue-2

Martinez, D., Martinez-Schuldt, R., & Cantor, G. (2017). Providing sanctuary or fostering crime? A review of the research on "Sanctuary cities" and crime. *Sociology Compass*. Advanced online publication. doi:10.1111/soc4.12547

Martinez, D. E., Martinez-Schuldt, R. D., & Cantor, G. (2018). "Sanctuary cities" and crime. In H. V. Miller & A. Peguero (Eds.), *Routledge handbook on immigration and crime* (pp. 270–283). New York, NY: Routledge.

Martinez, R., & Lee, M. T. (2000). On immigration and crime. In G. LaFree, R. J. Bursik, Jr., J. F. Short, Jr. and R. B. Taylor (Eds.), *The nature of crime: Continuity and change* (Volume 1, pp. 485–524). Washington DC: National Institute of Justice.

Martinez, R., Stowell, J. I., & Cancino, J. M. (2008). A tale of two border cities: Community context, ethnicity, and homicide. *Social Science Quarterly, 89*, 1–16. doi:10.1111/ssqu.2008.89.issue-1

Martinez, R. J. (2002). *Latino homicide: Immigration, community, and violence*. New York, NY: Simon & Schuster.

Martinez, R. J. (2010). Economic conditions and racial/ethnic variations in violence: Immigration, the Latino paradox, and future research. *Criminology & Public Policy, 9*, 707–713. doi:10.1111/j.1745-9133.2010.00663.x

Martinez, R. J., & Stowell, J. I. (2012). Extending immigration and crime studies: National implications and local settings. *The Annals of the American Academy of Political and Social Science, 641*, 174–191. doi:10.1177/0002716212437363

Martinez, R. J., Stowell, J. I., & Lee, M. T. (2010). Immigration and crime in an era of transformation: A longitudinal analysis of homicides in San Diego neighborhoods, 1980–2000. *Criminology, 48*, 797–829. doi:10.1111/crim.2010.48.issue-3

Martinez-Schuldt, R. D., & Martinez, D. E. (2017). Sanctuary policies and city-level incidents of violence, 1990 to 2010. *Justice Quarterly, 36*, 567–593. doi:10.1080/07418825.2017.1400577

Massey, D., Alarcon, R., Durand, J., & Gonzalez, H. (1990). *Return to Aztlan: The social process of international migration from Western Mexico*. Berkeley: University of California Press.

Mears, D. P. (2002). Immigration and crime: What's the connection? *Federal Sentencing Reporter, 14*, 284–288. doi:10.1525/fsr.2002.14.5.284

Menjívar, C., & Alvord, D. (2018). The expansion of "crimmigration," mass detention, and deportation. *Sociology Compass, 12*, 1–15. doi:10.1111/soc4.12573

Menjívar, C., & Lakhani, S. M. (2016). Transformative effects of immigration law: Immigrants' personal and social metamorphoses. *American Journal of Sociology, 121*, 1818–1855. doi:10.1086/685103

Moehling, C., & Piehl, A. M. (2009). Immigration, crime, and incarceration in early twentieth-century America. *Demography, 46*, 739–763. doi:10.1353/dem.0.0076

Morenoff, J. D., & Astor, A. (2006). Immigrant assimilation and crime: Generational differences in youth violence in Chicago. In R. J. Martinez & A. J. Valenzuela (Eds.), *Immigration and crime: Race, ethnicity, and violence* (pp. 36–63). New York: New York University Press.

Mukherjee, S., Molina, L. E., & Adams, G. (2013). "Reasonable suspicion" about tough immigration legislation: Enforcing laws or ethnocentric exclusion? *Cultural Diversity and Ethnic Minority Psychology, 19*, 320–331. doi:10.1037/a0032944

Nagasawa, R., Qian, Z., Wong, P., & Wong, P. (2001). Theory of segmented assimilation and the adoption of marijuana use and delinquent behavior by Asian pacific youth. *The Sociological Quarterly, 42*, 351–372. doi:10.1111/j.1533-8525.2001.tb02405.x

Nielsen, A. L., Lee, M. T., & Martinez Ramiro, J. (2005). Integrating race, place and motive in social disorganization theory: Lessons from a comparison of black and Latino homicide types in two immigrant destination cities. *Criminology, 43*, 837–872. doi:10.1111/j.0011-1348.2005.00025.x

Nowrasteh, A. (2018a). *Criminal immigrants in Texas: Illegal immigrant conviction and arrest rates for homicide, sex crimes, larceny, and other crimes* (Immigration Research and Policy Brief No. 4). Washington, DC: Cato Institute.

Nowrasteh, A. (2018b). *Another confusing federal report on immigrant incarceration*. Cato Institute. Retrieved from https://www.cato.org/blog/another-confusing-federal-report-immigrant-incarceration

Olson, C. P., Laurikkala, M. K., Huff-Corzine, L., & Corzine, J. (2009). Immigration and violent crime: Citizenship status and social disorganization. *Homicide Studies, 13*, 227–241. doi:10.1177/1088767909336202

Ousey, G. C., & Kubrin, C. E. (2009). Exploring the connection between immigration and violent crime rates in U.S. cities, 1980–2000. *Social Problems, 56*, 447–473. doi:10.1525/sp.2009.56.3.447

Ousey, G. C., & Kubrin, C. E. (2014). Immigration and the changing nature of homicide in U.S. cities, 1980–2010. *Journal of Quantitative Criminology, 30*, 453–483. doi:10.1007/s10940-013-9210-5

Ousey, G. C., & Kubrin, C. E. (2018). Immigration and crime: Assessing a contentious issue. *Annual Review of Criminology, 1*, 63–84. doi:10.1146/annurev-criminol-032317-092026

Painter-Davis, N. (2016). Immigration effects on violence contextualized: The role of immigrant destination type and race/ethnicity. *Sociological Perspectives, 59*, 130–152. doi:10.1177/0731121415588152

Petersilia, J., & Cullen, F. T. (2015). Liberal but not stupid: Meeting the promise of downsizing prisons. *Stanford Journal of Criminal Law and Policy, 2*, 1–43.

Philbin, M. M., Flake, M., Hatzenbuehler, M. L., & Hirsch, J. S. (2018). State-level immigration and immigrant-focused policies as drivers of Latino health disparities in the United States. *Social Science and Medicine, 199*, 29–38. doi:10.1016/j.socscimed.2017.04.007

Piquero, A. R., Bersani, B. E., Loughran, T. A., & Fagan, J. (2016). Longitudinal patterns of legal socialization in first-generation immigrants, second-generation immigrants, and native-born serious youthful offenders. *Crime & Delinquency, 62*, 1403–1425. doi:10.1177/0011128714545830

Portes, A. (1996). Children of immigrants: Segmented assimilation and its determinants. In A. Portes (Ed.), *The economic sociology of immigration: Essays on networks, ethnicity, and entrepreneurship* (pp. 248–279). New York, NY: Russell Sage Foundation.

Portes, A., Fernández-Kelly, P., & Haller, W. (2005). Segmented assimilation on the ground: The new second generation in early adulthood. *Ethnic and Racial Studies, 28*, 1000–1040. doi:10.1080/01419870500224117

Portes, A., & Jensen, L. (1992). Disproving the enclave hypothesis. *American Sociological Review, 57*, 418–420. doi:10.2307/2096246

Portes, A., & Rumbaut, R. (2001). *Legacies: The story of the immigrant second generation*. Berkeley: University of California Press.

Portes, A., & Rumbaut, R. G. (2014). *Immigrant America: A portrait*. Berkeley: University of California Press.

Portes, A., & Stepick, A. (1993). *City on the edge: The transformation of Miami*. Berkeley: University of California Press.

Portes, A., & Zhou, M. (1993). The new second generation: Segmented assimilation and its variants. *American Academy of Political and Social Science, 530*, 74–96. doi:10.1177/0002716293530001006

Pryce, D. K. (2018). U.S. citizens' current attitudes toward immigrants and immigration: A study from the general social survey. *Social Science Quarterly, 9*, 1467–1483. doi:10.1111/ssqu.12514

Ramey, D. M. (2013). Immigrant revitalization and neighborhood violent crime in established and new destination cities. *Social Forces, 92*, 597–629. doi:10.1093/sf/sot085

Reid, L. W., Weiss, H. E., & Adelman, R. M. (2005). The immigration-crime relationship: Evidence across US metropolitan areas. *Social Science Research, 34*, 757–780. doi:10.1016/j.ssresearch.2005.01.001

Rojas-Gaona, C. E., & Madero-Hernandez, A. (2018). Latino immigration and crime. In H. V. Miller & A. Peguero (Eds.), *Routledge handbook on immigration and crime* (pp. 133–149). New York, NY: Routledge.

Romero, M. (2018). Trump's immigration attacks, in brief. *Contexts, 17*, 34–41. doi:10.1177/1536504218766549

Rosenbloom, R. E. (2018). Beyond severity: A new view of crimmigration. *Lewis & Clark Law Review, 22*, 663–708.

Rumbaut, R. G., & Ewing, W. A. (2007). *The myth of immigrant criminality and the paradox of assimilation: Incarceration rates among native and foreign-born men*. Washington, DC: American Immigration Council.

Sabogal, F., Marin, G., Otero-Sabogal, R., Marin, B. V., & Perez-Stable, E. J. (1987). Hispanic familism and acculturation: What changes and what doesn't? *Hispanic Journal of Behavioral Sciences, 9*, 397–412. doi:10.1177/07399863870094003

Salas-Wright, C. P., Vaughn, M. G., Schwartz, S. J., & Córdova, D. (2016). An "immigrant paradox" for adolescent externalizing behavior? Evidence from a national sample. *Social Psychiatry and Psychiatric Epidemiology, 51*, 27–37. doi:10.1007/s00127-015-1115-1

Sampson, R. J. (2008). Rethinking crime and immigration. *Contexts, 7*, 28–33. doi:10.1525/ctx.2008.7.1.28

Sampson, R. J., Morenoff, J. D., & Raudenbush, S. (2005). Social anatomy of racial and ethnic disparities in violence. *American Journal of Public Health, 95*, 224–232. doi:10.2105/AJPH.2004.045799

San Francisco Administrative Code. (2016). Retrieved from https://sfgov.org/oceia/sanctuary-city-ordinance-0

Schwartz, I. (2015, June 16). Trump: Mexico not sending us their best; criminals, drug dealers and rapists are crossing border. *RealClear Politics CNN*. Retrieved from https://www.realclearpolitics.com/video/2015/06/16/trump_mexico_not_sending_us_their_best_criminals_drug_dealers_and_rapists_are_crossing_border.html

Sessions, J. (2017). *Attorney General Jeff sessions delivers remarks in Las Vegas, to federal, state, and local law enforcement about sanctuary cities and efforts to combat violent crime*. Retrieved from https://www.justice.gov/opa/speech/attorney-general-jeff-sessions-delivers-remarks-las-vegas-federal-state-and-local-law

Shaw, C., & McKay, H. (1942). *Juvenile delinquency and urban areas*. Chicago, IL: University of Chicago Press.

Shihadeh, E. S., & Barranco, R. E. (2010a). Latino employment and black violence: The unintended consequence of U.S. immigration policy. *Social Forces, 88*, 1393–1420. doi:10.1353/sof.0.0286

Shihadeh, E. S., & Barranco, R. E. (2010b). Latino immigration, economic deprivation, and violence: Regional differences in the effect of linguistic isolation. *Homicide Studies, 14*, 336–355. doi:10.1177/1088767910371190

Shihadeh, E. S., & Winters, L. (2010). Church, place, and crime: Latinos and homicide in new destinations. *Sociological Inquiry, 80*, 628–649. doi:10.1111/soin.2010.80.issue-4

Skogan, W. G., & Steiner, L. (2004). *CAPS at ten: Community policing in Chicago*. Chicago, IL: Illinois Criminal Justice Information Authority.

Stansfield, R. (2013). Safer cities: A macro-level analysis of recent immigration, Hispanic-owned businesses, and crime rates in the United States. *Journal of Urban Affairs, 36*, 503–518. doi:10.1111/juaf.12051

Stowell, J. I., Messner, S. F., McGeever, K. F., & Raffalovich, L. E. (2009). Immigration and the recent violent crime drop in the United States: A pooled, cross-sectional time-series analysis of metropolitan areas. *Criminology, 47*, 889–928. doi:10.1111/crim.2009.47.issue-3

Stumpf, J. (2006). The crimmigration crisis: Immigrants, crime, and sovereign power. *American University Law Review, 56*, 367–419.

Stupi, E. K., Chiricos, T., & Gertz, M. (2016). Perceived criminal threat from undocumented immigrants: Antecedents and consequences for policy. *Justice Quarterly, 33*, 239–266. doi:10.1080/07418825.2014.902093

Suárez-Orozco, C., Rhodes, J., & Milburn, M. (2009). Unraveling the immigrant paradox. *Youth & Society, 41*, 151–185. doi:10.1177/0044118X09333647

Suárez-Orozco, C., Yoshikawa, H., Teranishi, R. T., & Suárez-Orozco, M. M. (2011). Growing up in the shadows: The developmental implications of unauthorized status. *Harvard Educational Review, 81*, 438–473. doi:10.17763/haer.81.3.g23x203763783m75

Sullivan, E. (2019, April 12). Trump says he is considering releasing migrants in "Sanctuary cities". *The New York Times*. Retrieved from https://www.nytimes.com/2019/04/12/us/politics/trump-sanctuary-cities.html?module=inline

Tramonte, L. (2011). *Debunking the myth of "sanctuary cities": Community policing policies protect American communities*. Washington, DC: Immigration Policy Center.

Treyger, E., Chalfin, A., & Loeffler, C. (2014). Immigration enforcement, policing, and crime: Evidence from the secure communities program. *Criminology & Public Policy, 13*, 285–322. doi:10.1111/1745-9133.12085

United States Immigration and Customs Enforcement. (2018). *Fiscal year 2018 ICE enforcement and removal operations report*. Retrieved from https://www.ice.gov/doclib/about/offices/ero/pdf/eroFY2018Report.pdf

United States Office of Immigration Statistics. (2017). *2017 Yearbook of immigration statistics*. Washington, DC: U.S. Department of Homeland Security, Office of Immigration Statistics.

Valdez, I. (2016). Punishment, race, and the organization of U.S. immigration exclusion. *Political Research Quarterly, 69*, 640–654. doi:10.1177/1065912916670515

Van Hook, J., & Balistreri, K. S. (2006). Ineligible parents, eligible children: Food stamps receipt, allotments, and food insecurity among children of immigrants. *Social Science Research, 35*, 228–251. doi:10.1016/j.ssresearch.2004.09.001

Van Sant, S. (2019). Border security funding talk stalled, government shutdown looms. *NPR*. Retrieved from https://www.npr.org/2019/02/10/693135144/border-security-funding-talks-stalled-government-shutdown-looms

Vargas, E. D. (2016). Immigration enforcement and mixed-status families: The effects of risk of deportation on medicaid use. *Children and Youth Services Review, 57*, 83–89. doi:10.1016/j.childyouth.2015.07.009

Vaughn, M. G., Salas-Wright, C. P., DeLisi, M., & Maynard, B. R. (2014). The immigrant paradox: Immigrants are less antisocial than native-born Americans. *Social Psychiatry and Psychiatric Epidemiology, 49*, 1129–1137. doi:10.1007/s00127-013-0799-3

Vázquez, Y. (2017). Crimmigration: The missing piece of criminal justice reform. *University of Richmond Law Review, 51*, 1093–1147.

Vélez, M. B. (2009). Contextualizing the immigration and crime effect. *Homicide Studies, 13*, 325–335. doi:10.1177/1088767909337238

Wacquant, L. (2010). Crafting the neoliberal state: Workfare, prisonfare and social insecurity. Why prison? *Sociological Forum, 25*, 65–86. doi:10.1111/j.1573-7861.2010.01173.x

Wadsworth, T. (2010). Is immigration responsible for the crime drop? An assessment of the influence of immigration on changes in violent crime between 1990 and 2000. *Social Science Quarterly, 91*, 531–553. doi:10.1111/(ISSN)1540-6237

Waldinger, R. (2018). Immigration and the election of Donald Trump: Why the sociology of migration left us unprepared … and why we should not have been surprised. *Ethnic and Racial Studies, 41*, 1411–1426. doi:10.1080/01419870.2018.1442014

Wang, X. (2012). Undocumented immigrants as perceived criminal threat: A test of the minority threat perspective. *Criminology, 50*, 743–776. doi:10.1111/crim.2012.50.issue-3

Wong, T. K. (2017). *The effects of sanctuary policies on crime and the economy*. Retrieved from https://www.americanprogress.org/issues/immigration/reports/2017/01/26/297366/the-effects-of-sanctuary-policies-on-crime-and-the-economy/

Xie, M., & Baumer, E. P. (2018). Reassessing the breadth of the protective benefit of immigrant neighborhoods: A multilevel analysis of violence risk by race, ethnicity, and labor market stratification. *Criminology, 56*, 303–332. doi:10.1111/1745-9125.12172

Xie, Y., & Greenman, E. (2005). Segmented assimilation theory: A reformulation and empirical test. *Population Studies, 41*, 1–56.

Yoshikawa, H., & Kalil, A. (2011). The effects of parental undocumented status on the developmental contexts of young children in immigrant families. *Child Development Perspectives, 5*, 291–297. doi:10.1111/cdep.2011.5.issue-4

Zayas, L. H., & Bradlee, M. H. (2014). Exiling children, creating orphans: When immigration policies hurt citizens. *Social Work, 59*, 167–175. doi:10.1093/sw/swu004

Part III

Affecting America

Will Black Lives Matter to the Police? African Americans' Concerns about Trump's Presidency

Hannah D. McManus, Francis T. Cullen, Cheryl Lero Jonson, Alexander L. Burton, and Velmer S. Burton Jr.

ABSTRACT

Based on a 2017 national survey of 1,000 Black Americans, perceptions regarding the implications of Donald Trump's election as President on race relations, police-minority relations, and police treatment of Black citizens in the United States were examined. Findings suggest the existence of a "Trump Effect." With minor variation across demographic groups, the survey respondents expressed overall negative perceptions concerning the effects of President Trump's election. In particular, they expressed the belief that his presidency shows that the United States is a racist society, will strain police-minority relationships, and will create a climate in which African Americans are more likely to be arrested or subjected to police violence. At issue is not just African Americans' distrust of President Trump but, importantly, whether his emphasis on "law and order" and dismissal of minority-group concerns attenuates the legitimacy of law enforcement in the eyes of African Americans.

On July 28, 2017, President Donald Trump stood before an audience of local, state, and federal law enforcement personnel in Long Island, New York to publicize his administration's efforts to crack down on gang violence and illegal immigration in the eradication of the gang Mara Salvatrucha (MS-13). President Trump's speech included common rhetoric from his presidential campaign and early months in office. He emphasized his support for law enforcement and reiterated the need for law and order in the United States, highlighting the significant role of police in keeping citizens safe (Berman, 2017; Bump, 2017). His remarks departed from past speeches, however, when advocating the use of force in the apprehension and management of suspects (Bump, 2017). President Trump joked that police officers should not be concerned about preventing physical harm to people being taken into custody. Noting that the laws were typically "stacked against police," President Trump requested that officers not be "too nice," giving them permission to "take the hand away" when placing suspects into a vehicle. These statements were met with laughter and applause by many officers in the audience (Herreria, 2017b).

This speech created a frenzy within American media, where writers were disturbed both by President Trump's comments and by the reactions of some of the uniformed law enforcement within the crowd (see, e.g., Chiusano, 2017). Representatives across media outlets viewed President Trump's statements as explicitly encouraging police to use violence – likely illegally – against suspects (Blake, 2017; Cobb, 2017; Graham, 2017b; Lind, 2017b). Many pundits suggested that his rhetoric regarding law enforcement called in to question the "hallmarks" of the American justice system, such as due process and equal protection under the law (Graham, 2017b; Haberman, 2017). In juxtaposition to President Trump's statements insinuating that the police are too "soft," the media pointed to recent events where police violence and violation of civil rights had created a national outcry against law enforcement (Blake, 2017). Indeed, the idea of roughing up suspects in transit was viewed as "distressingly common," particularly following the death of Freddie Carlos Gray, Jr. in Baltimore after a spinal injury that occurred in the back of a police van (Blake, 2017; Sparrow, 2016).

Law enforcement agencies – such as the Suffolk County Police Department (Long Island), the New York Police Department, and the Los Angeles Police Department – were quick to distance themselves from the President's statements (Cobb, 2017; Herreria, 2017a; Manchester, 2017; Tracy & Fanelli, 2017). The International Association of Chiefs of Police (IACP) released a formal statement emphasizing law enforcement efforts to ensure that "any use of force is carefully applied and objectively reasonable considering the situation confronted by the officers." The IACP's statement assured that officers are trained to treat all individuals with dignity and respect (Herreria, 2017b). Despite these responses, many officials pointed to the undermining effects of President Trump's speech on the efforts of law enforcement agencies around the country to address police misconduct and build community trust, particularly in minority neighborhoods where, historically, police-community relations have been strained (Berman, 2017; Stokes, 2017).

President Trump's speech in Long Island is just one example of his controversial statements concerning issues related to crime and justice. The persistence and weight of these statements may have significant implications for public attitudes toward the police, particularly among minority citizens. Although police executives may seek to distance their agencies from the visage of law enforcement that Trump presents, the rhetoric of his administration regarding race and policing in America is potentially consequential. As Druckman and Jacobs (2009) point out, presidents position themselves to seem responsive to the public, sometimes the citizenry as a whole and sometimes specific constituencies. To the extent that President Trump seeks to appeal to his political base and certain segments of White America, his remarks – whether in speeches or tweets – can be interpreted as unsympathetic to people of color. His general depiction of Mexican immigrants, Muslims, and offenders as "the other" – all to be treated harshly and with little sensitivity for their legal rights – may cause his presidency to diminish perceptions among minorities of equal treatment by government agencies and inclusiveness in the United States.

In this regard, the current project conducted a 2017 national survey to examine whether the Trump presidency is experienced as a cause of concern by African Americans. Specifically, the goal is to explore whether the nation's Black population believes that Trump's election negatively impacts expressions of racism in American society, police conduct, and the future of police-minority relations. That is, has there been a "Trump Effect," and, if so, what has it been? Variation in opinions among African Americans is also examined. As a prelude to this analysis, the following section discusses the recent crisis in police legitimacy, the election of Donald Trump as the President of the United States, and the potential effects of his election on Black Americans' perceptions of policing, law, and justice in America.

Policing in the era of the Trump Presidency

Police innovation and critique

The past three decades have witnessed a significant era of change and innovation in American policing (Engel & Eck, 2015; National Research Council, 2004; Weisburd & Braga, 2006). Seeking to move beyond the view that police are unable to have a meaningful effect on crime (Bayley, 1994; Sherman, 1993), police practitioners have redefined and reprioritized their fundamental mission, core strategies, and nature of their relationships with the communities they serve (National Research Council, 2004; Weisburd & Braga, 2006). Driven by the work of researchers such as Goldstein (1979, 1990)), Wilson and Kelling (1982), and others, American policing entered a period in the 1990s where strategic innovations emphasized proactive approaches such as problem-solving, order maintenance, and the focus of police resources on specific types of crimes, criminals, and crime places (National Research Council, 2004; Weisburd & Eck, 2004). In general, these strategies targeted inner-city neighborhoods experiencing the greatest amount of violence and disorder, causing many proponents of these approaches to suggest that police efforts were being made (in essence) to save Black lives (Hayes, 2017). The simultaneous reduction in crime during this era, particularly in New York City, was remarkable (Fagan, Zimring, & Kim, 1998; Zimring, 2012). After experiencing high levels of crime for almost three decades, crime rates began dropping in 1993 in almost all categories nationwide. By the start of the 21st century, most serious crime rates had dropped by 35% (Zimring, 2007). While there is debate concerning how much of the crime reduction was a product of the significant changes in policing during this era, research consistently suggests that police have made at least some difference in crime prevention and control (Eck & Maguire, 2000; Engel & Eck, 2015; Zimring, 2007, 2012).

Despite this tremendous amount of police innovation and the dramatic reduction in violence and disorder in cities across the country, citizens, particularly Black Americans, have expressed a growing amount of discontent regarding the nature of police practices in the United States (Engel & Eck, 2015; Meares & Tyler, 2017). Specifically, the concentration of police activity and resources in inner-city communities has had collateral consequences, spurring tensions between the police and the communities they serve and provoking a crisis in police legitimacy. These consequences have taken two major forms: accusations of racial bias in aggressive policing tactics and the "second great awakening" (Sherman, 2018) concerning police use of deadly force that has motivated a "new conversation" regarding police reform (Walker, 2018).

Perceptions of racial bias in policing became salient with the use of aggressive police practices – such as pretext stops, stop-question-and-frisk tactics, and zero-tolerance policing – which reached epic proportions across cities, particularly New York City, in the 1990s (Zimring, 2007, 2012). Critics observe that minorities, particularly poor, Black Americans, bore the brunt of police strategies targeting violence and disorder in the inner-city (Figures & Legewie, 2019; Gelman, Fagan, & Kiss, 2007; Rosenbaum, 2006; Taylor, 2006; Weitzer, 2000). Black Americans were frequently and disproportionately subjected to stops, searches, and ultimately arrest, suggesting that while aggressive enforcement models may have tremendous benefits for some, they confer "widespread harassment and misery" on others (Butler, 2017; Epp, Maynard-Moody, & Haider-Markel, 2014; Hayes, 2017). Although initially supported by key Black politicians and community leaders (e.g., Eric Holder's support of aggressive investigatory stops in D.C.'s Operation Ceasefire as the U.S. Attorney for the District of Colombia; Forman, 2017), over time, the costs of reducing violence and maintaining order by means of aggressive enforcement seemed too high. Even as their neighborhoods became safer, Black citizens argued that they were giving up too much (Engel & Eck, 2015). The realities of constant surveillance by police (Brayne, 2017; Butler, 2017), the suspicion and indignity experienced in police encounters (Brunson & Weitzer, 2008; Gau & Brunson, 2010; Tyler, Jackson, & Mentovich, 2015), and the long-term implications for Black Americans' increased likelihood of contact with and penetration into the criminal justice system caused many to call for an end to the "psychological warfare" of aggressive enforcement (Butler, 2017; Forman, 2017; Hayes, 2017).

More recently, the United States has experienced a "second great awakening" concerning fatal police shootings (Sherman, 2018). A series of incidents involving the deaths of unarmed Black men at the hands of police officers has once again brought the quality and nature of policing in America into question (Nix, Campbell, Byers, & Alpert, 2017; Sparrow, 2016; Weitzer, 2015). Fed by a stream of online videos, the nation witnessed police-involved shootings first-hand (Graham, McManus, Cullen, Burton, & Jonson, 2019; Russel-Brown, 2017). The multitude of incidents, occurring in a short period of time, shifted public perceptions of police use of deadly force. Eric Garner in New York City (July 2014), Michael Brown in Ferguson, MO (August 2014), Tamir Rice in Cleveland, OH (November 2014), Walter Scott in North Charleston, SC (April 2015), Freddie Carlos Gray, Jr. in Baltimore, MD (April 2015) – no longer were these deaths viewed as isolated events, but instead as evidence of a larger national problem (Zimring, 2017). From consistent observations of police use of excessive force against Black Americans, a national movement emerged asserting that police misconduct and violence are systemic, and racial animus is often the motive (Weitzer, 2015). Eventually formalized as the Black Lives Matter movement, these individuals seek to shed light on police excessive use of force. They aim to broaden the conversation around state violence to include all ways in which Black citizens are intentionally left powerless at the hands of the state, and to demand criminal and social justice for this population (Garza, 2014; https://blacklivesmatter.com/about/what-we-believe/).

Policing in the Obama administration

Amid this crisis, the Obama administration sought to examine the state of policing in America. Recognizing the danger and difficulty faced by law enforcement officers every day, President Obama assured police officers across the nation that they had the support of his administration (Somanader, 2016). However, he also recognized that "No institution is entirely immune [to racism], and that includes our police departments" (Donella, 2016). The Obama administration increased the oversight of state and local law enforcement agencies. Under the then U.S. Attorney General, Eric Holder, the investigation of the "pattern or practice" of discrimination in law enforcement became a top priority (Weichselbaum, 2015). In the eight years of the Obama administration, the Department of Justice entered 12 consent decrees with different police agencies across the United States – a significant increase from the work of previous presidential administrations (Civil Rights Division, 2017). In further response to the series of high-profile police use-of-force incidents involving minority citizens, President Obama signed an executive order on December 18, 2014 to establish the Task Force on 21st Century Policing (Obama, 2017). This task force was created to identify best practices in policing and to offer recommendations on ways police agencies might promote effective crime reduction while building public trust. Importantly, in their final report, the Task Force highlighted the need for law enforcement agencies to acknowledge the role of policing in injustice and discrimination – both in the past and present (President's Task Force on 21st Century Policing, 2015).

While many police leaders responded to this initiative by taking steps toward reform, some conservative commentators argued that the "incessant drumbeat against the police" present in news and social media since the Summer of 2014 – following the death of Michael Brown in Ferguson, MO – held dangerous implications for policing and public safety in the United States (Mac Donald, 2016; see also Maguire, Nix, & Campbell, 2017). The idea of a "Ferguson effect" suggests that the "onslaught of anti-police rhetoric" makes police officers reluctant to engage in proactive enforcement due to fear of criticism and/or lawsuits regarding racial discrimination and excessive use of force (Mac Donald, 2016; see also Nix, 2017; Pyrooz, Decker, Wolfe, & Shjarback, 2015; Wolfe & Nix, 2016). As police hesitate to enforce the law, criminals feel more empowered, allowing crime rates to increase over time (Mac Donald, 2016). The most vocal supporters of the "Ferguson effect" suggest that until the nationwide criticism of law enforcement declines and police agencies are provided the trust and support of the federal government to resume proactive policing strategies – largely referring to broken windows and zero-tolerance policing – crime will continue to take over America's cities (Mac Donald, 2016).

President Trump, race, and policing

Since announcing his intent to run for President in the 2016 election, President Trump has taken a decidedly different stance from the Obama administration on policing and criminal justice in the United States. Diverging from the "reformist agenda" of the Obama administration, President Trump spent his time on the campaign trail as the ultimate "law-and-order" candidate and champion of the police (Haberman, 2017; Swaine, 2017). Through his campaign, President Trump actively endorsed aggressive crime-fighting strategies, such as stop-and-frisk policing, often suggesting that police officers should be given more discretion in their activities (Dwyer, 2016; Hee Lee, 2016; Nelson, 2016). Additionally, he has consistently supported the Blue Lives Matter Movement. Often presented as a contrast to the more liberal-dominated Black Lives Matter Movement, the Blue Lives Matter Movement advertises to support law enforcement by fighting "broad-brushed" accusations of institutionalized racism, brutality, and misconduct (Bacon, 2016; https://www.themaven.net/bluelivesmatter). This movement also emphasizes the protection and safety of police officers, seeking to end the "war on cops" – exemplified by violent incidents against police, such as in Dallas, TX and Baton Rouge, LA in July of 2016 (Fernandez, Pérez-Peña, & Bromwich, 2016; Visser, 2016; see also Mac Donald, 2016).

In his first year of presidency, President Trump made several executive decisions affecting policing in the United States. For example, fulfilling a promise made during his campaign, President Trump signed an executive order in February 2017 directing the Justice Department to explore new legislation that will make attacks on police officers a federal crime – a move supported by many states' "Blue Lives Matter Bills" (Casteel, 2017; Craven, 2017). Additionally, President Trump lifted the Obama-era ban on the transfer of surplus military equipment to police departments – a ban that first came into effect following the "battlefield-style" responses to rioting in Ferguson, MO four years earlier (Johnson, 2017). He has also publicly pardoned a high-ranking police official, the former Sheriff of Maricopa County (AZ), Joe Arpaio, who was found to repeatedly engage in racial profiling. President Trump suggested that Arpaio had been convicted "simply for doing his job" (Haberman, 2017).

Furthermore, under the leadership of the former U.S. Attorney General, Jeff Sessions, the Trump administration questioned the utility of federal intervention in state and local law enforcement (Melber, 2017). Specifically, Sessions ordered a review of the Justice Department's police reform activities and consent decrees (Office of the Attorney General, 2017). Having previously suggested that consent decrees forcing reforms on law enforcement agencies can "undermine respect for police officers," Sessions cited the purpose of this review as an assurance that agreements do not work against the Trump administration's goals of fighting crime while protecting officer safety and morale (Berman, 2017; Levenson, 2017). One year later, as one of his final acts while in office, Jeff Sessions signed an order limiting the Justice Department's use of consent decrees to monitor and adjust the actions of local law enforcement agencies (Benner, 2018; Norwood, 2018).

Donald Trump's time in office has also borne witness to powerful social justice debates concerning the confluence of race and policing. For example, following the highly publicized shootings of unarmed Black men at the hands of the police, a series of peaceful protests to police brutality by National Football League (NFL) players drew the attention of the nation (Mindock, 2017). This protest began in the 2016 NFL preseason when, in recognition of police violence, Colin Kaepernick, then quarterback for the San Francisco 49ers, chose to sit – and later kneel – during the national anthem preceding football games (Branch, 2017). As Kaepernick stated in a press conference:

> I am not going to stand up to show pride in a flag for a country that oppresses black people, and people of color. To me, this is bigger than football, and it would be selfish on my part to look the other way. There are bodies in the street, and people getting paid leave, and getting away with murder. (Wyche, 2016)

Although several NFL players joined Kaepernick in the 2016 NFL season, this form of protest did not gain traction until the 2017 season (Mindock, 2017). Specifically, President Trump became a "catalyst" for this movement when, at a campaign rally in September 2017, he suggested that NFL players who protest should be fired. Rebranding the protest as one against the American flag, President Trump commented, "Wouldn't you love to see one of these NFL owners, when somebody disrespects our flag, to say, 'Get that son of a bitch off the field right now, out, he's fired. He's fired!'" (Shelbourne, 2017). His comments spurred widespread demonstrations by NFL players across the country in a show of solidarity against his criticism (Hoffman, Mather, & Fortin, 2017). While President Trump would later argue that his criticisms had "nothing to do with race," many commentators noted the divisive nature of his statements (Graham, 2017a).

Throughout his campaign, election, and presidency, Trump's actions and rhetoric appear to have done little to garner African Americans' trust and support. Prior to the election, public opinion polls suggested that Trump's campaign message was doing little to sway Black voters. For example, ABC News and the Washington Post released a poll on June 15, 2016 reporting that 94% of Black adults surveyed held negative views of Trump (ABC News/Washington Post, 2016). Despite findings such as these, Trump insisted he would do well among minority voters (Hellmann, 2016). The results from election exit polls, however, show that Hillary Clinton held an 80-point advantage among African Americans, collecting 88% of the Black vote compared to Trump's eight percent (Tyson & Maniam, 2016). Although comparable to the percent of African American votes captured by previous Republican candidates (e.g., 9% captured by George W. Bush in 2000), Trump was elected with less support from Hispanic and Asian American voters than any president in at least 40 years (Eisler, 2016). As will be noted later, Black citizens' limited support for the president remains firm today.

Research strategy

In this context, this study examines whether the election of Donald Trump as president – given his rhetoric and policies on race and criminal justice – affects African Americans' views of the police and race relations in the United States. That is, is there a "Trump Effect" on Black Americans perceptions? Using a national survey of 1,000 Black Americans, we explore this issue, focusing on three concerns. First, we assess most generally whether the respondents believe that Trump's election shows that the United States is a racist society and will provide a license for the expression of racial hatred toward minorities. Second, we examine whether the respondents perceive President Trump's election as potentially straining police-minority relationships. Third, we consider whether the respondents are fearful that Trump's presidency will provide a climate in which African Americans will be more likely to be arrested, subjected to police violence, or experience a police shooting. At issue is not just African Americans' distrust of President Trump but, more importantly, whether his "law and order" politics and general dismissal of the concerns about Black lives further attenuates the legitimacy of law enforcement in the eyes of African Americans.

Methods

Sample

The data for this study are drawn from a national survey designed by the research team and conducted from June 8 to 19, 2017 by YouGov America, Inc., an opt-in internet panel survey company. YouGov employs a pool of approximately 1.8 million U.S. residents (at the time this survey was conducted) who have agreed to participate in online surveys in exchange for small incentives (e.g., small charitable donation on their behalf, sweepstake entry for a small prize, small cash payment) (YouGov, 2016). To complete survey research, YouGov uses a three-phase sampling strategy: (1) constructing a pseudo sampling frame using high-quality probability surveys and large-scale, commercially available databases (e.g., lists of registered voters), (2) matching YouGov panel members to this frame based on several demographic and behavioral variables, and (3) adjusting biases in the sample through propensity score weighting (Rivers, 2006; Thielo, 2017). Note that evidence exists that findings from YouGov surveys generalize to the U.S. population and that opt-in surveys rival the effectiveness of probability polls (Ansolabehere & Schaffner, 2014; Kennedy et al., 2016; Sanders, Clarke, Stewart, & Whiteley, 2007; Simmons & Bobo, 2015; Thielo, Graham, & Cullen, in press).

In the present study, the pseudo sampling frame was constructed from a random sample of adults who participated in the U.S. Census Bureau's 2010 American Community Survey (ACS). YouGov used simple random sampling with strata by weighted sampling with replacements (using the person weights on the public use file for the full 2010 ACS sample). Data on voter registration status and turnout (retrieved from the November 2010 Current Population Survey) and interest in politics and party identification (retrieved from the 2007 Pew Religious Life Survey) were matched to this frame. YouGov interviewed 1,214 African American panel members who were matched to the sampling frame based on gender, age, education, party identification, ideology, and political interest. These matched cases were then weighted to the sampling frame using propensity scores. The propensity score function included age, gender, years of education, and ideology. These propensity scores were grouped into deciles of the estimated propensity score in the frame and post-stratified according to those deciles. Ultimately, the 1,214 African American respondents were matched down to a sample of 1,000.

In this final sample, 45.5% of the respondents were male. The average age of the respondents was approximately 44 years (43.7), with most respondents falling within the 25–44 (38.1%) and 45–64 (34.1%) age categories. The majority of the respondents (41.9%) were high school graduates. Though a quarter of respondents (25%) reported completing some college, while another quarter (25.5%) indicated completing either a two-year degree, four-year degree, or post-graduate school. The average annual household income for the sample was between $20,000 and $39,999. Finally, among the respondents identifying their political ideology, the majority identified themselves as either liberal (30.9%) or moderate (37.4%), with only 15% identifying as conservative.

Public opinion measures

African Americans' perceptions of a "Trump Effect" were assessed in several ways. Survey respondents were asked for their opinions regarding the impact and implications of Donald Trump's election as President of the United States on a number of outcomes measured through eight individual survey items. These items assessed respondents' perceptions of the effects and implications of President Trump's election for general race relations in the United States, police-minority relations, and the likelihood of police mistreatment of African Americans. The exact items used are contained in Tables 1 and 2, which are presented in the Results section. The respondents were asked to use a six-point Likert-scale ranging from "strongly disagree" to "strongly agree" to rate the eight items. The description and frequencies of responses across these eight items are discussed in greater detail below.

To facilitate the investigation of variation in African Americans' opinions regarding the impact of President Trump's election, the eight survey items were examined in two additional ways. First, the items were combined and their scores averaged to develop the overall "Trump Effect" scale ($\alpha = .864$). Higher scores on this scale indicate greater perceptions of the negative effects and implications of President Trump's election. Next, the eight items were divided into a series of subscales to assess African Americans' perceptions of the impact of President Trump's election on (1) race relations in the United States, (2) police-minority relations, and (3) police mistreatment of African Americans.

The *impact on race relations* scale is a two-item measure assessing respondents' belief that the election of Donald Trump shows that the United States is still a racist society and that the Trump presidency has increased hate toward African Americans and other minorities ($\alpha = 0.852$). Higher scores on this scale indicate stronger beliefs that the Trump presidency has negative effects on race relations in the United States. Next, the *impact on police-minority relations* scale is a two-item measure assessing respondents' beliefs that President Trump's election will not have any effect on police-minority relations and that President Trump might help improve police-minority relations ($\alpha = .627$).[1] Higher scores on this scale indicate greater perceptions that Trump's presidency will neither impact nor improve police-minority relations. Finally, the *impact on police mistreatment of African Americans* scale is a three-item measure assessing respondents' beliefs that with Trump as President, more Black Americans will be arrested or victimized by the police ($\alpha = .888$). Higher scores on this scale indicate greater perceptions of the likelihood of police mistreatment of Black Americans during the Trump Presidency.

Independent variables

The survey assessed each respondent's sex, age, highest level of education, annual household income, political ideology, and the current area they live. These variables are included in the multivariate analyses. The purpose of these analyses is to explore whether deep cleavages or a general consensus exists among African Americans of varying groups in their perceptions of a "Trump effect." *Sex* is a dichotomous measure (0 = Female; 1 = Male). *Age* is a continuous measure calculated from the respondent's date of birth. *Highest level of education* is a categorical measure consisting of six categories ranging from "No High School" to "Post Grad." *Annual household income* is a categorical measure consisting of seven categories ranging from "\$0-\$9,999" to "\$100,000 + ." *Political ideology* is a dichotomous measure (0 = other; 1 = conservative or very conservative). Finally, *current area living* is a dichotomous measure (0 = Other; 1 = Urban Area with Crime).

Results

To assess African Americans' perceptions, we first examine the descriptive data on survey participants' responses to the eight survey items used to measure their beliefs regarding the impact and implications of President Trump's election. Second, multiple linear regression is used to analyze the relationship between the respondents' demographic characteristics and their perceptions of the effects of Donald Trump's election and presidency on the scales described above.

African Americans' perceptions of the impact of President Trump's election

Eight survey items were used to measure the respondents' beliefs regarding the impact and implications of Donald Trump's election as president of the United States. As shown in

Table 1. Perceived impact of Trump Presidential Election on race and police-minority relations (N = 1,000).

Item	% Total Agree	% Total Disagree	% Strongly Agree	% Agree	% Slightly Agree	% Slightly Disagree	% Disagree	% Strongly Disagree
Impact on Race Relations								
1. Donald Trump's election shows that the United States is still a racist society. (n = 973)	84.5	15.4	55.8	16.8	11.9	6.1	4.0	5.3
2. I believe that the Trump presidency has increased hate toward African Americans and other minorities. (n = 992)	82.4	17.6	47.4	23.1	11.9	8.0	4.9	4.7
Impact on Police-Minority Relations								
3. Most police officers probably voted for Donald Trump. (n = 975)	75.7	24.4	26.4	25.1	24.2	13.5	8.7	2.2
4. Although many African Americans do not like Trump, I do not believe that his being electedpresident will have any effect on how police and Blacks get along. (n = 991)	47.4	52.6	14.8	16.4	16.2	17.5	14.3	20.8
5. I think that President Trump will reach out to Blacks and might even improve police- minority relations. (n = 988)	23.5	76.5	4.2	9.4	9.9	12.6	17.5	46.4

*Percentages reported may be affected by rounding. The number of respondents answering each question differs and is listed.

Table 2. Perceived impact of Trump Presidential Election on police mistreatment of African Americans (N = 1,000).

Item	% Total Agree	% Total Disagree	% Strongly Agree	% Agree	% Slightly Agree	% Slightly Disagree	% Disagree	% Strongly Disagree
1.With Trump as President, I am fearful that more Black people will be arrested and sent to prison. (n = 988)	71.2	28.8	30.8	23.4	17.0	12.6	9.7	6.5
2. With Trump as President, I am more fearful that I or a family member will be a victim of police violence. (n = 986)	67.0	33.0	29.6	18.8	18.6	13.4	9.5	10.1
3. With Trump as President, shootings of unarmed Black men by the police are likely to increase. (n = 977)	70.6	29.3	31.8	23.2	15.6	16.4	8.3	4.6

[a]Percentages reported may be affected by rounding. The number of respondents answering each question differs and is listed.

Tables 1 and 2, the distribution of responses across these eight items reveals overall negative perceptions regarding the effects of President Trump's election on race relations, police-minority relations, and the mistreatment of African Americans by the police. For example, regarding the impact on race relations in the United States, a substantial majority of the respondents – 84.5% and 82.4% respectively – agreed that Donald Trump's election shows that the United States is still a racist society and that the Trump presidency has increased hate toward African Americans and other minorities (see Items 1 and 2 in Table 1). Notably, for both of these race-relations items, approximately half of the respondents (55.8% and 47.4%) strongly agreed with the statements presented.

Regarding police-minority relations, the majority of the respondents (75.7%) indicated their belief that most police officers probably voted for Donald Trump and their disbelief (76.5%) that

President Trump will reach out to Blacks and might even improve police-minority relations (see Items 3 and 4 in Table 1). In contrast, the final item assessing the respondents' perceptions of the impact of the Trump presidency on police-minority relations showed greater variation in responses (see Item 5 in Table 1). Almost half (47.4%) of the respondents suggested that they did not believe President Trump's election will have any effect on how police and Blacks get along. Still, a slight majority (52.6%) of the respondents disagreed with this statement, including about 1 in 5 who strongly disagreed. This finding suggests that Trump's election will negatively impact police-minority relations for a meaningful segment of the African American citizenry.

As seen in Table 2, the respondents consistently expressed concern that a Trump presidency would potentially increase police mistreatment of African Americans. Thus, with Trump as president, a high proportion of African Americans expressed concern that more Black people would be arrested and imprisoned (71.2%, Item 1), that a family member would be a victim of police violence (67.0%, Item 2), and that more unarmed Black men would be shot (70.6%, Item 3). Across each of these three items, about 3 in 10 respondents selected "strongly agree," indicating a notable intensity in African Americans' concerns about President Trump's adverse influence on police responses to Blacks in the United States.

Multivariate analyses

An important issue is whether the attitudes expressed in Tables 1 and 2 are broadly shared by African Americans or whether specific subgroups depart from the generally negative view of the Trump presidency and express positive sentiments. To explore this issue, we examined whether perceptions varied by sex, age, education, income, political ideology, and living in an urban area with crime. Table 3 presents the findings across four models. Model 1 examines the effect of the respondents' characteristics on the full "Trump Effect" scale, whereas Models 2, 3, and 4 examine the impact of these characteristics on the race relations, police-minority relations, and mistreatment of Blacks subscales.

The findings from Model 1 indicate that sex and political ideology are the only characteristics significantly associated with the respondents' perceptions of a "Trump Effect." Specifically, male respondents were found to report more positive views regarding the impact and implications of President Trump's election than female respondents. Similarly, the respondents that identified politically as either "conservative" or "very conservative" were less likely to perceive the effects of Trump's election and presidency as adverse.

Table 3. Impact of African Americans' characteristics on perceptions of Trump effect (Standardized coefficients reported; unstandardized coefficients in parentheses).

Independent Variables	Model 1 Trump Effect Scale (N = 906)	Model 2 Race Relations (N = 920)	Model 3 Police-Minority Relations (N = 937)	Model 4 Mistreatment of Blacks (N = 926)
Male	−.102* (−.234)	−.079* (−.210)	−.117* (−.329)	−.052 (−.147)
Age	.045 (.003)	.039 (.003)	.110* (.009)	−.015 (−.001)
Education	−.007 (−.007)	−.013 (−.013)	−.001 (−.001)	−.027 (−.029)
Income	.056 (.038)	.073* (.058)	.131* (.112)	−.021 (−.017)
Conservative	−.209* (−.684)	−.168* (−.633)	−.215* (−.857)	−.149* (−.594)
Living in Urban Area With Crime	.019 (.043)	.017 (.46)	.041 (.116)	−.016 (−.045)
R Square	0.063	0.043	0.100	0.028

*p < .05

In the evaluation of the Trump subscales, political ideology – that is, identifying as conservative – remained statistically significant across the three models. Sex maintained statistical significance in Models 2 and 3 but had no significant effect on the respondents' perceptions of the impact of the Trump presidency on police mistreatment of African Americans (Model 4). Annual household income became statistically significant in Models 2 and 3, with Blacks of higher income expressing greater negative perceptions of the implications of the Trump presidency on both race relations and police-minority relations. Finally, age was statistically significant in Model 3, with younger respondents expressing the belief that Trump's presidency will neither effect nor improve police-minority relations in the United States.

Although significant findings occurred, it is instructive to note that, taken as a whole, the independent variables accounted for only a limited amount of variation. Specifically, in the full "Trump Effect" model (Model 1), respondents' characteristics accounted for only 6.3% of the variation. Across the remaining three models, the percent of variation accounted for by these characteristics ranged between about three percent and 10% (R^2 = .043; .100; .028 respectively).

To further explore potential opinion gaps among African Americans, we examined the responses to the eight "Trump Effect" items by political ideology and sex, the only two demographic characteristics that were found statistically significant in the majority of the multivariate models above (see Table 3). For this analysis, we first combined the agree responses (slightly agree, agree, strongly agree) and the disagree responses (slight disagree, disagree, strongly disagree). Then, we assessed how attitudes across the eight Trump items differed by conservatives versus non-conservatives (Table 4) and males versus females (Table 5).

With regard to political ideology, the salience of any cleavages on the basis of political ideology are diminished by the fact that conservative respondents comprise only 15% of the sample. Regardless, two conclusions can be drawn from Table 4. First, political ideology

Table 4. Perceived impact of Trump Presidential Election by political ideology (Percentages reported).

	Conservative (*N* = 150)		Other (*N* = 850)		
Item	Agree	Disagree	Agree	Disagree	Difference
Impact on Race Relations					
1. Donald Trump's election shows that the United States is still a racist society.	66.5	33.6	87.8	12.3	21.3
2. I believe that the Trump presidency has increased hate toward African Americans and other minorities.	66.6	33.3	85.1	15.0	18.5
Impact on Police-Minority Relations					
3. Most police officers probably voted for Donald Trump.	88.5	11.5	73.4	26.7	15.1
4. Although many African Americans do not like Trump, I do not believe that his being elected president will have any effect on how police and Blacks get along.	60.9	36.9	44.6	55.4	16.3
5. I think that President Trump will reach out to Blacks and might even improve police-minority relations.	46.6	53.4	19.5	80.5	27.1
Police Mistreatment of African Americans					
6. With Trump as President, I am fearful that more Black people will be arrested and sent to prison.	52.3	47.7	74.6	25.4	22.3
7. With Trump as President, I am more fearful that I or a family member will be a victim of police violence.	55.7	44.3	69.0	15.0	13.3
8. With Trump as President, shootings of unarmed Blackmen by the police are likely to increase.	54.3	45.6	73.6	26.3	19.3

*Percentages reported may be affected by rounding. The number of respondents answering each question varies.

Table 5. Perceived impact of Trump Presidential Election by sex (Percentages reported).

Item	Male (*N* = 455)		Female (*N* = 545)		
	Agree	Disagree	Agree	Disagree	Difference
Impact on Race Relations					
1. Donald Trump's election shows that the United States is still a racist society.	80.7	19.3	87.8	12.2	7.1
2. I believe that the Trump presidency has increased hate toward African Americans and other minorities.	79.7	20.4	84.5	15.5	4.8
Impact on Police-Minority Relations					
3. Most police officers probably voted for Donald Trump.	80.1	19.9	71.8	28.2	8.3
4. Although many African Americans do not like Trump, I do not believe that his being elected president will have any effect on how police and Blacks get along.	50.7	49.3	44.4	55.6	6.3
5. I think that President Trump will reach out to Blacks and might even improve police-minority relations.	30.5	69.6	17.7	82.3	12.8
Police Mistreatment of African Americans					
6. With Trump as President, I am fearful that more Black people will be arrested and sent to prison.	69.8	30.2	72.3	27.7	2.5
7. With Trump as President, I am more fearful that I or a family member will be a victim of police violence.	66.1	33.9	67.8	32.1	1.7
8. With Trump as President, shootings of unarmed Black men by the police are likely to increase.	64.4	35.5	75.8	24.2	11.4

*Percentages reported may be affected by rounding. The number of respondents answering each question varies.

affects Blacks' opinions. Across the items, the average percentage-point difference between conservatives and others was 19.2. Second, although this gap is not trivial, in 7 of the 8 items, a majority of the two political groups answered in the same direction (Item 4 in Table 4 being the exception). Take, for example, Item 1, which proposed that Donald Trump's election shows the United States is still a racist society. Although the difference between groups was 21.3 percentage points, two-thirds of conservative respondents still agreed with this statement (66.5% versus 87.8% for non-conservatives). Similarly, when asked to indicate their agreement with the statement "With Trump as President, I am more fearful that I or a family member will be a victim of police violence," the agree responses were 55.7% for conservatives versus 69% for non-conservatives (Item 7). Thus, even among conservative African Americans, concern about the Trump presidency is clearly present.

Differences between males and females were even less pronounced. Across the eight items in Table 5, the average percentage-point difference was only 6.9. Again, the responses by group aligned in the same direction. Females were more negative in assessing the impact of the Trump presidency, but the males were similarly concerned. Collectively, the study's findings suggest limited cleavages in African Americans' perceptions of a "Trump Effect." In general, there appears to be far more consensus than disagreement that the election of Donald Trump as president has negatively impacted race relations and increases Blacks' vulnerability to arrest and police violence.

Discussion

The Trump effect

The ability of presidents to shape public opinion in the United States has been well established in research. This influence on the public's attitudes and policy preferences has been attributed to the tendency of Americans to view the president as the principal policymaker and representative of the country (see, e.g., Cohen, 1995, 1997; Lawrence, 2004). Indeed, evidence of the impact of presidential speeches and general dialog have led some commentators to suggest that the most potent tool for shaping public opinion is a president's rhetoric (Druckman & Jacobs, 2009; Tulis, 1987). While historically presidents have concentrated their efforts in swaying public opinion in their favor, it appears that President Trump may be intensifying worry among the public – in many cases making his political beliefs personal concerns for segments of the American population. Indeed, recent studies suggest that the political climate and the future of the nation following the election of President Trump are significant sources of stress for many Americans (see, e.g., American Psychological Association, 2017, 2018; Ray, 2019) – particularly minorities (Gemmill et al., 2019; Krupenkin, Rothschild, Hill, & Yom-Tov, 2019; Wan & Bever, 2019). For African Americans, it is possible that President Trump's strong remarks regarding crime and justice, including his rigid support for "law and order" and "tough on crime" policies, could be consequential for perceptions of police and race relations in the United States.

Our data seem to confirm the presence of this "Trump Effect." Specifically, findings from our national survey illustrate the substantial consensus among Black Americans regarding their perceptions of the impact and implications of Donald Trump's presidency. With a few minor exceptions, the survey's respondents consistently expressed concern regarding the Trump Presidency, noting the negative effects of Donald Trump's election on race relations, police-minority relations, and police mistreatment of Black citizens in the United States. These concerns were apparent in the survey respondents' beliefs that Donald Trump's election shows that the United States is still a racist society (84.5% agreed) and that the Trump Presidency has increased hate toward African Americans and other minorities (82.4% agreed). As noted above, relatively few of the survey respondents (23.5%) expressed their belief that President Trump will reach out to Blacks and might even improve police-minority relations. In contrast, the survey findings suggest that African Americans perceive the Trump Presidency as likely to increase police mistreatment of Black citizens – with more than two-thirds of the survey respondents expressing their fear that more Black people will be arrested and sent to prison (71.2%), that they or a family member will be a victim of police violence (67.0%), and that shootings of unarmed Black men by the police are likely to increase (70.6%) with Donald Trump as President. Lacking longitudinal data, we cannot definitively conclude that the election of Donald Trump in 2016 caused these perceptions to worsen. Still, it is clear that the vast majority of Black Americans believe that his presidency will have wide-ranging negative implications for both social and criminal justice.

It is instructive to note that this national survey was administered prior to several highly publicized race-related events in the United States. These events include the Unite the Right Rally in Charlottesville, Virginia (August 2017). This rally resulted in a clash between White nationalists and counter-protesters and ultimately the death of one woman and injury of several others as a White nationalist drove his car into a crowd of pedestrians following the march. Described as "a day of racial rage, hate, violence, and death," President Trump provided an equivocal response. He condemned the "display of hatred, bigotry, and violence *on many sides*" and then later suggested that there was blame *on both sides* of the protest (Desjardins, 2018; Heim, 2017; Politico Staff, 2017).

The current survey also preceded the controversy of the NFL 2017 season described previously. President Trump's characterization of the players' protests as disrespectful to the American flag – including attacks on specific African American players – caused many commentators to accuse him of purposefully misrepresenting the players' cause in a racially divisive way (Graham, 2017a; Shelbourne, 2017). Given these events – as well as his recent anti-immigrant policies and rhetoric targeting people of color – it seems likely that the viewpoints captured by our survey have, if anything, been solidified if not intensified (see, e.g., Lopez, 2019; Pew Research Center, 2019; Rogers, 2019; Romo, 2019).

An examination of public opinion poll data would lend credence to this conclusion. From the beginning, perceptions of the Trump presidency have been found to be divided among racial lines (Dugan, 2018). By January 2018, a Gallup Poll exploring Americans' approval of President Trump revealed that only nine percent of Black Americans expressed approval of how he handles his job (Dugan, 2018). A public opinion poll published by Quinnipiac University (2017) further exemplifies this racial divide. In this poll, only three percent of African Americans indicated their approval of the way President Trump is handling race relations in the United States (compared to 41% of White Americans). Further, fully 79% of Black respondents indicated that they think President Trump is racist (compared to 44% of White Americans). These findings are reiterated in a recent public opinion poll published by the Pew Research Center (Horowitz, Brown, & Cox, 2019). Specifically, this poll reports that 56% of the individuals surveyed suggest President Trump has made race relations in the United States worse. Among those individuals, the majority of Black (73%), Hispanic (69%), and Asian (65%) respondents held this view, compared to 49% of White respondents

Policy implications

President Trump entered office at a point in history when tensions between law enforcement and Black Americans had escalated to a high level (see, e.g., Butler, 2017; Forman, 2017; Hayes, 2017; Mac Donald, 2016). Upon taking office, an opportunity existed for a "Nixon-goes-to China" moment – when a politician whose credentials supporting the police would have provided the political capital to bridge police-minority cleavages. As in many other areas, however, President Trump not only did not seek to bind the citizenry together but doubled down on his right-leaning views (Bobo, 2017). Indeed, since his election, his rhetoric and political standpoints appear to have done more to stoke the fire of adversity between law enforcement agencies and communities of color, rather than extinguish the flames – doing little to alleviate Black Americans' concerns regarding the potential injustices they may experience at the hands of the police (Rucker, 2018). Specifically, President Trump's emphasis on "law and order" and being "tough on crime," while appealing to his largely White political base, may appear to many Black Americans as creating a permissive climate for the mistreatment of Black citizens at the hands of the police. Recall him giving law enforcement officers the license to "take the hand away."

Combined with recent observations noting the reluctance of the Trump administration to speak out against racial violence (see, e.g., Bouie, 2018; Diamond, 2018), the lack of concern for Black lives in the United States appears to be a characterizing feature of the Trump presidency. Notably, this insensitivity is likely to fuel the Black Lives Matter Movement, making their claims regarding social injustice and violence against Black communities particularly salient and the overall mission of the organization more viable. In this context, President Trump's statements and embrace of the police will continue to attenuate the legitimacy of law enforcement in the eyes of Black Americans. As such, the risk exists that the efforts of law enforcement agencies across the nation to build trust and improve relations within communities of color will be made more difficult, if not undermined in a serious way.

The exact views of rank-and-file law enforcement officers regarding President Trump and his message are largely unknown, though anecdotal evidence may suggest they are receptive (see; e.g., Balto, 2017; Kaste, 2016; Lind, 2017a). Importantly, however, many law enforcement executives have expressed that President Trump's rhetoric regarding race and policing is misguided and often damaging in their work to establish closer, more trusting relationships with the minority communities they serve (Sanchez, 2017; Wootson & Berman, 2017). It appears that to mitigate further threats to police legitimacy in the United States, police leaders will need to dissociate their agencies from the views and policies of the Trump administration. That is, in the post-Ferguson and Trump era, police officials must choose whose side they are on – Trump or their community. Indeed, police executives have already challenged policies laid down by the Trump administration. For example, in 2017, many law enforcement executives came forward, opposing President Trump's stance on sanctuary cities (Campbell, 2017). While expressing their opposition to the Presidential Executive Order: Enhancing Public Safety in the Interior of the United States (2017) risked law enforcement agencies' access to much-needed federal funds, it was deemed necessary by many police executives to ameliorate the negative effects (i.e., increased fear and distrust of police) caused by the Trump administration's anti-immigrant rhetoric in the minority communities they serve (Jackman, 2017; Magnus, 2017).

Given the historically strained relationships between law enforcement and Black communities in the United States, it is likely that altering Black Americans' perceptions of police will require more than law enforcement executives' public statements refuting their agency's alliance with the Trump administration. Law enforcement agencies across the United States should invest in their relationships with their community, demonstrating their prioritization of equity in policing, in addition to effectiveness in crime prevention and control (Engel & Eck, 2015; President's Task Force on 21st Century Policing, 2015). This prioritization of equity will require greater transparency – openness and visibility into the strategic, operational, and tactical decision-making processes – within police agencies at both the administrative-level and officer-level (Engel & Eck, 2015), as well as active communication and collaboration between police agencies and the public (President's Task Force on 21st Century Policing, 2015).

Notably, survey research can assist in law enforcement efforts to connect with their community – providing agencies insight on the perceptions of the citizens they serve. However, this research on public attitudes of police must probe the views of African Americans more intimately, moving beyond general questions regarding "satisfaction with" or "confidence in" police to generate a more nuanced understanding of the experiences and expectations of individuals in the communities most often receiving police attention (see, e.g., La Vigne, Fontaine, & Dwivedi, 2017). Police executives may also consider the development or continuation of reform efforts within their agency designed to enhance the equity, fairness, and legitimacy of policing in the communities they serve. This type of voluntary reform is not unheard of. For example, law enforcement agencies, such as the San Francisco Police Department, have chosen to continue with state-level oversight though the United States Justice Department has discontinued their involvement (Berman, 2018; Sernoffsky, 2018). Collectively, the completion and publication of these efforts can play an important role in demonstrating that, regardless of the Trump administration's policies and proclamations regarding crime and justice in the United States, Black lives do indeed matter to the police.

Note

1. The impact on police-minority relations scale was originally constructed as a three-item measure, including an item assessing respondents' beliefs that "most police officers probably voted for Donald Trump." However, this item was removed due to its negative effect on the Cronbach's alpha for the scale (α = .476).

Disclosure statement

No potential conflict of interest was reported by the author.

References

ABC News/Washington Post. (2016). Trump's unfavorable spike, but Clinton's challenged, too (poll). *Lange Research Associates*. Retrieved from http://www.langerresearch.com/wp-content/uploads/1144-57Clinton-TrumpFavorability.pdf

American Psychological Association. (2017). *Stress in America: Coping with change*. Washington, DC: Author.

American Psychological Association. (2018). *Stress in America: Generation Z*. Washington, DC: Author.

Ansolabehere, S., & Schaffner, B. F. (2014). Does survey model still matter? Findings from a 2010 multi-mode comparison. *Political Analysis*, *22*, 285–303. doi:10.1093/pan/mpt025

Bacon, P., Jr. (2016). Trump and other conservatives embrace 'blue lives matter' movement. *NBC News*. Retrieved from https://www.nbcnews.com/storyline/2016-conventions/trump-other-conservatives-embrace-blue-lives-matter-movement-n615156

Balto, S. (2017). Why many police cheered Trump's dark speech: Rank-and-file officers have long been drawn to demagogues. *Washington Post*. Retrieved from https://www.washingtonpost.com/news/made-by-history/wp/2017/07/31/why-police-officers-cheered-trumps-dark-speech/?utm_term=.a1be59213185

Bayley, D. H. (1994). *Police for the future*. New York, NY: Oxford University Press.

Benner, K. (2018). Sessions, in last-minute act, sharply limits use of consent decrees to curb police abuses. *New York Times*. Retrieved from https://www.nytimes.com/2018/11/08/us/politics/sessions-limits-consent-decrees.html

Berman, M. (2017). Trump tells police not to worry about injuring suspects during arrests. *Washington Post*. Retrieved from https://www.washingtonpost.com/news/post-nation/wp/2017/07/28/trump-tells-police-not-to-worry-about-injuring-suspects-during-arrests/?utm_term=.67a47036f885

Berman, M. (2018). San Francisco's police force will be under state oversight after Justice Dept. rolls back federal program. *The Washington Post*. Retrieved from https://www.washingtonpost.com/news/post-nation/wp/2018/02/06/san-franciscos-police-force-will-be-under-state-oversight-after-justice-dept-rolls-back-federal-program/?utm_term=.15dc29c7537c

Blake, A. (2017). Trump's continued, not-so-subtle suggestion of violence. *The Washington Post*. Retrieved from https://www.washingtonpost.com/news/the-fix/wp/2017/07/28/president-trump-encourages-violence-yet-again-this-time-by-police/?utm_term=.4e2ced150c14

Bobo, L. (2017). Racism in Trump's America: Reflections on culture, sociology, and the 2016 US presidential election. *British Journal of Sociology*, *68*, S85–S104. doi:10.1111/1468-4446.12324

Bouie, J. (2018). What the President won't say: Donald Trump breaks with precedent by not speaking out against racial violence. *Slate*. Retrieved from https://slate.com/news-and-politics/2018/03/donald-trump-refuses-to-speak-out-against-racial-violence.html

Branch, J. (2017). The awakening of Colin Kaepernick: In college, Kaepernick began a journey that led him to his position as one of the most prominent, divisive, social activists in sports. *New York Times*. Retrieved from https://www.nytimes.com/2017/09/07/sports/colin-kaepernick-nfl-protests.html

Brayne, S. (2017). Big data surveillance: The case of policing. *American Sociological Review, 82*, 1–32. doi:10.1177/0003122417725865

Brunson, R. K., & Weitzer, R. (2008). Police relations with black and white youths in different urban neighborhoods. *Urban Affairs Review, 44*, 858–885. doi:10.1177/1078087408326973

Bump, P. (2017). Trump's speech encouraging police to be 'rough,' annotated. *Washington Post*. Retrieved from https://www.washingtonpost.com/news/politics/wp/2017/07/28/trumps-speech-encouraging-police-to-be-rough-annotated/?utm_term=.2b27877c38d2

Butler, P. (2017). *Chokehold: Policing black men; A renegade prosecutor's radical thoughts on how to disrupt the system*. New York, NY: The New Press.

Campbell, A. F. (2017). US police chiefs are fighting the crackdown on "sanctuary cities." *Vox*. Retrieved from https://www.vox.com/policy-and-politics/2017/8/18/16130954/police-sanctuary-cities

Casteel, K. (2017). Would Trump's 'blue lives matter' effort really help protect police? *FiveThirtyEight*. Retrieved from https://fivethirtyeight.com/features/would-trumps-blue-lives-matter-effort-really-help-protect-police/

Chiusano, M. (2017). Donald Trump's speech was made more disturbing as Suffolk County cops cheered the idea of police brutality. *Newsday*. Retrieved from http://www.newsday.com/opinion/columnists/mark-chiusano/donald-trump-s-speech-was-made-more-disturbing-as-suffolk-county-cops-cheered-the-idea-of-police-brutality-1.13864824

Civil Rights Division. (2017). *The civil rights division's pattern and practice reform work: 1994-present*. Washington, DC: U.S. Department of Justice.

Cobb, J. (2017). Donald Trump is serious when he "jokes" about police brutality. *The New Yorker*. Retrieved from http://www.newyorker.com/news/news-desk,donald-trump-is-serious-when-he-jokes-about-police-brutality

Cohen, J. E. (1995). Presidential rhetoric and the public agenda. *American Journal of Political Science, 39*, 87–107. doi:10.2307/2111759

Cohen, J. E. (1997). *Presidential responsiveness and public policy*. Ann Arbor, MI: University of Michigan Press.

Craven, J. (2017). 32 blue lives matter bills have been introduced across 14 states this year. The wave of legislation, which classifies violent attacks on police as hate crimes, exposes an appetite to provide political sanctuary to an already protected class. Huffington Post. Retrieved from https://www.huffingtonpost.com/entry/blue-black-lives-matter-police-bills-states_us_58b61488e4b0780bac2e31b8

Desjardins, L. (2018). Every moment in Trump's charged relationship with race. *PBS News Hour*. Retrieved from https://www.pbs.org/newshour/politics/every-moment-donald-trumps-long-complicated-history-race

Diamond, J. (2018). White House calls police shootings of black men 'a local matter'. *CNN*. Retrieved from https://www.cnn.com/2018/03/28/politics/alton-sterling-white-house-reaction/index.html?sr=twCNN032818alton-sterling-white-house-reaction0744PMVODtop

Donella, L. (2016). 'Bias remains:' A week of strong words on race. *NPR*. Retrieved from http://www.npr.org/sections/codeswitch/2016/07/16/486155522/bias-remains-a-week-of-strong-words-on-race

Druckman, J. N., & Jacobs, L. R. (2009). Presidential responsiveness to public opinion. In G. C. Edwards & W. G. Howell (Eds.), *The Oxford handbook of the American presidency* (pp. 160–181). New York, NY: Oxford University Press.

Dugan, A. (2018). Party, ideology and race play key roles in Trump approval. *Gallup*. Retrieved from https://news.gallup.com/poll/226091/party-ideology-race-play-key-roles-trump-approval.aspx

Dwyer, J. (2016). What Donald Trump got wrong on stop-and-frisk. *New York Times*. Retrieved from https://www.nytimes.com/2016/09/28/nyregion/what-donald-trump-got-wrong-on-stop-and-frisk.html

Eck, J. E., & Maguire, E. R. (2000). Have changes in policing reduced violent crime? An assessment of the evidence. In A. Blumstein & J. Wallman (Eds.), *The crime drop in America* (pp. 207–265). New York, NY: Cambridge University Press.

Eisler, P. (2016). Trump won with lowest minority vote in decades, fueling division. *Reuters*. Retrieved from https://www.reuters.com/article/us-usa-trump-polarization-analysis/trump-won-with-lowest-minority-vote-in-decades-fueling-divisions-idUSKBN13I10B

Engel, R. S., & Eck, J. E. (2015). Effectiveness vs. equity in policing: Is a tradeoff inevitable? *Ideas in American Policing, 18*, 1–12.

Epp, C. R., Maynard-Moody, S., & Haider-Markel, D. (2014). *Pulled over: How police stops define race and citizenship*. Chicago, IL: The University of Chicago Press.

Executive order 13678. (2017). Enhancing public safety in the interior of the United States. *Federal Register, 82*, 8799–8803.

Fagan, J., Zimring, F. E., & Kim, J. (1998). Declining homicide in New York City: A tale of two trends. *Journal of Criminal Law & Criminology, 88*, 1277–1324. doi:10.2307/1144257

Fernandez, M., Pérez-Peña, R., & Bromwich, J. E. (2016). Five Dallas officers were killed as payback, police chief says. *New York Times*. Retrieved from https://www.nytimes.com/2016/07/09/us/dallas-police-shooting.html

Figures, K. D., & Legewie, J. (2019). Visualizing police exposure by race, gender, and age in New York City. *Socios, 5* 237802311982891. Advances online publication. doi:10.1177/2378023119828913.

Forman, J. J. (2017). *Locking up our own: Crime and punishment in black America*. New York, NY: Farrar, Strauss, & Giroux.

Garza, A. (2014). A herstory of the #BlackLivesMatter movement. *Feminist Wire*. Retrieved from http://www.thefeministwire.com/2014/10/blacklivesmatter-2/

Gau, J. M., & Brunson, R. K. (2010). Procedural justice and order maintenance policing: A study of inner-city young men's perceptions of police legitimacy. *Justice Quarterly, 27*, 255–279. doi:10.1080/07418820902763889

Gelman, A., Fagan, J., & Kiss, A. (2007). An analysis of the New York City police department's "stop-and-frisk" policy in the context of claims of racial bias. *Journal of the American Statistical Association, 102*, 813–823. doi:10.1198/016214506000001040

Gemmill, A., Catalano, R., Casey, J. A. M., Karasek, D., Alcalá, H. E., Elser, H., & Torres, J. M. (2019). Association of preterm births among US Latina women with the 2016 presidential election. *JAMA Network, 2*, e197084. Advanced online publication. doi:10.1001/jamanetworkopen.2019.7084.

Goldstein, H. (1979). Improving policing: A problem-oriented approach. *Crime and Delinquency, 25*, 236–258. doi:10.1177/001112877902500207

Goldstein, H. (1990). *Problem-oriented policing*. New York, NY: McGraw Hill Inc.

Graham, A., McManus, H. D., Cullen, F. T., Burton, J. V., & Jonson, C. L. (2019). Videos don't lie: African Americans support for body-worn cameras. *Criminal Justice Review, 44*, 284–303. doi:10.1177/0734016819846229

Graham, B. A. (2017a). Trump blasts NFL anthem protesters: 'Get that son of a bitch off the field.' *The Guardian*. Retrieved from https://www.theguardian.com/sport/2017/sep/22/donald-trump-nfl-national-anthem-protests

Graham, D. A. (2017b). Trump's vision of lawless order: The president suggests he sees the rule of law as an impediment to getting tough on crime. *The Atlantic*. Retrieved from https://www.theatlantic.com/politics/archive/2017/07/trump-long-island-ms-13/535317/

Haberman, M. (2017). Trump's brand of law and order leaves leeway on the law. *The New York Times*. Retrieved from https://www.nytimes.com/2017/08/27/us/politics/trump-law-order-police-arpaio.html

Hayes, C. (2017). *A Colony in a nation*. New York, NY: W.W. Norton & Company.

Hee Lee, M. Y. (2016). Trump's false claim that stop and frisk in NYC wasn't ruled unconstitutional. *Washington Post*. Retrieved from https://www.washingtonpost.com/news/fact-checker/wp/2016/09/28/trumps-false-claim-that-stop-and-frisk-was-not-ruled-unconstitutional/?utm_term=.82092f1c5043

Heim, J. (2017). Recounting a day of rage, hate, violence and death: How a rally of white nationalists and supremacists at the University of Virginia turned into a "tragic, tragic weekend." *Washington Post*. Retrieved from https://www.washingtonpost.com/graphics/2017/local/charlottesville-timeline/?noredirect=on&utm_term=.98f95cb3f606

Hellmann, J. (2016). Poll: Trump has 94 percent unfavorable rating with blacks. *The Hill*. Retrieved from http://thehill.com/blogs/ballot-box/presidential-races/283744-poll-trump-has-94-percent-unfavorable-rating-with-blacks

Herreria, C. (2017a). NYPD call unreasonable use of force 'irresponsible' after Trump's speech. The department said suggestions for using another standard for use of force "sends the wrong message". *Huffington Post*. Retrieved from http://www.huffingtonpost.com/entry/nypd-responds-to-trump-speech-use-of-force_us_597cf58be4b02a8434b6d20e

Herreria, C. (2017b). Police chiefs defend 'respect' after Trump appears to endorse brutality. The international association of police chiefs sends out a timely lesson on use of force. *Huffington Post*. Retrieved from http://www.huffingtonpost.com/entry/international-police-chief-association-respond-trump-brutality-speech_us_597bfc86e4b02a4ebb759b22

Hoffman, B., Mather, V., & Fortin, J. (2017). After Trump blasts N.F.L., players kneel and lock arms in solidarity. *New York Times*. Retrieved from https://www.nytimes.com/2017/09/24/sports/nfl-trump-anthem-protests.html

Horowitz, J. M., Brown, A., & Cox, K. (2019). *Race in America 2019: Public has negative views of the country's racial progress; more than half say Trump has made race relations worse*. Washington, DC: Pew Research Center.

Jackman, T. (2017). Police chiefs' immigration task force outlines opposition to Trump policy. *Washington Post*. Retrieved from https://www.washingtonpost.com/news/true-crime/wp/2017/03/01/police-chiefs-immigration-task-force-outlines-opposition-to-trump-policy/?noredirect=on&utm_term=.de399400e0ec

Johnson, K. (2017). Trump lifts ban on military gear to local police forces. *USA Today*. Retrieved from https://www.usatoday.com/story/news/politics/2017/08/27/trump-expected-lift-ban-military-gear-local-police-forces/606065001/

Kaste, M. (2016). How the perceived 'war on cops' plays into politics and policing. *NPR*. Retrieved from https://www.npr.org/2016/12/29/507249260/how-the-perceived-war-on-cops-plays-into-politics-and-policing

Kennedy, C., Mercer, A., Keeter, S., Hatley, N., McGeeney, K., & Gimenez, A. (2016). *Evaluating online nonprobability surveys*. Washington, DC: Pew Research Center.

Krupenkin, M., Rothschild, D., Hill, S., & Yom-Tov, E. (2019). President Trump stress disorder: Partisanship, ethnicity, and expressive reporting of mental distress after the 2016 election. *Public Opinion Quarterly*. Advanced online publication. doi: 10.1177/2158244019830865.

La Vigne, N., Fontaine, J., & Dwivedi, A. (2017). *How do people in high-crime, low-income communities view the police?* Washington, DC: Urban Institute, Justice Policy Center.

Lawrence, A. B. (2004). *Does it matter what the presidents say? The influence of presidential rhetoric on the public agenda, 1946–2003* (Unpublished Doctoral Dissertation). University of Pittsburgh, Pittsburgh, PA.

Levenson, E. (2017). Here's why police consent decrees were made in the first place. *CNN*. Retrieved from http://www.cnn.com/2017/04/04/politics/jeff-sessions-consent-decree-roundup/index.html

Lind, D. (2017a). How police officers became the culture-war heroes of the Trump era: An identity politics that conservatives could love. *Vox*. Retrieved from https://www.vox.com/policy-and-politics/2017/12/29/16826152/trump-police-immigration-blue-lives-matter

Lind, D. (2017b). Trump just delivered the most chilling speech of his presidency. The President of the United States is explicitly encouraging police violence. *Vox*. Retrieved from https://www.vox.com/policy-and-politics/2017/7/28/16059486/trump-speech-police-hand

Lopez, G. (2019). Donald Trump's long history of racism from the 1970s to 2019. *Vox*. Retrieved from https://www.vox.com/2016/7/25/12270880/donald-trump-racist-racism-history

Mac Donald, H. (2016). *The war on cops: How the new attack on law and order makes everyone less safe*. New York, NY: Encounter Books.

Magnus, C. (2017). Tucson's police chief: Sessions's [sic] anti-immigrant policies will make cities more dangerous. *New York Times*. Retrieved from https://www.nytimes.com/2017/12/06/opinion/tucson-police-immigration-jeff-sessions.html

Maguire, E. R., Nix, J., & Campbell, B. A. (2017). A war on cops? The effects of Ferguson on the number of U.S. police officers murdered in the line of duty. *Justice Quarterly, 34*, 739–758. doi:10.1080/07418825.2016.1236205

Manchester, J. (2017). Long Island police department responds to Trump: We don't tolerate roughing up prisoners. *The Hill*. Retrieved from http://thehill.com/blogs/blog-briefing-room/news/344402-long-island-police-department-responds-to-trump-we-dont

Meares, T., & Tyler, T. (2017). Policing: A model for the 21st century. In A. J. Davis (Ed.), *Policing the black man: Arrest, prosecution, and imprisonment* (pp. 161–177). New York, NY: Pantheon Books.

Melber, A. (2017). 100 days of Trump and the police. *NBC News*. Retrieved from https://www.nbcnews.com/storyline/president-trumps-first-100-days/100-days-trump-police-n752281

Mindock, C. (2017). Taking a knee: Why are NFL players protesting and when did they start to kneel? Critics say that sports should be clear of politics, but athletes have used their platform to protest before. *Independent*. Retrieved from http://www.independent.co.uk/news/world/americas/us-politics/taking-a-knee-national-anthem-nfl-trump-why-meaning-origins-racism-us-colin-kaepernick-a7966961.html

National Research Council. (2004). *Fairness and effectiveness in policing: The evidence*. Washington, DC: The National Academies Press.

Nelson, L. (2016). Trump calls for nationwide 'stop-and-frisk' policy. *Politico*. Retrieved from http://www.politico.com/story/2016/09/donald-trump-stop-and-frisk-228486

Nix, J. (2017). American policing in the post-Ferguson Era. *Fordham Urban Law Review*. Retrieved from http://urbanlawjournal.com/american-policing-in-the-post-ferguson-era/

Nix, J., Campbell, B. A., Byers, E. H., & Alpert, G. P. (2017). A bird's eye view of civilians killed by police in 2015. *Criminology & Public Policy, 16*, 309–340. doi:10.1111/1745-9133.12269

Norwood, C. (2018). Are cops 'off the hook'? How police reform has changed under Trump. *Governing*. Retrieved from https://www.governing.com/topics/public-justice-safety/gov-trump-sessions-consent-decrees-police-reform.html

Obama, B. (2017). Commentary: The President's role in advancing criminal justice reform. *Harvard Law Review, 130*, 811–866.

Office of the Attorney General. (2017). *Memorandum for heads of department components and United States attorneys: Supporting federal, state, local, and tribal enforcement*. The United States Department of Justice. Retrieved from https://www.justice.gov/opa/pr/attorney-general-sessions-memorandum-supporting-federal-state-local-and-tribal-law

Pew Research Center. (2019). *Majority says Trump has done 'too little' to distance himself from white nationalists*. Washington, DC: Author.

Politico Staff. (2017). Full text: Trump's comments on white supremacists, 'alt-left' in Charlottesville. *Politico*, Retrieved from https://www.politico.com/story/2017/08/15/full-text-trump-comments-white-supremacists-alt-left-transcript-241662

President's Task Force on 21st Century Policing. (2015). *Final report of the president's task force on 21st century policing*. Washington, DC: Office of Community Oriented Policing Services

Pyrooz, D. C., Decker, S. H., Wolfe, S. E., & Shjarback, J. A. (2015). Was there a Ferguson effect on crime rates in large U.S. cities? *Journal of Criminal Justice, 46*, 1–8. doi:10.1016/j.jcrimjus.2016.01.001

Quinnipiac University. (2017). Trump is not fit to be president, American voters say, Quinnipiac University National Poll Finds; Voter disapprove 2-1 of his handling of race relations. *Quinnipiac University*. Retrieved from https://poll.qu.edu/national/release-detail?ReleaseID=2487

Ray, J. (2019). Americans' stress, worry and anger intensified in 2018. *Gallup*. Retrieved from https://news.gallup.com/poll/249098/americans-stress-worry-anger-intensified-2018.aspx

Rivers, D. (2006). *Sample matching—Representative sampling from internet panels.* Palo Alto, CA: YouGovPolimetrix.

Rogers, K. (2019). The painful roots of Trump's 'go back' comment. *New York Times.* Retrieved from https://www.nytimes.com/2019/07/16/us/politics/aoc-trump-tlaib-omar-pressley.html?module=inline

Romo, V. (2019). Trump administration moves to speed up deportations with expedited removal expansion. *NPR.* Retrieved from https://www.npr.org/2019/07/22/744177726/trump-administration-moves-to-speed-up-deportations-with-expedited-removal-expan

Rosenbaum, D. P. (2006). The limits of hot spots policing. In D. Weisburd & A. A. Braga (Eds.), *Police innovation: Contrasting perspectives* (pp. 245–263). New York, NY: Cambridge University Press.

Rucker, P. (2018). 'A blowtorch to the tinder': Stoking racial tensions is a feature of Trump's presidency. *Washington Post.* Retrieved from https://www.washingtonpost.com/politics/a-blowtorch-to-the-tinder-stoking-racial-tensions-is-a-feature-of-trumps-presidency/2018/06/20/e95e71dc-73d9-11e8-805c-4b67019fcfe4_story.html?noredirect=on&utm_term=.8eb7d29e3772

Russel-Brown, K. (2017). Making implicit bias explicit. In A. J. Davis (Ed.), *Policing the black man: Arrest, prosecution, and imprisonment.* (pp. 135–160). New York, NY: Pantheon Books.

Sanchez, R. (2017). Police push back against Trump's law-and-order speech. *CNN Politics.* Retrieved from https://www.cnn.com/2017/07/29/politics/trump-police-remarks-reaction/index.html

Sanders, D., Clarke, H. D., Stewart, M. C., & Whiteley, P. (2007). Does mode matter for modeling political choice? Evidence from the 2005 British Election Study. *Political Analysis, 15,* 257–285. doi:10.1093/pan/mpl010

Sernoffsky, E. (2018). State to take on reform oversight at SF police department. *San Francisco Chronicle.* Retrieved from https://www.sfchronicle.com/news/article/State-to-take-on-reform-oversight-at-SF-Police-12550865.php

Shelbourne, M. (2017). Trump says criticism of NFL 'has nothing to do with race.' *The Hill.* Retrieved from http://thehill.com/homenews/administration/352171-trump-says-criticism-of-nfl-protests-has-nothing-to-do-with-race

Sherman, L. W. (1993). Why crime control is not reactionary. In D. Weisburd & C. Uchida (Eds.), *Police innovation and control of the police* (pp. 171–189). New York, NY: Springer.

Sherman, L. W. (2018). Reducing fatal police shootings as system crashes: Research, theory, and practice. *Annual Review of Criminology, 1,* 421–449. doi:10.1146/annurev-criminol-032317-092409

Simmons, A. D., & Bobo, L. D. (2015). Can non-full-probability internet surveys yield useful data? A comparison with full-probability face-to-face surveys in the domain of race and social inequality attitudes. *Sociological Methodology, 45,* 357–387. doi:10.1177/0081175015570096

Somanader, T. (2016). Read President Obama's open letter to America's law enforcement community. *The White House.* Retrieved from https://obamawhitehouse.archives.gov/blog/2016/07/19/read-president-obamas-open-letter-americas-law-enforcement-community

Sparrow, M. (2016). *Handcuffed: What holds policing back and the keys to reform.* Washington, DC: The Brookings Institution.

Stokes, S. (2017). Trump remarks eclipse Sessions' talk before black law enforcement group. *NPR.* Retrieved from http://www.npr.org/2017/08/02/541061862/trump-remarks-eclipse-sessions-talk-before-black-law-enforcement-group

Swaine, J. (2017). Trump breaks from Obama with crime crackdown and 'blue lives matter' protections. President's plan represents sharp about-turn from moderately progressive proposals by Obama amid unrest over fatal police shootings in past two years. *The Guardian.* Retrieved from https://www.theguardian.com/us-news/2017/feb/09/trump-criminal-justice-reform-police-protections-obama

Taylor, R. B. (2006). Incivilities reduction policing, zero tolerance, and the retreat from coproduction: Weak foundations and strong pressures. In D. Weisburd & A. A. Braga (Eds.), *Police innovation: Contrasting perspectives* (pp. 98–114). New York, NY: Cambridge University Press.

Thielo, A. J. (2017). *Redemption in an era of penal harm: Moving beyond offender exclusion* (Unpublished doctoral dissertation). University of Cincinnati, Cincinnati, OH.
Thielo, A. J., Graham, A., & Cullen, F. T. (in press). Opt-in internet surveys. In J. C. Barnes & D. R. Forde (Eds.), *The encyclopedia of research methods and statistical techniques in criminology and criminal justice*. New York, NY: Wiley.
Tracy, T., & Fanelli, J. (2017). International police condemn President Trump's MS-13 speech pushing use of force on gang suspects. *New York Daily News*. Retrieved from http://www.nydailynews.com/news/politics/international-cops-condemn-trump-speech-pushing-force-article-1.3367489
Tulis, J. (1987). *The rhetorical presidency*. Princeton, NJ: Princeton University Press.
Tyler, T. R., Jackson, J., & Mentovich, A. (2015). The consequences of being an object of suspicion: Potential pitfalls of proactive police contact. *Journal of Empirical Legal Studies, 12*, 602–636. doi:10.1111/jels.2015.12.issue-4
Tyson, A., & Maniam, S. (2016). Behind Trump's victory: Divisions by race, gender, and education. *Pew Research Center*. Retrieved from http://www.pewresearch.org/fact-tank/2016/11/09/behind-trumps-victory-divisions-by-race-gender-education/
Visser, S. (2016). Baton Rouge shooting: 3 officers dead; shooter was Missouri man, sources day. *CNN*. Retrieved from https://www.cnn.com/2016/07/17/us/baton-route-police-shooting/index.html
Walker, S. (2018). "Not dead yet": The national police crisis, a new conversation about policing, and the prospects for accountability-related police reform. *University of Illinois Law Review, 2018*, 1777–1841.
Wan, W., & Bever, L. (2019). Trump's presidency may be making Latinos sick. *Washington Post*. Retrieved from https://www.washingtonpost.com/health/trumps-presidency-may-be-making-latinos-sick/2019/07/19/4e89b9f0-a97f-11e9-9214-246e594de5d5_story.html?noredirect=on&utm_term=.6efc428305c6
Weichselbaum, S. (2015). The problems with policing the police: As the Justice Department pushes reform, some push back. *Time*. Retrieved from http://time.com/police-shootings-justice-department-civil-rights-investigations/
Weisburd, D., & Braga, A. A. (2006). *Police innovation: Contrasting perspectives*. New York, NY: Cambridge University Press.
Weisburd, D., & Eck, J. E. (2004). What can police do to reduce crime, disorder, and fear? *The Annals of the American Academy of Political and Social Science, 593*, 42–65. doi:10.1177/0002716203262548
Weitzer, R. (2000). Racialized policing: Residents' perceptions in three neighborhoods. *Law & Society Review, 34*, 129–155. doi:10.2307/3115118
Weitzer, R. (2015). American policing under fire: Misconduct and reform. *Social Science and Modern Society, 52*, 475–480.
Wilson, J. Q., & Kelling, G. L. (1982). The police and neighborhood safety: Broken windows. *Atlantic Monthly*, pp. 29–38
Wolfe, S. E., & Nix, J. (2016). The alleged "Ferguson Effect" and police willingness to engage in community partnership. *Law and Human Behavior, 40*, 1–10. doi:10.1037/lhb0000164
Wootson, C. R., Jr., & Berman, M. (2017). U.S. police chiefs blast Trump for endorsing 'police brutality'. *Washington Post*. Retrieved from https://www.washingtonpost.com/news/post-nation/wp/2017/07/29/u-s-police-chiefs-blast-trump-for-endorsing-police-brutality/?utm_term=.d57694713b65
Wyche, S. (2016). Colin Kaepernick explains why he sat during national anthem. *NFL*. Retrieved from http://www.nfl.com/news/story/0ap3000000691077/article/colin-kaepernick-explains-why-he-sat-during-national-anthem
YouGov. (2016). *Survey procedures: Information related to the treatment of human subjects*. Redwood City, CA: Author.
Zimring, F. E. (2007). *The great American crime decline*. New York, NY: Oxford University Press.
Zimring, F. E. (2012). *The city that became safe: New York's lessons for urban crime and its control*. New York, NY: Oxford University Press.
Zimring, F. E. (2017). *When police kill*. Cambridge, MA: Harvard University Press.

Harming America: Corporate Crime in a Context of Deregulation

Michael L. Benson, William A. Stadler, and Henry N. Pontell

ABSTRACT

Like many Republican presidential candidates before him, Donald J. Trump campaigned on a pro-business, anti-regulation platform, and since his election in November 2016, he has directed his administration to move forward with deregulation in many arenas, including consumer financial protections, environmental controls, and workplace safety among others. Past efforts to roll back regulations governing certain industries, such as the savings and loan and the mortgage industries, have had harmful consequences for the general public or for specific interest groups. In this study, we review what the Trump administration has accomplished with regard to deregulation to date. Then, based on past deregulatory fiascos, we theorize the harmful collateral consequences that may result from this most recent swing of the regulatory-deregulatory pendulum.

Although the criminal justice system can play an important role in controlling corporate crime, responsibility for the day-to-day oversight and control of corporate misconduct falls primarily on regulatory agencies. By promulgating and enforcing regulations that govern business activities, agencies seek to ensure that corporations conduct their activities in a manner that is as safe and as fair for workers, consumers and the general public as possible within the limits of economic feasibility. Regulations are necessary because history has shown that when left to their own devices, some corporate leaders have a tendency to prioritize profits and convenience over safety and fairness. Hence, whenever regulatory agencies and regulatory rules come under attack, it raises the specter that workers, consumers, and the general public will eventually see more, rather than less, harm at the hands of corporate actors. After his election as President in 2016, Donald Trump commenced just such an attack.

Like many Republican candidates for political office, Trump campaigned on an anti-regulation, pro-business platform, and as soon as he was in office, he began to follow through on his campaign promises, directing his administration to start reviewing and rolling back regulations in a number of different arenas. As we show below, he has had some success. However, he has also encountered push back and hold ups on many fronts, because the process of changing regulations is itself governed by law and regulation, regardless whether the changes are meant to weaken or strengthen them. As a result, deregulation often takes time and cannot be put into effect with the simple stroke of a pen.

In addition, deregulation and regulatory rollback can take different forms, some of which are easier to accomplish than others. Thus, even though Trump has been in office for over three years now, his progress on the deregulation front has been mixed and the potential effects, harmful, benign or helpful, of his deregulatory efforts are still emerging. However, the historical record on deregulation suggests that it is likely that deregulation fostered by Trump will have unanticipated and unintended consequences that harm certain segments of American society.

In this article, we review the status of Trump's deregulatory initiatives, focusing on three specific areas: the environment, workplace safety, and consumer financial protection. We focus on these areas because deregulation in them would seem to carry greater potential for corporations to impose real physical or financial harm on individuals than it does in other areas, such as education or trade.[1] We begin by describing the different ways in which deregulation or regulatory rollback, as it is often called, can be achieved. Next, we shift to the specific areas noted above, beginning with environmental and workplace safety, and describe the current state of affairs in each area. Since regulatory rollback sometimes happens when Presidents use their prerogatives to appoint agency leaders who are actively hostile to an agency's mission, we then describe some of the key players in what we call Trump's war on white-collar crime enforcement. Finally, we conclude by drawing comparisons between what has happened in the past when sectors of the economy have been deregulated and what might happen in the future as Trump's agenda moves forward.

Mechanisms of regulatory rollback

President Trump and his administration have at their disposal four different mechanisms that can be used to ease the regulatory burden on corporations, and all of them have been tried in the areas under examination here. From the point of view of those interested in promoting deregulation, each of the mechanisms has its strengths and weaknesses. First, the President can issue executive orders that are informal declarations and overarching directives meant to dictate policy approaches for agencies within the federal government (Potter, Rudalevige, Thrower, & Warber, 2019). Presidents can and often do issue a series of such orders immediately after they have taken office. For example, President Trump's very first executive order (13765) was issued on January 20, 2017 and was designed to weaken protections associated with the Patient Protection and Affordable Care Act passed under President Obama. Although executive orders are easy to issue, their constitutionality can be challenged in court and their actual implementation can be delayed or prevented altogether. Executive orders also can be replaced by new orders whenever a new president is elected. Hence, as a mechanism of deregulation, the effectiveness and longevity of an executive order is always uncertain.

Second, besides issuing executive orders, Presidents can also appoint people to lead a regulatory agency who are actively hostile to an agency's original mandate. This form of deregulation is often called agency capture, wherein the agency comes to serve the interests of the industry it is supposed to regulate instead of the interests of the public. The appointees can take steps to undermine the execution of existing policies by ignoring enforcement precedent and procedural justice, issuing "non-action assurances" in regard to existing regulations, or refusing to refer allegations of misconduct for civil resolution or criminal prosecution. As with executive orders, the longevity of such actions depends on the administration staying in power and the agency leaders maintaining their positions.

Third, a president can also attempt to reduce the power of regulatory agencies through budget cuts, workforce reductions, or restrictions on an agency's scope or authority. Reducing an agency's budget is certainly a powerful and effective way to reduce its ability to pursue its mission and protect the public, but it depends in part on the willingness of Congress to go along with the president's budgetary priorities. As with the first two mechanisms, this one is also subject to the ebb and flow of political power in Washington. A new administration with different budgetary priorities can undo whatever its predecessor has accomplished with this mechanism.

Finally, the most powerful and long-lasting regulatory effects can be achieved via the implementation of formal rule changes, in which federal regulatory agencies themselves abolish existing regulations or issue formal amendments to them. But removing or formally amending regulations requires an agency to successfully navigate a legal process that is both highly technical and highly political and that can take years to complete in the case of complex regulations, such as many of those that govern the environment, workplace safety, and consumer financial security. However, once such formal changes are on the books, they are protected by the very process that made them difficult to establish in the first place. Thus, as a mechanism of deregulation, formal rule changes are likely to have the most long-lasting effects. Nevertheless, because it is easier to reduce the flow of new regulations than it is to remove existing regulations, the Trump administration so far has chosen to focus on slowing down the pace of new regulations and using the other tactics described above to undermine those that are already on the books.

Environmental and workplace deregulation

President Donald J. Trump, who campaigned on a promise to deregulate America, has been openly hostile to industry rules and regulations (Krisberg, 2017), and as a result, is dramatically changing labor and environmental policy for the United States. His administration, which includes a veritable who's who of pro-business agency leaders and advisors opposed to industry regulation, has systematically engaged in an all-out assault to dismantle federal rules enacted by previous administrations. Over his first term, Trump has introduced shocking and disruptive reforms through the four broad maneuvers discussed above, all in an attempt to eliminate "job-killing regulations" (Trump, 2017) and weaken the power of federal agencies. Some of his efforts have been squarely targeted at labor policies, which have clear implications for workplace safety (Meier & Ivory, 2017), and many more have been directed at environmental regulations, which are intended to protect nature and the health of the public (Fredrickson et al., 2018). According to The Brookings Institution (2019), which tracks the status of deregulation across a number of industries in the Trump administration, there are currently more than 180 proposed or completed actions as of July 2019, thirteen of which are directly intended to limit or expunge industrial regulations designed to protect U.S. workers. Similarly, *The New York Times* has cited at least 83 proposed rollbacks of environmental regulations that could result in dire consequences, including increases in greenhouse gas emissions, poorer water and air quality, and even thousands of human deaths (Popovich, Albeck-Ripka, & Pierre-Louis, 2019).

Because a plurality of proposed Trump administration regulatory rollbacks are linked with the environment, the most conspicuous federal body under assault is the Environmental Protection Agency (EPA). It is here where the President has brazenly reversed course away from decades of precedent set by previous administrations to establish policies that explicitly favor the very industries the EPA is charged with regulating (Dillon et al., 2018). This practice, termed by social scientists as "regulatory capture," occurs when "regulation is ... directed away from the public interest and toward the interest of the regulated industry" (Carpenter & Moss, 2013, p. 73). Recent deregulation tactics employed by the Trump administration represent bold efforts to shift the balance of power away from government intrusion into the free market. Yet, many of this administration's actions may be haphazardly putting the public's health and safety at risk while teetering on the verge between politically motivated gamesmanship and outright public collusion with industry. Clearly, the administration's war-like efforts to eviscerate existing environmental and workplace regulations are political, but they may arguably be of questionable legality, as well (Davis Noll & Grab, 2017).

Unilateral executive actions

As a testament to his disillusionment with what he considers to be industry-suffocating rules, Trump has exhibited a combative willingness to issue broad-sweeping executive orders, memoranda, and proclamations designed to demolish Obama's legacy, forcefully asserting his anti-regulation agenda, and providing contrary guidance to federal agencies with industry oversight. In the first weeks of his presidency, and with much spectacle, Trump began his siege by signing Executive Order 13771 in 2017 that sought to reduce regulatory burdens across a variety of industries by requiring federal agencies to eliminate two old regulations for each newly proposed rule (EPA, 2017). This was followed shortly by Executive Order 13777, which requires each federal agency to designate a "regulatory reform officer" and "task force" to enforce the President's regulatory agenda (Ballotpedia, 2017). Though both of these initial declarations were intended to apply more broadly, they are emblematic of the President's views on industry oversight and signify his desire to shift regulatory agency policy toward a laissez-faire approach. These initial moves also set a clear trajectory for his presidency and laid the groundwork for his many future attacks on regulations designed to protect the environment and workplace safety.

From the Oval Office of The White House, President Trump waged his first battle on the environment by proudly signing and issuing a memorandum to approve completion of the embattled Trans-Canada Keystone Oil Pipeline, a controversial project that the Obama administration had blocked due to its potential environmental impact (Thrower, 2018). Later, with even greater pomp and circumstance from the Rose Garden of The White House, he announced his intention to withdraw the U.S. from the Paris Climate Agreement (Mooney, 2018), a multinational environmental accord, years in the making, that is designed to protect the world from the harms caused by manmade climate change. These two announcements represented the beginning of what has become a literal onslaught of unilateral actions aimed squarely at dismantling existing environmental and labor policies.

Review of the federal register indicates that more than halfway through his term, Trump has signed eleven additional Executive Orders that explicitly reshape environmental policy and two exclusively focused on American worker safety. The environmental decrees issued by Trump have directed agencies to review existing rules or repeal Executive Orders issued under previous administrations (see EO's 13778, 13792, 13840, and 13867), expand industry access, such as mining and drilling, to previously protected regions (see EO's 13795 and 13817), achieve greater speed in conducting environmental and regulatory reviews (see EO's 13707 and 13807), promote industry increases in efficiency, development, and productivity (see EO's 13834 and 13868), and reduce impediments to energy production (see EO 13783). Similarly, the two aimed at labor policy have revoked Obama-era orders that sought to protect workers by creating a federal labor-management relations council (see EO 13812) and establishing a minimum wage for contracted federal workers (see EO 13838). Although presidential actions such as these carry limited authority and scope, they predominantly serve as formal guidance for agencies with respect to how they should generally adopt and enforce regulations. And from the perspective of the Trump administration, these actions are generally intended to minimize regulatory disruption into numerous industries, though they also signify his willful intent to restrict federal agency directives and their capacity to perform oversight and checks and balances on the industries they have responsibility for regulating.

Agency funding and structure

If his record on executive orders leaves any doubt as to Trump's mission of deprioritizing environmental and workplace regulation, a look at his administration's plans for agency appropriations and organization should eliminate lingering uncertainty. Under the guise of fiscal responsibility and curtailing government overreach, the administration has sought to further weaken the authority and regulatory power of many federal agencies through three related mechanisms: slashing agency budgets, reducing agency workforces, and reshaping agency missions. Trump's proposed 2020 budget for the EPA includes a 31% reduction in spending (more than $650 million), on top of already deep cuts proposed in 2019 of more than 25% (Green, 2019; Tankersley & Tackett, 2019). If Congress were to approve proposed budget cuts at the EPA (which, thankfully, is unlikely) it would decimate climate science research and environmental enforcement capabilities of the agency (Green, 2019), providing further evidence of President Trump's pre-election vow to reduce the EPA to "little tidbits" (Davenport, 2016).

On the labor side, Trump's fiscal year 2019 budget sought a 21% reduction in the Department of Labor budget, along with the elimination of several programs designed to provide job and safety training to workers (Morath, 2018). The proposed 2020 budget – also unlikely to be adopted – seeks cuts of nearly $1 Billion, or 10%, of the department's current budget. Despite draconian budget proposals from the Trump administration and the significant risks they pose, to date, Congress has been unwilling to acquiesce but has instead continued to provide relatively stable funding for both the EPA and Department of Labor in recent years. Still, the risks of significant budget cuts loom over the heads of many who work in these agencies, and the proposals offered by this administration thus far should provide a clear indication of Trump's deliberate attempt to reduce the size and scope of federal regulatory agencies.

Unfortunately, some regulatory agency workforces have not been lucky enough to avoid Trump's wrath. Headcounts at the EPA have declined markedly in the Trump era. Before his ouster as head of the agency, Scott Pruitt oversaw efforts to cut its workforce in half by 2020 through hiring freezes, buyouts, office closures, and "workforce reshaping" (O'Grady, 2018). Eighteen months into the Trump presidency, at about the same time as Pruitt's departure, the EPA workforce had fallen by 8% to historically low levels not seen since the Reagan administration – and many expect it to fall further under new EPA director, Andrew Wheeler (Dennis, Eilperin, & Ba Tran, 2018). The office of Enforcement and Compliance Assurance within the EPA saw an even more precipitous decline in its workforce, losing 131 full-time employees, or nearly 18% of its staff, over the last two years (Volcovici, 2019). The number of EPA criminal investigators has tumbled under Trump, dropping by more than 20% since 2012 to 140 by April of 2018, well below the minimum of 200 agents required by the U.S. Pollution Prosecution Act of 1990 (Public Employees for Environmental Responsibility, 2018).

The employee headcount at the Department of Labor has also fallen during Trump's era. According to internal data, the labor department employed nearly 18,000 people in 2016 (Department of Labor, 2017), but at the publication of its most recent 2020 budget proposal, the workforce had fallen to approximately 15,500 employees (Department of Labor, 2019b). The workforce at OSHA has also experienced "unprecedented atrophy" under the Trump Administration – in 2016, OSHA had 952 employees, but by year-end 2018 that number had fallen to a 48-year low of 875 personnel (Chen, 2019). Like budget proposals, ongoing workforce reductions such as these represent the clear intent of the current administration to moderate the power, limit the scope, and diminish the capacity of agencies responsible for monitoring and enforcing workplace safety and environmental regulations.

Formal rule proposals

Lastly, in addition to unilateral chief executive actions, appointments provoking differential compliance and enforcement activities, and fiscal changes prompting workforce reductions and losses in regulatory strength, agencies under the current administration have directly proposed the revision or reversal of existing rules to counteract Obama-era regulations. These efforts are also intended to drastically tip the scales of regulatory agency work in favor of the free market. For example, rules that protect worker safety but are viewed by Trump as limiting hiring and job growth in traditional industries such as manufacturing and coal mining have recently been rolled back following initial delays (Kullgren, 2018). Such was the case for a rule proposed by the Mine Safety and Health Administration under Obama, which was supposed to go into effect in 2017. The Department of Labor first delayed implementation of this rule that required mine operators to examine workplace safety and record any adverse health and safety conditions prior to miners beginning their shifts (Nutzman, 2019). During the delay, the MHSA then revised and issued an amended rule in 2018 that relaxed previously adopted safety check and record-keeping requirements to provide greater flexibility and less burdensome standards for mine operators (Lopez, 2019). This move is indeed controversial because it could pose a real danger to workers and reduce the level of transparency in reporting mine safety concerns. Using similar tactics, OSHA delayed, failed to enforce, revised, and reissued a rule originally created under the Obama administration that required large employers to systematically track and electronically submit workplace injuries and illnesses to the agency (Lanham, Duvall, & Vitris, 2019). The new rule, which is predicated on the common Trump administration deregulation refrain that employers, rather than the government, are best positioned to engage in self-policing with respect to identifying and rectifying workplace safety issues, rescinds the electronic reporting requirement under the auspices of protecting worker privacy.

Similarly, the Trump administration has revised a number of other rules established during the Obama-era that have direct implications to both environmental protection and workplace safety. Following the Deep Water Horizon disaster of 2010, which polluted the Gulf of Mexico with millions of barrels of oil and killed 11 offshore drilling workers, the Obama administration implemented heightened safety checks and standards on offshore oil rig equipment to prevent future disasters (Fears, 2019). However, the Bureau of Safety and Environmental Enforcement in the Department of the Interior issued a revised rule in 2019 that is expected to result in hundreds of millions in cost savings for oil companies but at the possible expense of worker and environmental safety (Kullgren, 2018). Another recently rescinded regulation is the Obama enacted EPA Clean Power Plan (EPA, 2016), which was subsequently replaced by Trump's EPA Affordable Clean Energy Rule (EPA, 2019). Obama's plan sought to aggressively limit human-induced climate change antecedents, such as carbon emissions, and the subsequent dangers posed by a warming planet, air pollution, and rising seas. However, Trump's plan greatly weakens the rules set forth under Obama's in favor of efficiency and cost-savings for the energy industry and consumers. Several similar draft EPA rules are anticipated to be released in the summer of 2019, including one that is expected to eliminate the existing ability of concerned communities to appeal EPA decisions to issue so-called "pollution permits" to industrial sites, one which would weaken restrictions on pollution from vehicle tailpipes, and one which would diminish regulations on greenhouse gas pollution (Davenport, 2019a).

Consumer financial protection

The Trump administration has pursued financial deregulation in a number of areas, but according to The Brookings Institution's (2019) deregulation tracker, the administration's efforts in five specific areas are most noteworthy. Three areas relate directly to consumer financial protection. They include the Fiduciary Rule, the Arbitration Rule, and the Automobile Dealer Markup Guidance. In each of these areas, the Trump administration is attempting to modify or repeal existing regulations in such a way as to take power away from consumers and expose them to a greater risk of being financially exploited or abused by corporate criminals.

The fiduciary rule was issued during President Obama's term. It required all financial professionals who work with retirement assets or provide retirement planning advice to put the interests of their clients above their own and to not conceal conflicts of interest (Grant, 2019). Prior to the Obama rule registered retirement investment advisors were required to meet this fiduciary standard, but others who work in retirement planning were only required to meet a "suitability standard," which is more lenient and gives advisors more leeway to steer clients toward particular investments that may be more in the interest of the advisors. The fiduciary standard would have required all retirement investment advisors to disclose conflicts of interests, fees, and commissions for their advice. The suitability standard only requires advisors to make recommendations about financial products that are suitable in terms of the investors stated investment goals (e.g., capital growth versus income) and stated level of risk tolerance (e.g., aggressive versus conservative). Under the suitability standard, an investment advisor can recommend that a client choose a product that is suitable but not necessarily in the best financial interests of the client. For example, an advisor might recommend a product that cost the client more but gave the advisor a bigger commission than another similarly suitable product. With the support of the Trump administration, the Fiduciary Rule has been repealed. The Securities and Exchange Commission (SEC) has issued a new suitability standard that is better than the old one, but it is still not as stringent as the fiduciary standard.

Both the fiduciary rule and the suitability standard are designed to correct what economists call information asymmetries in financial markets. Such asymmetries, in which the advisor has more information than the client, are inherent in all agent-client relationships (Shapiro, 2005). The less an agent, such as an investment advisor, has to disclose about their interests when working for a client, the easier it is for the agent to pursue their own interests at the expense of their clients. Unfortunately, the number of individuals at risk of being financially exploited by financial advisors has grown in recent decades, because as governments have withdrawn from welfare provisions, financial markets have become an increasingly important source of financial security for everyone. People can no longer depend upon pensions or government stipends to support themselves in old age. Hence, they must plan to take care of themselves through personal savings and investments. In the United States between 1970 and 2003, the proportion of household savings held in financial products, such as stocks, bonds, and mutual funds, increased from 17% to 38% (Group of Ten, 2005). Thus, households are increasingly exposed to risks that lie in financial markets (Maloney, 2010) and this risk is exacerbated by the Trump administration's repeal of the fiduciary rule.

The Arbitration Rule was issued by the Consumer Financial Protection Bureau (CFPB) in July, 2017. It barred selected financial companies from demanding that consumers submit to mandatory arbitration if they wanted to use a company's products, such as a credit card or checking account. The rule was supposed to make it easier for consumers to pursue alternative legal remedies if they were wronged by a financial company, especially class action lawsuits. In theory, the threat of a large penalty as a result of a successful class-action lawsuit can deter financial companies from engaging in deceptive and exploitative practices. The Treasury Department, along with many financial companies, vehemently opposed the rule, arguing that it only benefitted trial lawyers, not consumers. With support from Trump, the Republican-controlled Congress passed a law repealing the rule under the Congressional Review Act, and Trump signed it, nullifying the rule. By effectively removing the threat of class-action lawsuits, the Trump administration has made it possible for enormous financial companies, such as Citibank and Wells Fargo, to continue dealing with consumer complaints on a case-by-case basis. Even if a consumer happens to win in an arbitration hearing, which is unlikely given the way the hearings are structured and the legal and financial resources at the disposal of corporate behemoths, the penalty imposed on the company is so negligible that it provides absolutely no incentive for a company to change its practices, no matter how unfair they may be to consumers.

Finally, The Equal Credit Opportunity Act (ECOA) prohibits lenders from discriminating against lenders on the basis of race. In March 2018, the CFPB issued guidance for compliance with the (ECOA). The guidance was aimed at "dealer markups" in which an automobile dealer charges additional interest above what a third party lender has approved for a particular buyer. Research has shown that this practice disproportionately affects people of color (National Consumer Law Center, 2015). Congress has the authority to review regulatory rules and to repeal them, which after some legislative maneuvering is exactly what the GOP controlled Congress did in May of 2018, and Trump signed the bill. So, the rule established by the CFPB has been repealed (Lane, 2018a).

Taken together, the repeal of the fiduciary, arbitration, and dealer markup regulations represent a series of steps that take power away from consumers and give it to financial professionals and business corporations. Each of these repeals and nullifications makes it harder for individual consumers to protect themselves against self-serving financial professionals, such as investment advisers, as well as profit-hungry banks and credit card companies, not to mention shady auto dealers. Coupled with the increasing complexity of financial products and the naivety and inexperience so many household investors, financial deregulation under the Trump administration has certainly increased opportunities for self-dealing by the financial industry and outright fraud against consumers.

The other two noteworthy areas of financial deregulation relate to the rules governing federal programs designed to improve business and economic activity within designated communities, usually disadvantaged ones via Opportunity Zone (OZ) regulations and the Community Reinvestment Act (CRA). It is harder to identify exactly how regulatory rollback in this area will affect individual consumers, but they raise the risk that they will enable wealthy people and wealthy corporations to benefit while not providing much in the way of benefits to disadvantaged communities.

As part of the 2017 tax cuts (Tax Cuts and Jobs Act), Opportunity Zones were created in economically distressed areas selected by states and designated to receive federal tax subsidies for investment. In brief, the subsidies give tax breaks (e. g., partial forgiveness of capital gains taxes) to investors who invest in economic projects within the zones. In May 2019, Treasury clarified the rules governing this program and it expects the proposed rules when final to be an E.O. (13771) deregulatory action. In principle, reducing taxes on funds invested in Opportunity Zones seems like a good way to spur investment in businesses in economically disadvantaged areas. But the question remains: Do the rules as written really spur economic development, or are they just another way for wealthy people to avoid paying taxes and hence get wealthier? In other words, does this program merely create a new form of tax shelter for the wealthy rather than new economic opportunities for local residents? The Center on Budget and Policy Priorities (CBPP) suggests the result will be the former rather than the latter (Jacoby, 2019). The new rules make it possible for an investor to qualify for tax breaks without really doing anything to help the local community. For example, an investor can buy land that does not have any structures on it and not invest any money to improve the land. Of course, the investor is required to use the land as part of a business, but this requirement can be met by simply using the land for a parking lot, which could be automated and have very few employees. After ten years, if the land rises in value, the investor can then sell it to a developer tax-free. The local community gets minimal new business activity out of this scenario. The new rules do give the IRS authority to combat abuse if it thinks the funds are not being used to increase business activity, but the level of business activity is not well-defined and the IRS is obviously understaffed and under-resourced to enforce the anti-abuse rule anyway.

The Community Reinvestment Act (CRA) has been in existence since 1977. It was originally designed to curb discriminatory lending practices by banks who fail to meet the credit needs of the communities in which they operate, especially low and moderate-income communities (called LMI lending). Among the main issues is how to measure the amount of LMI lending a bank is doing and what kinds of communities should qualify for CRA credit. With the rise of online banking, defining where a bank is located has gotten complicated, and the Trump administration is proposing to change the way in which the LMI lending of a bank is measured. Currently, banks are evaluated based on geographic assessment areas, so they are required to engage in a certain amount of CRA activity in the bank's brick and mortar market area – that is, the communities that surround their branch locations. The Office of the Comptroller of the Currency (OCC) has proposed replacing geographically based assessment areas with what is called the "one-ratio rule." Under the one-ratio rule, the CRA activity of a bank would be evaluated by the fraction of the bank's total assets that are invested in community development. Banks love the new rule as setting a clear and objective standard that they can meet, but community advocates argue that the one-ratio rule will reduce transparency and eventually result in banks not being held accountable to invest in local communities (Kaushal & Mitchell, 2019). At this time, the rule is pending.

Deregulation via agency capture

As we noted earlier, one of the main mechanisms that President Trump can use to pursue deregulation is to capture an agency by simply delivering it to someone who opposes its mission. Thus, in order to fully consider the effects of deregulation on the potential for corporate lawbreaking, it is paramount to consider those who head major agencies. These individuals, appointed by the president as cabinet secretaries, set the regulatory agenda that largely determines the enforcement of administrative codes and referral of criminal cases. They also work directly with those industries, groups, and organizations subject to their agency's control in order to meet the stated missions of their organizations and to serve the public interest. Thus, both the backgrounds and actions of these persons directly determine the degree to which regulators act as "the corporate cops on the beat." Many of the individuals appointed by President Trump have already resigned, being forced out of office due to numerous personal and agency scandals. Here are some of the main players in the ongoing attempt to gut environmental, workplace safety, and consumer financial protection regulations.

Ryan Zinke, former Secretary of the Interior, was the first Cabinet member from Montana (Chaney, 2018). He resigned on December 15, 2018 (Chaney, 2018). According to its stated mission, The Department of the Interior (U. S. Department of Interior, n.d.) conserves and manages the Nation's natural resources and cultural heritage for the benefit and enjoyment of the American people, provides scientific and other information about natural resources and natural hazards to address societal challenges and create opportunities for the American people, and honors the Nation's trust responsibilities or special commitments to American Indians, Alaska Natives, and affiliated island communities to help them prosper.

Zinke resigned amidst controversies regarding conflict(s) of interests and questionable actions about how he spent taxpayer money (Eilperin, Dawsey, & Fears, 2018). One example involved his work with Halliburton's chairman to complete a land deal in his hometown in Montana. Founded in 1919, Halliburton works extensively in the oil field industries and other environmentally harmful practices like drilling (About Halliburton, 2019). In addition to deals with Halliburton, he rolled back legislation to protect the environment, including neutering the Migratory Bird Treaty Act that protects about a thousand species from human interference and opening up offshore oil and natural-gas extraction along much of the U. S. coastline. These actions demonstrate that Zinke was acting in the interest of private, big businesses, and not at all in conjunction with the stated mission of the regulatory protection agency he headed (Binelli, 2018).

Besides opening the way for predatory acts on the natural environment by private business interests, Zinke mixed his political and private life at taxpayer expense, resulting in more than fifteen ongoing corruption investigations. He allegedly allowed his wife to use government vehicles and, while vacationing in Turkey, had an expensive government security detail, the cost of which was billed to taxpayers. He also had a personal real estate deal with a company that was regulated by the Department of the Interior (Eilperin et al., 2018).

Rick Perry, Secretary of Energy at the U.S. Department of Energy (DOE), heads an agency whose official mission "is to ensure America's security and prosperity by addressing its energy, environmental and nuclear challenges through transformative science and technology solutions" ("Rick Perry," n.d.). The DOE website claims that Perry's tenure as governor of Texas showed that "economic growth and protection of the environment can be achieved simultaneously," as he was able to add more jobs and reduce carbon dioxide and other gases in the air ("Rick Perry," n.d.). Perry allocated $38 million into hydrogen and fuel research and technology (Fuel Cells Bulletin, 2018), a very small fraction of the $30 billion DOE budget (Jacobs, Dlouhy, & Natter, 2019). This small investment into new energy sources is in sharp contrast with Perry's stated desire to save "unprofitable coal and nuclear plants," which is antithetical to the DOE's official mission (Jacobs et al., 2019).

Perry's past negative statements and lack of educational credentials cast severe doubt on his qualifications as DOE chief. He has been a vociferous foe of the agency, going so far as to propose abolishing it altogether during his previous bid for the Republican presidential nomination. Unlike his predecessors, Perry does not hold a doctorate in physics but rather a bachelor's degree in animal science (Jacobs et al., 2019). Finally, when Perry was governor of Texas in 2014, he was indicted on charges of "coercion of a public servant and abuse of his official capacity" (CNN, 2019). These charges were eventually dropped in 2016, but they certainly raise questions regarding his qualifications to be Secretary of the DOE.

Former Environmental Protection Agency (EPA) Secretary Scott Pruitt resigned his official position in July 2018 (Diamond, Watkins, & Summers, 2018). The EPA's mission is "to protect human health and the environment" (EPA, 2019). During his short tenure, Pruitt had wood declared a "carbon-neutral fuel," allowing it to become eligible for beneficial treatment under tax, trade, and environmental regulations. This change was designed to increase logging activity, which would lead to an increase in carbon emissions and a decrease in the environment's biodiversity (Daley, 2018), denying the stated mission of the EPA.

Before accepting the cabinet post, Pruitt was a well-known critic of the EPA, having sued them on multiple occasions (Diamond et al., 2018). Until his eventual resignation, he was able to weather more scandals than other Trump appointees, as he set on stripping EPA's regulations and weakening the agency overall. His personal scandals while in office included incurring over $168,000 in luxurious travel expenses and "accepting below-market-rate housing from a deep-pocketed Washington lobbyist" that does business with the EPA (Zurcher, 2018). He removed climate change as a major issue of the EPA, loosened regulations for chemical plants, and eliminated policies or delayed new laws designed to protect clean air and water (Milman, 2018).

Thus, beyond the promulgation of Executive Orders, President Trump has ignited great controversy over his leadership nominations for various agencies responsible for protecting workers and the environment. Trump's controversial pick for Secretary of Labor, a fast-food executive with an anti-labor track record, eventually withdrew from consideration after widespread concerns over his past practices related to worker rights, failure to pay taxes for an undocumented immigrant that he employed, and allegations of domestic violence (Everett & Levine, 2017; Salam, 2017). Similarly, the announcement of Scott Pruitt to head the Environmental Protection Agency was seen by many as a slap in the face to environmental regulation, since Pruitt built his career as Oklahoma Attorney General suing the EPA over its environmental rules (Davenport, 2017). He subsequently left Trump's administration amid scandal after approximately 18 months at the helm of the EPA, leaving Andrew Wheeler, a former coal industry lobbyist, to take over as acting head of the agency. Likewise, Ryan Zinke's appointment to lead the Department of the Interior was also contentious, due to his anti-regulation and pro-energy agenda that reduced protections for wildlife, shrunk the size of national monuments, and expanded mining and fossil fuel extraction on public lands (Turkewitz & Davenport, 2018). However, like Pruitt, Zinke's tenure was short-lived, due to multiple ongoing investigations into his conduct in office (Eilperin et al., 2018). His successor at the Department of the Interior, David Bernhardt, is yet another polarizing, pro-energy figure and former oil industry lobbyist who has stricken climate change reports from being made public, advocated for relaxing methane rules for energy companies, and promoted a rollback of endangered species protections (Hegyi, 2019). Several of Trump's other nominees to cabinet positions for these and other agencies have also been contentious, resulting in a litany of unfilled positions. Additionally, Trump's failure to even nominate prospective appointees, along with the Senate's inability to confirm others, has engendered significant reliance during the Trump administration on "acting" agency leaders, a fact which Trump touts as positive because it gives him more flexibility to act quickly with respect to agency functioning (Naylor, 2019).

Notwithstanding the many other leadership changes, which have plagued agencies under the Trump administration, nominees who have successfully ascended to leadership positions have consistently taken actions to reshape agency missions and significantly modify administrative guidance, or more explicitly, sabotage prevailing regulatory policies. To this end, the Trump administration has arguably gone further than others to overtly alter the purpose and priorities of several regulatory bodies and rebuke the policies of his predecessors. Though again, Trump's ire seems almost obsessively focused on dismantling the EPA, in particular, from the inside out, by appointing leaders who willfully ignore science, data, and the likely implications of deregulation actions to execute the President's priorities. To this end, both Pruitt and Wheeler have overseen efforts to drastically reshape the EPA by disbanding scientific advisory boards, ignoring scientific evidence, suppressing evidence and references to "climate change" from inclusion in EPA reports and actions, partnering with industry groups to question the veracity of climate change, changing calculations to downgrade estimates of environmental and public health harms caused by pollution, challenging prior regulatory decisions by U.S. courts, and adopting policies that patently favor the energy industry (Friedman, 2019; Friedman & Davenport, 2018).

Trump appointees have also taken direct aim at existing rules created under the Obama administration, by issuing directives to delay, suspend, or altogether eliminate rule compliance dates for at least fifty-six different Obama regulations promulgated in 2016 (Thrower, 2018). Such was the case when the Department of the Interior lifted restrictions on mining in Bristol Bay, Alaska, opened up offshore drilling in the Atlantic and Arctic Oceans, and reversed a moratorium on new federal coal extraction leases (Lipton, 2017). Trump's EPA has gone even further with its actions against Obama-era rules, including suspending emissions compliance requirements for heavy trucks known as "glider vehicles" that do not comply with the Clean Air Act (Chappell, 2017), delaying methane gas restrictions from taking effect that were intended to limit greenhouse gas emissions (Thrower, 2018), indefinitely postponing a ban on three toxic chemicals found in common consumer products (Kaplan, 2017), and completely lifting the summertime ban on the use of smog-producing E15 ethanol-gasoline mixtures (Davenport, 2019b). The Occupational Safety and Health Administration (OSHA) also joined in the deregulation movement by deferring a rule issued under Obama to lower worker exposure to a mineral associated with deadly lung disease while regulatory changes were being considered (Meier & Ivory, 2017). These delay tactics all fall under the umbrella of "no action assurances," which are intended to generally suspend compliance requirements for a given rule, thereby allowing industries to temporarily avoid following federal regulations while the agency seeks rule revision or full-scale repeal over the long-term (Teitelbaum, 2019).

Trump appointees have also curtailed prevailing compliance and enforcement actions for their agencies in other ways. Under the current administration, agencies have dramatically reduced activities such as workplace and environmental inspections, levying civil penalties, and issuing rule violation notifications, all of which are expressly designed to compel compliance with environmental rules and limit illegal behavior. As evidence of its shifting focus, the EPA's most recent annual report revealed that it only conducted 10,612 site inspections in 2018, the lowest number in at least a decade (U. S. EPA, Office of Enforcement and Compliance Assurance, 2019). Similar findings are revealed for both OSHA and the Mine Safety and Health Administration (MSHA) compliance and safety inspections, which also declined precipitously from the previous administration. OSHA inspections peaked at nearly 41,000 in fiscal year 2012 but fell to about 32,000 in fiscal year 2018, while MSHA inspections topped out near 49,000 in fiscal year 2009 and fell to just under 37,000 in fiscal year 2018 (U.S. Department of Labor, 2019a). Workplace hazard inspections conducted by OSHA for work-related illness, musculoskeletal disorders (ergonomics), workplace heat conditions, and dangerous chemicals like pesticides, have all fallen by one-half to two thirds during the Trump administration (Chen, 2019).

Further, an analysis of data by The New York Times found that the number of civil cases brought by the EPA has declined by nearly one-third, civil penalties have plummeted more than 60%, and total demands for injunctive relief, such as requiring factory repairs to cut pollution, have dropped by almost 90% since the Obama administration (Lipton & Ivory, 2017). Citations and civil penalties issued by OSHA and the MHSA have also declined significantly since the Obama administration. In 2010, the MHSA issued more than 170,000 citations and $162 million in penalties for mine workplace safety violations, but by the end of 2018, those numbers had dropped to approximately 98,000 citations and $54 million in penalties (U.S. Department of Labor, 2019a). At OSHA, sanctions in the highest-penalty category fell by half from 2016 to 2018 (Chen, 2019). Additionally, both the EPA and the OSHA have rolled back their notification practices known as "regulatory shaming" wherein the names of environmental and workplace safety violators are published for deterrent effect (Yadin, 2018). At OSHA, in particular, press releases of violators have dropped by more than two-thirds under the Trump administration from 470 to below 160 (Chen, 2019).

Criminal enforcement, particularly for environmental crime, also appears to have taken a big hit under Trump. In 2018, the EPA referred just 166 cases to the Department of Justice for criminal prosecution, less than half the number of just six years prior, with referrals for 2019 on pace toward a 25-year low (Abel, 2019). These trends are borne out in actual prosecutions and convictions, as well. According to Department of Justice data published by the Transaction Records Access Clearinghouse (2018) at Syracuse University, the number of criminal prosecutions by the federal government for environmental crime has declined substantially from previous administrations, falling almost 40% from five years ago. This trend across administrations has continued year-over-year throughout the Trump administration, despite officials arguing that they remain steadfastly focused on enforcement. In fiscal year 2018, there were only 109 environmental crime prosecutions, more than 10% fewer than in 2017 when there were 122 (Transactional Records Access Clearinghouse, 2018). Only 78 pollution cases were prosecuted in 2018, and at just 36 cases prosecuted by mid-2019, the EPA is on track for its lowest year ever (Abel, 2019). Similarly, 2018 saw the fewest number of convictions ever for environmental crimes at 62.

Given that regulation delays and suspensions have increased while compliance and enforcement activities have decreased – and remain comparatively low to previous administrations – it is difficult to argue by any common measure that the Trump administration places the same value on worker safety and environmental protection as previous administrations. More importantly, the unwillingness of this administration to sufficiently use civil and criminal enforcement as mechanisms of deterrence and control for workplace safety, industrial pollution, and other environmental harms could pose significant, long-term risks to the environment and public health.

Next, consider what the Trump administration has done to the Consumer Financial Protection Bureau (CFPB) that "regulates the offering and provision of consumer financial products or services under the federal consumer financial laws and educates and empowers consumers to make better informed financial decisions" (U. S. Consumer Financial Protection Bureau (n.d.). Mick Mulvaney was appointed as acting director of the CFPB, yet he is one of the most vocal critics of this agency (Puzzanghera, 2018). As a Congressman, he had previously introduced legislation to abolish the bureau (Arnold & Schneider, 2018). Consumer protections quickly eroded under his leadership (Ramirez, 2018).

For example, Mulvaney decided to not investigate the Equifax breach that exposed millions of Americans' private information (Ramirez, 2018). Mulvaney also tried to defang the agency's enforcement power and authority by trying to re-brand the agency's name, which would have cost millions of dollars, and restricting regulations on financial firms the CFPB oversees, which would also limit legal action against those businesses (Lane, 2018b).

Mulvaney also fired the Consumer Advisory Board (CAB) members comprised of subject matter experts who worked with struggling Americans (Arnold & Schneider, 2018). One CAB member, attorney Chi Chu Wu, claimed that by firing CAB members, CFPB was necessarily eroding consumer financial protections. It also implied that Mulvaney was not interested in working with subject matter experts to protect consumers, but that he would prefer to deal with industry lobbyists, who represent regulated firms (Arnold & Schneider, 2018).

Countervailing forces and a look forward

Despite some progress in President Trump's campaign to unwind the regulatory legacy of the Obama administration, proposed and executed Trump rollbacks have faced stiff public-opinion headwinds and will likely encounter a myriad of legal challenges from environmental and public health groups for years to come. Some of those challenges have already been successful in rebuffing President Trump's changes. Of the 83 proposed environmental rollbacks proposed under the Trump administration, by mid-year 2019, only forty-nine rule changes had been finalized and implemented, while thirty-four remain in progress (Popovich et al., 2019). Several of the efforts by the current administration to revise or rescind previously adopted rules have also been struck down by federal courts as violations of existing law (Lipton, 2017). For instance, a previously adopted rule concerning mining safety that the Department of Labor amended in favor of a less restrictive one was recently overturned by a federal appeals court as a violation of the Federal Mine Safety and Health Act (Nutzman, 2019). Midway through his first term, at least 10 other Trump administration regulatory rollbacks have either been vacated by federal courts or reversed through other mechanisms, including attempts by Trump's EPA to eliminate requirements for states to monitor greenhouse gas emissions, delay a rule regulating the application of pesticides, rescind rules designed to reduce asthma-inducing ozone pollution and toxic mercury water contamination, and attempts by both the EPA and Department of the Interior to delay compliance rules for oil and gas companies "flaring" excess methane (Lipton, 2017; Popovich et al., 2019). Many of the other proposed rollbacks are currently mired in the lengthy bureaucracy of the rule-making process or the back-logged court system. So, it can be argued that opponents of Trump's policies are mounting an admirable defense of environmental and labor protections already in place.

Notwithstanding the limited success he has been able to achieve thus far, the proposed and enacted deregulation actions launched by Trump and his administration are emblematic of a systemic shift in domestic policy through the exercise of "regulatory capture" – that is, toward industry and arguably away from the public good. For example, Trump himself has claimed that climate change is "very expensive … bullshit" and a hoax perpetrated by the Chinese to reduce U.S. manufacturing competitiveness in the global economy (Phillips, 2016). This shift has led some to express that "the public and environmental health consequences of regulatory capture of the EPA will probably be severe and far-reaching" (Dillon et al., 2018, p. 589). To this end, many of the executive actions, leadership changes, funding reductions, and formal rule changes described above represent a clear and present danger to workers, the environment, and public health, because they so carelessly inhibit the ability of regulatory agencies to place checks on private sector actions, compel compliance with the law, create and enforce safety standards, and most importantly, protect both the environment and society from industry malfeasance.

Evidence of the dangers that Trump policies have created can already be seen in the labor force where workplace deaths have increased under Trump just as the number of inspectors has fallen – "a sign that the administration's effort to dismantle health and safety protections for workers has made many workplaces more deadly" (Chen, 2019). Growing cause for concern has also been revealed in the unlikeliest of places, from directly within Trump administration agencies. By the EPA's own internal estimates, replacing Obama's Clean Power Plan with Trump's Affordable Clean Energy Rule would produce an additional 36,000 deaths each decade (1,400 premature deaths each year (Friedman, 2019), and proposed EPA rollbacks of mercury and air toxics standards and glider vehicle restrictions are predicted to result in an additional 12,500 premature deaths (Waldman, 2018). Experts and researchers from the public health field have also weighed in on the likely effects of Trump's policies, suggesting a general concern for American's health and well-being (Krisberg, 2017) and estimating that up to 80,000 additional deaths will occur per decade (Cutler & Dominici, 2018). Others expect the consequences will impact "vulnerable social groups, such as low-income communities, farmworkers, and first responders" the most, but that "many more health consequences for all lie just over the horizon, especially if regulatory capture becomes more pronounced" (Dillon et al., 2018). Financial harms are also already beginning to occur as a result of Trump's deregulation policies. According to a report from the Consumer Federation of America, the CFPB, which was returning about $43 million in restitution from enforcement activities to consumers every week under the Obama administration is now only enforcing consumer protection rules to the tune of less than $1 million per week (Lazarus, 2019). In essence, these few examples suggest that the deregulation reforms initiated by this administration are draconian and far-reaching.

All told, we believe Trump's assault on "job-killing" regulations may be nowhere near complete. In fact, he has tweeted more than twenty-two times over the past 12 months about his ongoing commitment to deregulate American industries. For this reason, we anticipate the continued erosion of protections for American workers and consumers resulting from Trump's ambitious efforts to strip agencies of their regulatory authority and rollback existing environmental, workplace safety, and consumer finance rules. Even if many of these reforms do not stand the test of time, we believe that stripping workers, consumers, and the environment of federal protections, even in the short-term, will not be benign. On the contrary, this erosion will likely result in immediate and significant collateral consequences for the average American, possibly in diminished financial stability due to fewer rules governing banks and investment corporations, unsafe working conditions provoked by less stringent enforcement of labor laws, or poor health outcomes hastened by industrial polluters. Should even a small number of Trump's proposed or enacted reforms last beyond his presidency, the fallout will presumably result in real physical, emotional, and financial harm to the lives of American workers and the general public over the long-term.

Despite the siren song emanating from the media, not enough empirical research has been done to explore the real-world implications of the Trump administration's industry deregulation reforms and investigate possible alternatives for consideration. It is altogether possible that cynics in academia and the general public believe the actions of this administration are immune to the influence of the scientific community or public opinion. We believe this is a defeatist position to take and argue that a collective lack of action will only cultivate the status quo and subsequent harms likely to befall citizens of this country. Therefore, we call on others to empirically evaluate Trump's regulatory agenda and the possible consequences of his administration's actions so that we may sufficiently prepare for and address what is likely to come should Trump win a second term in office.

Note

1. But this is not to deny the importance of the potential harm that deregulation in other areas could also cause.

Acknowledgments

The authors wish to thank Nicole Le for her assistance on this article.

Disclosure statement

No potential conflict of interest was reported by the authors.

References

Abel, D. (2019, July 2). EPA prosecutions haven fallen sharply, especially in New England, advocacy group says. *Boston Globe*. Retrieved from https://www.bostonglobe.com/metro/2019/07/02/epa-prosecutions-decline-sharply-especially-new-england/OmzFCTr54k5qe6SifECnFN/story.html

"About Halliburton". (2019, May 27). *Halliburton*. Retrieved from www.halliburton.com/en-US/default.html

Arnold, C., & Schneider, A. (2018, June 6). Mick Mulvaney effectively fires CFPB advisory council. *National Public Radio*. Retrieved from www.npr.org/2018/06/06/617612219/mick-mulvaney-effectively-fires-cfpb-advisory-council

Ballotpedia. (2017). *Presidential executive order 13777* (Donald Trump, 2017). Retrieved from https://ballotpedia.org/Presidential_Executive_Order_13777_(Donald_Trump,_2017)

Binelli, M. (2018, August). Ryan Zinke's war on the Interior. *Rolling Stone*, Issue 1318, pp. 47–94. Retrieved from www.web.a.ebscohost.com/ehost/detail/detail?vid=6&sid=956b3e78-44d7-4b28-9839-4584a759bccc%40sdc-v-essmgr05&bdata=JnNpdGU9ZWhvc3QtbGl2ZSZzY29wZT1zaXRl#AN=130880008&db=a9h

The Brookings Institution. (2019). *Tracking deregulation in the Trump era*. Retrieved from https://www.brookings.edu/interactives/tracking-deregulation-in-the-trump-era/

Carpenter, D., & Moss, D. (Eds.). (2013). *Preventing regulatory capture: Special interest influence and how to limit it*. Cambridge, UK: Cambridge University Press.

Chaney, R. (2018, December 22). Zinke leaves mixed grades on Montana actions. *Missoulian*. Retrieved from www.missoulian.com/news/local/zinke-leaves-mixed-grades-on-montana-actions/article_67e083fd-0c34-5a15-b591-f2f4102352e4.html

Chappell, B. (2017, November 16). EPA moves to shield older semi-truck engines in "gliders" from emissions rules. *NPR*. Retrieved from https://www.npr.org/sections/thetwo-way/2017/11/16/564655569/epa-moves-to-shield-older-semi-truck-engines-from-emissions-rules

Chen, M. (2019, March 27). Declining Federal oversight of workplace safety could have fatal consequences. *The Nation*. Retrieved from https://www.thenation.com/article/workplace-injuries-osha-trump/

CNN Library. (2019, March 4). Rick Perry fast facts. *CNN*. Retrieved from www.cnn.com/2013/02/28/us/rick-perry-fast-facts/index.html

Cutler, D., & Dominici, F. (2018). A breath of bad air: Cost of the Trump environmental agenda may lead to 80,000 extra deaths per decade. *JAMA*, *319*(22), 2261. doi:10.1001/jama.2018.7351

Daley, J. (2018). The EPA declared that burning wood is carbon neutral. It's actually a lot more complicated. *SMARTNEWS*. Retrieved from https://www.smithsonianmag.com/smart-news/epa-declares-burning-wood-carbon-neutral-180968880/

Davenport, C. (2016, March 18). E.P.A. faces bigger tasks, smaller budgets and louder critics. *The New York Times*. Retrieved from https://www.nytimes.com/2016/03/19/us/politics/epa-faces-bigger-tasks-smaller-budgets-and-louder-critics.html?module=inline

Davenport, C. (2017, February 17). Senate confirms Scott Pruitt as E.P.A. head. *The New York Times*. Retrieved from https://www.nytimes.com/2017/02/17/us/politics/scott-pruitt-environmental-protection-agency.html

Davenport, C. (2019a, July 12). E.P.A. plans to curtail the ability of communities to oppose pollution permits. *The New York Times*. Retrieved from https://www.nytimes.com/2019/07/12/climate/epa-community-pollution-appeal.html

Davenport, C. (2019b, May 31). Trump administration lifts ethanol-fuel ban that was meant to cut smog. *The New York Times*. Retrieved from https://www.nytimes.com/2019/05/31/climate/trump-ethanol-fuel-ban.html

Davis Noll, B. A., & Grab, D. A. (2017). Deregulation: Process and procedures that govern agency decision making in an era of rollbacks. *Energy Law Journal*, *38*, 269–295.

Dennis, B., Eilperin, J., & Ba Tran, A. (2018, September 8). With a shrinking EPA, Trump delivers on his promise to cut government. *The Washington Post*. Retrieved from https://www.washingtonpost.com/national/health-science/with-a-shrinking-epa-trump-delivers-on-his-promise-to-cut-government/2018/09/08/6b058f9e-b143-11e8-a20b-5f4f84429666_story.html?utm_term=.2d0f3cee3e04

Diamond, J., Watkins, E., & Summers, J. (2018, July 5). EPA chief Scott Pruitt resigns amid scandals, citing "unrelenting attacks". *CNN*. Retrieved from www.cnn.com/2018/07/05/politics/scott-pruitt-epa-resigns/index.html

Dillon, L., Sellers, C., Underhill, V., Shapiro, N., Ohayon, J. L., Sullivan, M., … Wylie, S. (2018). The Environmental Protection Agency in the early Trump Administration: Prelude to regulatory capture. *American Journal of Public Health*, *108*(S2), S89–S94. doi:10.2105/AJPH.2018.304360

Eilperin, J., Dawsey, J., & Fears, D. (2018, December 15). Interior Secretary Zinke resigns amid investigations. *The Washington Post*. Retrieved from www.washingtonpost.com/national/health-science/interior-secretary-zinke-resigns-amid-investigations/2018/12/15/481f9104-0077-11e9-ad40-cdfd0e0dd65a_story.html?utm_term=.66fc3c3b063a

EPA. (2016). *Clean power plan for existing power plants: Regulatory actions*. Retrieved from https://archive.epa.gov/epa/cleanpowerplan/clean-power-plan-existing-power-plants-regulatory-actions.html

EPA. (2017). *Executive order 13771 – Reducing regulation and controlling regulatory costs*. Retrieved from https://www.epa.gov/laws-regulations/executive-order-13771-reducing-regulation-and-controlling-regulatory-costs

EPA. (2019). *EPA finalizes affordable clean energy rule, ensuring reliable, diversified energy resources while protecting our environment*. Retrieved from https://www.epa.gov/newsreleases/epa-finalizes-affordable-clean-energy-rule-ensuring-reliable-diversified-energy

Everett, B., & Levine, M. (2017, February 15). Labor nominee Puzder withdraws. *Politico*. Retrieved from https://www.politico.com/story/2017/02/senate-republicans-tell-white-house-to-withdraw-puzder-nomination-235062

Fears, D. (2019, May 2). Trump rolls back safety rules meant to prevent another Deepwater Horizon spill. *The Washington Post*. Retrieved from https://www.washingtonpost.com/climate-environment/2019/05/02/trump-rolls-back-safety-rules-meant-prevent-another-deepwater-horizon-spill/?utm_term=.88bf991d5c43

Fredrickson, L., Sellers, C., Dillon, L., Ohayon, J. L., Shapiro, N., Sullivan, M., … Wylie, S. (2018). History of US presidential assaults on modern environmental health protection. *American Journal of Public Health, 108*(S2), S95–S103. doi:10.2105/AJPH.2018.304396

Friedman, L. (2019, February 28). Andrew Wheeler, who continued environmental rollbacks, is confirmed to lead E.P.A. *The New York Times*. Retrieved from https://www.nytimes.com/2019/02/28/climate/andrew-wheeler-epa-confirmation.html

Friedman, L., & Davenport, C. (2018, May 8). Pruitt's plan for climate change debates: Ask conservative think tanks. *The New York Times*. Retrieved from https://www.nytimes.com/2018/05/08/climate/pruitt-epa-red-blue-team-debate-emails.html

Fuel Cells Bulletin. (2018). *US DOE awards $38m for 28 new hydrogen, fuel cell tech projects*. Retrieved from https://www.sciencedirect.com/science/article/pii/S1464285918303456?via%3Dihub

Grant, M. (2019, July 19). Everything you need to know about the DOL Fiduciary Rule. *Investopedia*. Retrieved from https://www.investopedia.com/updates/dol-fiduciary-rule/

Green, M. (2019, March 11). Trump proposes slashing EPA budget by 31 percent. *The Hill*. Retrieved from https://thehill.com/policy/energy-environment/433496-white-house-proposes-dramatic-cuts-to-energy-and-environment

Group of Ten. (2005). *Ageing and pension system reform: Implications for financial markets and econmic policies*. Retrieved from https://www.oecd.org/daf/fin/financial-markets/ageingandpensionsystemreformimplicationsforfinancialmarketsandeconomicpolicies.htm

Hegyi, N. (2019, January 2). The new acting Interior Secretary is an agency insider and ex-oil lobbyist. *NPR*. Retrieved from https://www.npr.org/2019/01/02/677390503/the-new-acting-interior-secretary-is-an-agency-insider-and-ex-oil-lobbyist

Jacobs, J., Dlouhy, J. A., & Natter, A. (2019, April 17). *Rick Perry planning his exit as Trump's Energy Secretary, sources say*. Retrieved from www.bloomberg.com/news/articles/2019-04-18/rick-perry-is-said-to-plan-his-exit-as-trump-s-energy-secretary

Jacoby, S. (2019). *Opportunity zone regulations favor investor flexibility over community protection*. Retrieved from https://www.cbpp.org/blog/opportunity-zone-regulations-favor-investor-flexibility-over-community-protection

Kaplan, S. (2017, December 19). E.P.A. delays ban on uses of hazardous chemicals. *The New York Times*. Retrieved from https://www.nytimes.com/2017/12/19/health/epa-toxic-chemicals.html

Kaushal, A., & Mitchell, D. (2019, January 15). *The Community Reinvestment Act and the future of financial inclusion*. Retrieved from https://www.aspeninstitute.org/blog-posts/the-community-reinvestment-act-and-the-future-of-financial-inclusion/

Krisberg, K. (2017). Regulatory changes ignore science, threaten public health: New administration eroding progress. *The Nation's Health, 47*(8). Retrieved from http://thenationshealth.aphapublications.org/content/47/8/1.3

Kullgren, I. (2018, September 3). Trump rolls back worker safety rules. *Politico*. Retrieved from https://www.politico.com/story/2018/09/03/trumps-worker-safety-regulations-protections-unions-806008

Lane, S. (2018a). *Senate repeals auto-loan guidance in precedent-shattering vote*. Retrieved from https://thehill.com/policy/finance/383751-senate-votes-to-repeal-cfpb-auto-loan-guidance

Lane, S. (2018b, December 12). Consumer Bureau morale plummeted under Mulvaney: Report. *The Hill*. Retrieved from https://thehill.com/policy/finance/421007-consumer-bureau-morale-plummeted-under-mulvaney-analysis

Lanham, J. A., Duvall, M. N., & Vitris, M. F. (2019, January 30). OSHA electronic form 300 submission rule rescinded. *National Law Review*. Retrieved from https://www.natlawreview.com/article/osha-finalizes-rule-rescinding-electronic-submission-certain-injury-and-illness

Lazarus, D. (2019, March 15). While campaigning, Trump said he'd be a consumer champion. Guess what's happened. *The Los Angeles Times*. Retrieved from https://www.latimes.com/business/lazarus/la-fi-lazarus-consumer-protection-declines-under-trump-20190315-story.html

Lipton, E. (2017, October 6). Courts thwart administration's effort to rescind Obama-era environmental regulations. *The New York Times*. Retrieved from https://www.nytimes.com/2017/10/06/climate/trump-administration-environmental-regulations.html

Lipton, E., & Ivory, D. (2017, December 10). Under Trump, E.P.A. has slowed actions against polluters, and put limits on enforcement officers. *The New York Times*. Retrieved from https://www.nytimes.com/2017/12/10/us/politics/pollution-epa-regulations.html

Lopez, M. S. (2019, June 25). Court rejects MSHA's revisions to workplace examination rule. *National Law Review*. Retrieved from https://www.natlawreview.com/article/court-rejects-msha-s-revisions-to-workplace-examination-rule

Maloney, N. (2010). Financial services and markets. In R. Baldwin, M. Cave, & M. Lodge (Eds.), *The Oxford handbook of regulation* (pp. 437–461). Oxford, UK: Oxford University Press.

Meier, B., & Ivory, D. (2017, March 13). Worker safety rules are among those under fire in Trump era. *The New York Times*. Retrieved from https://www.nytimes.com/2017/03/13/business/us-worker-safety-rules-osha.html

Milman, O. (2018, July 5). Scott Pruitt is out but his impact on the environment will be felt for years. *The Guardian*. Retrieved from www.theguardian.com/environment/2018/jul/05/scott-pruitt-epa-impact-on-environment-analysis

Mooney, C. (2018, June 1). Trump withdrew from the Paris climate deal a year ago. Here's what has changed. *The Washington Post*. Retrieved from https://www.washingtonpost.com/news/energy-environment/wp/2018/06/01/trump-withdrew-from-the-paris-climate-plan-a-year-ago-heres-what-has-changed/?utm_term=.4b2fade8b5a9

Morath, E. (2018, February 12). Trump's 2019 budget targets elimination of four Labor Department Programs. *The Wall Street Journal*. Retrieved from https://www.wsj.com/livecoverage/trumps-2019-budget-proposal-live-analysis/card/1518455382

National Consumer Law Center. (2015, June). *Racial disparities in auto loan markups state-by-state data*. Retrieved from https://www.nclc.org/images/pdf/car_sales/ib-auto-dealers-racial_disparites.pdf

Naylor, B. (2019, April 9). Trump relies on record number of acting positions. *NPR*. Retrieved from https://www.npr.org/2019/04/09/711094554/an-acting-government-for-the-trump-administration

Nutzman, J. M. (2019, June 14). Back to the drawing board (somewhat)—D.C. Circuit Court of Appeals invalidates workplace examination final rule. *National Law Review*. Retrieved from https://www.natlawreview.com/article/back-to-drawing-board-somewhat-dc-circuit-court-appeals-invalidates-workplace

O'Grady, J. (2018, February 16). The $79 million plan to gut EPA staff. *The Hill*. Retrieved from https://thehill.com/opinion/energy-environment/374167-the-79-million-plan-to-gut-epa-staff

Phillips, T. (2016, November 17). Climate change a Chinese hoax? Beijing gives Donald Trump a lesson in history. *The Guardian*. Retrieved from https://www.theguardian.com/us-news/2016/nov/17/climate-change-a-chinese-plot-beijing-gives-donald-trump-a-history-

Popovich, N., Albeck-Ripka, L., & Pierre-Louis, K. (2019, June 7). 83 Environmental rules being rolled back under Trump. *The New York Times*. Retrieved from https://www.nytimes.com/interactive/2019/climate/trump-environment-rollbacks.html

Potter, R. A., Rudalevige, A., Thrower, S., & Warber, A. L. (2019). Continuity trumps change: The first year of Trump's administrative presidency. *PS: Political Science & Politics*. Retrieved from https://www.cambridge.org/core/journals/ps-political-science-and-politics/article/continuity-trumps-change-the-first-year-of-trumps-administrative-presidency/354E5207418050F0CC8E913925884D32

Public Employees for Environmental Responsibility. (2018, June 21). EPA agents fighting eco-crime drop as securing detail grows. *Public Employees for Environmental Responsibility*. Retrieved from https://www.peer.org/news/press-releases/epa-agents-fighting-eco-crime-drop-as-security-detail-grows.html

Puzzanghera, J. (2018, December 6). Senate confirms new Consumer Financial Protection chief: Kathy Kraninger, protege of industry-friendly Mick Mulvaney". *Los Angeles Times*. Retrieved from www.latimes.com/business/la-fi-cfpb-kraninger-confirmation-20181206-story.html

Ramirez, K. (2018, November 20). House Democrats to investigate CFPB acting director Mick Mulvaney. *Housingwire.com*. Retrieved from www.housingwire.com/articles/47450-democrats-to-open-investigations-on-cfpb-acting-director-mick-mulvaney

Rick Perry. (n.d.). *Energy.gov*. Retrieved from www.energy.gov/contributors/rick-perry

Salam, M. (2017, April 27). Senate confirms R. Alexander Acosta as Labor Secretary. *The New York Times*. Retrieved from https://www.nytimes.com/2017/04/27/us/politics/r-alexander-acosta-labor-secretary-confirmed.html

Shapiro, S. (2005). Agency theory. *Annual Review of Sociology*, *31*, 263–284. doi:10.1146/annurev.soc.31.041304.122159

Tankersley, J., & Tackett, M. (2019, March 11). Trump proposes a record $4.75 trillion budget. *The New York Times*. Retrieved from https://www.nytimes.com/2019/03/11/us/politics/trump-budget.html?partner=rss&emc=rss

Teitelbaum, C. (2019, February 19). Lawyer talks Trump's environmental deregulation efforts. *The Michigan Daily*. Retrieved from https://www.michigandaily.com/section/campus-life/lawyer-discusses-trump's-environmental-deregulation-efforts

Thrower, S. (2018). Policy disruption through regulatory delay in the Trump administration. *Presidential Studies Quarterly*, *48*, 517–536. doi:10.1111/psq.12473

Transaction Records Access Clearinghouse. (2018). *Federal Prosecutions of Environmental Crimes Continues to Drop*. Retrieved from https://trac.syr.edu/tracreports/crim/534/

Trump, D. J. (2017, March 28). Remarks by President Trump at signing of executive order to create energy independence. *The White House*. Retrieved from https://www.whitehouse.gov/briefings-statements/remarks-president-trump-signing-executive-order-create-energy-independence/

Turkewitz, J., & Davenport, C. (2018, December 15). Ryan Zinke, face of Trump environmental rollbacks, es leaving Interior Department. *The New York Times*. Retrieved from https://www.nytimes.com/2018/12/15/us/ryan-zinke-interior-secretary.html?login=email&auth=login-email

U. S. Consumer Financial Protection Bureau. (n.d.). *About us*. Retrieved from https://www.consumerfinance.gov/about-us/

U. S. Department of Interior. (n.d.). *About*. Retrieved from https://www.doi.gov/whoweare

U. S. EPA, Office of Enforcement and Compliance Assurance. (2019). *EPA enforcement annual results 2018*. Retrieved from https://epa.maps.arcgis.com/apps/Cascade/index.html?appid=0b9d73f351d648698f63bba3f3b15114

U.S. Department of Labor. (2017). *FY 2016 Department of Labor budget in brief*. Retrieved from https://www.dol.gov/sites/dolgov/files/legacy-files/documents/general/budget/2016/FY2016BIB.pdf

U.S. Department of Labor. (2019a). *Enforcement data*. Retrieved from https://enforcedata.dol.gov/views/searchExplorer.php

U.S. Department of Labor. (2019b). *FY 2020 Department of Labor budget in brief*. Retrieved from https://www.dol.gov/sites/dolgov/files/general/budget/2020/FY2020BIB.pdf

Volcovici, V. (2019, February 26). U.S. EPA denies being soft on polluters as Democrats question enforcement. *Reuters*. Retrieved from https://www.reuters.com/article/us-usa-epa-enforcement/u-s-epa-denies-being-soft-on-polluters-as-democrats-question-enforcement-idUSKCN1QF185

Waldman, S. (2018, October 2). 3 environmental rollbacks could result in 13,900 deaths. *E&E News*. Retrieved from https://www.eenews.net/stories/1060100271

Yadin, S. (2018). Regulatory shaming. *Environmental Law*, *49*, 407–451.

Zurcher, A. (2018, July 5). Scott Pruitt resigns: The EPA's chief's long list of controversies. *BBC News*. Retrieved from www.bbc.com/news/world-us-canada-43677216.

Justice, Not Jailbreak: The Context and Consequence of the First Step Act

Derek M. Cohen

ABSTRACT
The First Step Act, a legislative endeavor half nearly a decade in the making and advocated for by President Trump, represented the most significant easing of federal criminal punishment to date. This article discusses the historical antecedents for the prison and sentencing reform legislation and discusses its path through the 115th Congress of the United States.

The First Step Act of 2018 is a duality. It is both the most ambitious and aggressive criminal justice reform in generations and somewhat lackluster. It is the largest wholesale retroactive and prospective sentencing reorganization, and upon taking effect it will provide for the release of at most 4,600, a paltry percentage of the federal prison system's near 180,000 inmates. Yet perhaps the most remarkable thing about the First Step Act is that it passed and was signed into law. After decades of ratcheting up punitive sanctions and both parties harvesting political fruit for being "tough-on-crime," President Donald Trump – whose candidacy was fulsome with rhetoric more native to the lips of Barry Goldwater or Richard Nixon – signed an overwhelmingly bipartisan criminal justice reform bill that he had personally called to be sent to his desk.

The reforms themselves are not unique, each having been passed by a plethora of states prior to federal consideration. Conservatives states often led the way on these policy initiatives, enjoying both the potential cost savings in reducing prison populations with no detriment to public safety (Cohen, 2017). Still, a niche issue like federal criminal justice reform had to overcome both staunch opposition and institutional sclerosis in order to make it to the Resolute Desk. In this article, I will explain the context, content, and passage of the First Step Act of 2018.

Context for reform

During the latter half of the 20th century, the southern United States slowly shifted from Democrat to Republican control. Equal parts fallout from Reconstruction-era policies and the dominant political party's then-positions on domestic issues, the postbellum South represented a monolithic Democrat voting bloc. This bloc was so strongly unified on the party-line voting preference that it was apocryphally known that Southern voters would sooner elect a "yellow dog" than Republican to public office (Conlin, 2013). The South's shift to the Republican Party is frequently attributed to the legacy of anti-black racial animus stemming from the antebellum South failing to align with the cosmopolitan values of the day's Democrat Party on issues of integration. However, the Democrat policy dissonance had been in effect for almost a full century spanning sundry issues such as faith, abortion, and tolerance of Communism (Trende, 2010).

Notwithstanding the genesis of the North/South Democrat schism, the gulf between the two factions prevented the national party apparatus from putting forth a unified position on how to address rapidly increasing crime rates. While Northern Democrats proposed that the federal government increase social spending, Southern Democrats sought to create federal analogs of or increase the penalties to certain violent and drug crimes. This internecine debate was roundly decided following Republican presidential candidate Barry Goldwater's 1964 failed – and Richard Nixon's 1968 successful – campaign for the White House that heavily emphasized "tough-on-crime" rhetoric and policy proposals. As this strategy started bearing unequivocal political fruit for the Republicans, the Democrats had little choice but to collectively follow suit or be relegated into regional parties (Cohen, 2017). This was buttressed by public sentiment, as nearly 90% of Gallup Poll respondents in 1992 identified that crime was worse in than in the previous year, and 83% felt that the criminal justice system was "not tough enough" in handling crime (Gallup, n.d.).

In 1984, Congress passed the Comprehensive Crime Control Act, a wide-ranging piece of legislation affecting federal criminal jurisprudence. Of note, the bill reinstated federal capital punishment post-*Gregg*,[1] abolished federal parole as part of the Sentencing Reform Act subcomponent, and increased penalties for using a weapon during criminal activity under the Armed Career Criminal Act. Similarly, the Anti-Drug Abuse Act of 1986 ratcheted up penalties for various drug offenses, including the controversial "100-to-1" disparity between powder cocaine and crack cocaine. The Anti-Drug Abuse Act of 1988 further increased penalties, as well as established the executive position of "Drug Czar" and the Office of National Drug Control Policy. Federal mandatory minimum sentences for possession and distribution of narcotics – created and enhanced by the Anti-Drug Abuse Acts of 1986 and 1988, respectively – are enumerated in 21 U.S.C. 841, apart from the vast majority of *in se* federal crimes.

Mandatory minimum sentencing laws, much like determinate sentencing schemes, were seen as a way to divest judges of their perceived biased discretion (whether leniency- or racially-based) and mete out sentences more akin to legislative prerogative. Mandatory sentencing statutes are those that remove judicial discretion, perceived to be excessively lenient, from the calculation of a sentence to be served. In practice, these laws established a firm floor on the lower boundary of a criminal sentence; if a defendant is found guilty of a charge bearing a mandatory minimum, the person will be given now fewer than the specified number of months or years. Mandatory sentencing laws are typically applied to crimes of violence, drug trafficking, or the combination of the two (Cohen, 2017).

The zenith of the era of "tough on crime" policy came when President Bill Clinton signed the Violent Crime Control and Law Enforcement Act of 1994, colloquially known as the "'94 Crime Bill." Following a decades-long increase in the national crime rate and lockstep increases in punitive changes in criminal justice policy, the Crime Bill sought to address multiple popularly-perceived sources of criminal activity cast against a backdrop seismic shifts in partisan politics.

Both parties found base-alienating flaws with the legislation, such as many Republicans explicitly condemning the gun control and antifederalist spending components while the Democrats lamented many of the penalty expansions and the elimination of Pell grants for inmates (Seelye, 1994). After contentious negotiations in the U.S. House of Representatives, the Crime Bill ultimately cleared the chamber on a vote of 235 to 195; 188 Democrats and 46 Republicans voting aye, and 64 Democrats and 131 Republicans voting nay to adopt the joint chamber conference report. The U.S. Senate adopted the conference report as well with a vote of 61 to 38; 54 Democrats and 7 Republicans voting aye, and 2 Democrats and 36 Republicans voting nay. This agreement sent the legislation to the desk of President Bill Clinton, who signed the bill into law on September 13th, 1994.

The contents of the 1994 Crime Bill fit the mold of the "tough-on-crime" policy movements that had been in vogue for the previous decade. In addition to a vast expansion of federal capital punishment-eligible offenses, the bill included a mandatory life sentence for repeat drug offenders. It also dedicated billions of dollars in spending on state and local police and corrections so long as the receiving jurisdiction was in compliance with newly-enacted "truth-in-sentencing" policies. The bill had several other constituent parts – such as the Violence Against Women Act – each warranting a robust debate on the component's value to crime control given the costs, but only the sentencing components were subsequently revisited in the First Step Act.

After the 1986, 1988, and 1994 bills were enacted, the prevailing mandatory minimum sentencing regime was that upon receiving a second conviction for a serious drug felony[2] would require a term of imprisonment no less than 20 years, while a third such conviction would require an immutable life sentence. In 2016, over half (55.7%) of the federal prison population was convicted of an offense that bore a mandatory minimum sentence. There is sparse data illustrating what sub-percentage of these offenders are subject to 21 U.S.C. 841-specific enhancements versus self-contained mandatory minimum enhancements for different offense classifications, such as the violence-only enhancements enumerated under 18 U.S.C. 3559. In 2018, of the 77,505 nonregulatory or traffic criminal cases filed in U.S. district court, 28%, were primarily drug offenses (U. S. Courts, n.d.). Typically, convictions under a mandatory minimum sentencing scheme carry a sentence of almost four times that of other federal offenses (U. S. Courts, n.d.).

Another product of the 1980s sentencing bills was the sentencing disparity in sentencing between analogous weights of crack powder cocaine and "crack" cocaine, the free base form of the drug. Crack was, as seen by Congress, more addictive than powder cocaine, distributed through violent criminal networks, harmful to the user and offspring, and low cost (Kimbrough v. United States, 2007). To combat the distribution and use of the drug, punitive measures in the 1986 legislation criminalized crack at a 100:1 weight ratio to powder cocaine. In short, every one gram of crack would be subject to the same criminal penalty thresholds as 100 grams of powder cocaine. This sentencing disparity disproportionately affected African-Americans, who made up 82% of federal cases in 2007 (Federal Cocaine Sentencing Laws, 2008).

Another ratcheting mandatory minimum enhancement was the penalty added on to an underlying offense if a firearm was used. Housed in 18 U.S.C. 924(c), this enhancement was created by the Gun Control Act of 1968 with elements strengthened in subsequent legislation. After the most recent addition to the 924(c) in 1998, the full statutory enhancement mandated a 5-year additional term of imprisonment if a "firearm is used or possessed in furtherance a federal crime of violence or drug trafficking" (Doyle, 2015). Higher penalties applied for brandishing, discharge, or possessing a firearm that met certain functional characteristics. The enhancement also had a provision applicable to habitual offenders. For every subsequent 924(c) conviction, an offender would be given a 25-year term of imprisonment to run consecutively.

The habitual offender provision has led to a controversial practice known as "stacking," where one criminal filing against a defendant can contain multiple 924(c)-eligible charges. The case of Weldon Angelos in 2004 is a quintessential example of how stacking can lead to sentences incommensurate with the underlying criminal behavior. Mr. Angelos, a music producer, was found guilty of selling $350 worth of marijuana to a federal informant across three separate occasions while (according to informant testimony) in possession of a firearm, although no firearm was found on his person. However, since a legal firearm was found at his residence and considered "in furtherance" of his criminal enterprise, the firearm applied to filing under 924(c), which contained three counts of "drug trafficking." Having been found guilty of the sales after rejecting a 15-year plea arrangement, Judge Paul Cassell – a conservative 2002 George W. Bush appointee – was left with little recourse than to issue Angelos a 55-year minimum sentence: five years for the first count and 25 years for the two subsequent counts. Cassell excoriated 924(c) scheme in the Angelos opinion and lobbied both Presidents Bush and Obama to commute Angelos's sentence, claiming the mandatory minimum law was "unjust, cruel and even irrational" (Horwitz, 2016). Cassell resigned from the federal bench in 2007.

While the Sentencing Reform Act of 1984 eliminated federal parole as a means of discretionary post-incarceration release as a reward for compliance and successful rehabilitation, it did create a system of "good time" credit that accrues automatically under good behavior and can be taken away administratively. In line with "truth-in-sentencing" policies of the day, it held in that no less than 85% of an issued sentence must be served, and conversely that no more than 15% of the overall time can be deducted from the underlying sentence. While preferable than parole, it offered an incentive for inmates to comply with the guard's instructions and provided for a modicum of population control.

However, implementation problems arose when the Bureau of Prisons (BOP) misinterpreted the legislative intent of the good time credits. Thus, 85% of one year is 312 days, meaning that 54 days (using a 366-day calculation) would be the maximum eligible of earned good time credit. However, the BOP erroneously interpreted the statute to apply to the minimum time an individual must serve, not the actual time that was served. Simply put, they calculated the eligible 15% deduction *only after* applying a 15% deduction to the 366 days, resulting in an overall maximum good time credit of 47 days each year (Cohen, 2019).

Attempts at reform

Early attempts at reform

The first substantive foray into criminal justice reform came in 2005 when former Senator Sam Brownback of Kansas and then-Representative Rob Portman of Ohio (both Republicans) introduced the Second Chance Act of 2004. Focusing squarely on reentry and recidivism reduction program, the legislation was a functional grant appropriations vehicle versus a bill that would amend sentencing or penal policy. Both pieces of 2004 legislation were introduced and referred to committees but never given hearings.

The Second Chance Act was reintroduced in 2007, although this time sponsored Democrat Senator Joe Biden of Delaware and Representative Danny Davis of Illinois. Similar in approach to the previous attempt, the created grant pathways to support direct service providers and state agencies seeking to reduce returns to prison. The legislation unanimously passed the Senate and overwhelmingly passed the House on suspension 347–62. President Bush signed the Second Step Act – the first reform-oriented criminal justice bill in decades – into law on April 9, 2008.

Since the passage of the Anti-Drug Abuse Act of 1986, the crack/powder cocaine disparity had been extensively scrutinized. Administratively, the United States Sentencing Commission (USSC) had proposed reducing the disparity to between 2:1 and 15:1 as early as 1997, only three years after the passage of the 1994 Crime Bill. In Congress, members in both parties and both chambers proposed different approaches to tightening the disparity, including a 2007 proposal by Utah Republican senator and former Judiciary Committee chairman Orrin Hatch.

The sentencing disparity was also challenged before the Supreme Court of the United States (SCOTUS), most notably in Kimbrough v. United States (2007). In 2004, Derrick Kimbrough was indicted on four counts of trafficking both crack and powder cocaine. Under the applicable mandatory minimum sentencing guidelines, Kimbrough was subject to a sentence of no less than 15 years imprisonment to life. This range was later reduced to 228 to 270 months. However, had Kimbrough been trafficking only powder cocaine, the minimum sentence would have been 97 to 106 months. Kimbrough was ultimately given 180 months during district court sentencing. This confusion over the applicability of sentencing ranges and disparate application of mandatory minimums for two chemically similar substances ultimately elevated to the SCOTUS, where it was held the guidelines – while complicated and difficult to interpret – are advisory and the sentencing judge should take the disparity into account when applying the mandatory minimums. *Kimbrough* did not functionally alter the guidelines or the disparity (Kimbrough v. United States, 2007). Despite attempts in all three branches of government to reduce the disparity and soften the application of the mandatory sentences, no substantive progress was made.

The first major blow to the crack/powder cocaine disparity came in 2010 when President Barrack Obama signed the Fair Sentencing Act (FSA). Perhaps the most impactful legislative criminal justice effort of his administration, the FSA lowered the ratio to 18:1. A bipartisan effort, the bill was sponsored by the Senate Judiciary Committee Chairman Dick Durbin (D-Illinois) and cosponsored by conservative Republicans such as former senators Tom Coburn, Orrin Hatch, and former Attorney General of the United States Jeff Sessions; 16 Democrats, six Republicans, and one Independent in all. The FSA passed the Senate on unanimous consent and the House on a voice vote. The bill was not universally supported, with law enforcement and a handful of conservative House members in opposition. However, the provisions of the FSA were not retroactive, meaning that those sentenced before the law took effect were subject to the original 100:1 disparity (Anderson, 2018).

First attempt at First Step Act

The first attempt at First Step Act-style reform was filed in 2013 during the 113th Congress by Texas Republican Senator John Cornyn. Elected to the U.S. Senate in 2002 following the resignation of political fixture Phil Gramm, Cornyn had previously served as a district court judge, an associate justice of the Texas Supreme Court, and ultimately as Texas's Attorney General from 1985 to 2002. Deemed the Federal Prison Reform Act of 2013, Cornyn secured co-sponsorships from the conservative Utah delegation – Orrin Hatch and former Assistant United States Attorney Mike Lee – as well as the ranking member of the Senate's Committee on the Judiciary Chuck Grassley. This legislation sought to implement a post-adjudicatory risk assessment for the entirety of the Federal Bureau of Prisons and use the assessment's results to inform placement and reward decisions. However, this bill was never granted a committee hearing by then-Chairman Patrick Leahy. Broader criminal justice reform efforts were discussed during the 113th Congress, though ultimately none were passed.

Control of the United States Senate shifted during the 2014 midterm elections from 55–45 Democrat majority (53 elected party members with two registered Independents caucusing with the Democrats) to a 54–46 Republican senate. Cornyn, who served as Minority Whip during the 113th Congress, assumed the role of Assistant Leader and Majority Whip and maintained his position on the Judiciary Committee alongside Hatch and Lee. Similarly, Grassley became the committee's chairman.

Cornyn refiled the legislation as "Corrections Oversight, Recidivism Reduction, and Eliminating Costs for Taxpayers In Our National System Act of 2015," or the CORRECTIONS Act, alongside liberal Rhode Island Democrat Senator Sheldon Whitehouse. This bill was not heard but later was fully subsumed in Grassley's "Sentencing Reform and Corrections Act," or SRCA. The new legislation would have not only implemented the prison reforms but also reformed some violence- and drug-related mandatory sentences. Despite bipartisan support and popular appeal, Congress was unable to pass the legislation due to partisan splits and infighting spurred on by the approaching 2016 presidential election (Hulse, 2016).

The 2016 presidential election was ultimately won by Republican nominee Donald J. Trump. During his campaign and even in his inaugural address, Trump evoked images of "American carnage" and suggested that, while crime rates had been steadily declining since the mid-1990s, the slight uptick observed in 2015 and 2016 was a lead indicator of another nationwide crime wave (Johnson, 2017). Most in the criminal justice community viewed his election as a major setback to prospects of reform, while others observed that Trump's nonpolitical, business-oriented background might present a yet-unforeseen opportunity (Schuppe, 2016).

The First Step Act

Moving forward

In 2017, Cornyn again filed the CORRECTIONS Act without the sentencing additions that served as a political lightning rod during the 114th Congress. Focused entirely on the incarcerated population, this legislation again sought to create and promulgate a common risk assessment and to use the assessment's output to diagnose suitability for prerelease custody. Chairman Grassley, too, reintroduced his SRCA in October of 2017. In the House, Representative Doug Collins, a conservative pastor from Georgia, filed the Prison Reform and Redemption Act, a bill substantively related to Cornyn's CORRECTION'S Act. Both proposals were largely in line with both parties' platforms heading into the 2016 presidential election (Deason & Tolman, 2018).

This dissonance between the Cornyn/Collins and Grassley bills illustrated the difficulty in advancing criminal justice reform policy. While most would agree that a modicum of reform was needed to address issues of population control, rehabilitation, and fundamental justice, the policy solutions were radically different. Grassley, once a staunch opponent to most forms of sentencing reform, had slowly shifted his views on punishment. He believed that while mandatory minimum sentences still acted as a "valuable tool for law enforcement," they could easily and mistakenly target lower-level offenders rather than the intended kingpins (Office of Senator Chuck Grassley, 2018). However, each policy proposal had detractors. Lawmakers and activists on the Left believed that the Cornyn/Collins legislation was insufficient to meaningfully address issues of mass incarceration and racial disparity (Leadership Conference, 2018). A small portion of those on the Right felt that the Grassley (and some even the Cornyn/Collins approach) was too lenient and soft on crime and criminals (e.g., Horowitz, 2018). Despite one-party control of both Congress and the White House, the mere existence of legislative headwinds on an issue that had since fallen out of the public consciousness (Gallup, n.d.). Collins' and Cornyn's bills were not granted a hearing, and in February of 2018 Grassley's bill was ordered to be favorably reported without amendment from his committee, and advanced no further.

White House involvement

Early in his term, President Trump announced the creation of the "White House Office of American Innovation," or OAI. A new addition to the West Wing, the OAI is intended to complement the roles of the Domestic Policy Council, the Council of Economic Advisors, and other executive institutions. Moreover, this organization was tasked with soliciting input and recommendations from the private sector and "external thought leaders" (White House, 2017). Jared Kushner, the President's son-in-law, was tasked with running the OAI. Kushner's father, Charles Kushner, was convicted of several federal white-collar crimes in 2005 and spent 14 months in federal prison, allowing Jared the opportunity to see firsthand the realities of incarceration. It was Kushner himself – alongside Brooke Rollins and Deputy Assistant to the President Ja'Ron Smith – that focused the Administration's attention and efforts on passing a measure of criminal justice reform in the President's first term.

On September 15, 2017, the OAI hosted its first "listening session" on criminal justice issues. Focusing almost entirely on reentry, this gathering solicited legislative and executive proposals that could better streamline the process of inmates leaving federal prisons and halfway houses and effectively transition back into society. Those in attendance included business leaders like Mark Holden of Koch Industries and Republican Donor Doug Deason, as well as Governors Matt Bevin of Kentucky and Sam Brownback of Kansas, whose states had gone through the criminal justice reinvestment process. The meeting was also attended by Brooke Rollins, president of the Texas Public Policy

Foundation (TPPF), one of the conservative organizations that had started advocating for state-level criminal justice reform over a decade prior (Cohen, 2017; Ward, 2017). Subsequent discussions were held with conservative stakeholder groups on the role the White House could play in advancing criminal justice reform.

On February 16, 2018, it was announced that Rollins was leaving TPPF to join the OAI as Advisor to the President, replacing Reed Cordish who had assumed the position shortly after the creation of the office (Svitek, 2018). While Rollins's issue portfolio was not solely confined to criminal justice, the initial movement of reform legislation in Congress made the matter a primary focus. On March 7, 2018, President Trump announced he would be reconstituting the Federal Interagency Reentry Council from the Obama Administration. Now titled the Federal Interagency Council on Crime Prevention and Improving Reentry, the revamped organization now had a two-part mandate: preventing crime and lowering recidivism through cooperation between executive branch agencies (White House, 2018a). On May 18, the OAI hosted its first White House Prison Reform Summit. With roundtables in the morning followed by a presidential address in the East Room that highlighted in-prison treatment and reentry, the Trump Administration's mirrored the Cornyn/Collins approach.

Advancing the FIRST STEP Act

While the Trump Administration was making headway on what could be done administratively or by executive fiat, the House of Representatives reached a decision to proceed with the Cornyn/Collins proposal. By early April, leftwing groups had started to mobilize against the Prison Reform and Redemption Act, claiming the legislation was insufficient and perhaps even racially discriminatory. This started a war-of-words between them and conservative activists who would have accepted a modest reform in lieu of no reform. While the rightwing advocates would have accepted some sentencing reform, it was viewed in the House as a needlessly difficult political battle (West, 2018).

On May 7, 2018, Rep. Collins filed the "Formerly Incarcerated Reenter Society Transformed Safely Transitioning Every Person Act," or FIRST STEP Act. The new legislation conformed largely to Cornyn's CORRECTIONS Act in order to ease the inter-chamber legislative process. It was immediately referred to House Judiciary Committee and, two days later, was marked up and ordered to be reported with amendments. It was voted out 25–5, opposed by the lone Republican Steve King (IA) joined by Ranking Member Jerry Nadler (NY), Shelia Jackson-Lee (TX), Jamie Raskin (MD), and Pramila Jayapal (WA). These four Democrats again claimed that the legislation was not substantive enough. On May 22, 2018, the FIRST STEP Act was heard on the floor of the House. The limited bill was met with vocal bipartisan support including Congressional Black Caucus chairman Cedric Richmond; several Democrats rose to lay out their objections to the bill. Ultimately, the legislation passed the House by an overwhelming 360–59 vote, with King joined by Michigan Republican Bill Huizenga and 57 Democrats.

True to Congressional tradition, that which flies through House unhindered is often greatly slowed in the institutional trappings of the Senate. Despite the overwhelming margin of engrossment, there was only selective interest in dedicating committee and floor time to advancing criminal justice legislation. Further, the bill faced two additional obstacles: the chairman of the relevant committee (Grassley's Judiciary) having already advanced his preferred policy solution over Cornyn's conforming legislation, and a very small-but-vocal opposition from Senators Tom Cotton (AR) and John Kennedy (LA), both conservative Republicans with very traditional views on crime and punishment. Grassley and Ranking Member Dick Durbin were resolute in refusing to advance legislation that did not include sentencing reform, such as those included in the SRCA. Eventually, all parties arrived at an agreement that portions of the sentencing bill will be included in the FIRST STEP Act.

Negotiations between leadership in both chambers, bill authors, and White House personnel on advancing the FIRST STEP Act were progressing but wholly ceased on June 27th, 2018 when SCOTUS Associate Justice Anthony Kennedy announced his retirement, functionally consuming the entirety of the Senate Judiciary's work time. By the time his replacement, Associate Justice Brett Kavanaugh, was confirmed by the full Senate on October 6th, 2018, there was no longer the requisite time needed to negotiate and advance legislation prior to the 2018 midterm elections. However, earlier in August, Senate Majority Leader Mitch McConnell (KY) committed to advancing the FIRST STEP Act during the "lame duck" session after the midterm elections (Kight, 2018). When the legislature reconvened in November, sponsors returned with a fully negotiated legislative package. The agreed-upon language was a hybrid of the Cornyn/Collins and Grassley legislation that incorporated not only prison reform and reentry but also rolled back some of the more pernicious sentencing practices of the past several decades. The details will be discussed in a later section.

Durban, the Ranking Member of the Judiciary and Minority Whip, was able to secure ayes from the entirety of the Democrat Caucus in the Senate. However, a contingent of Republicans still opposed this negotiated language that now contained sentencing reform. Senators Cotton and Kennedy were frequent guests on cable news and radio talk shows excoriating the bill and how it would "jailbreak" violent and sexual offenders, despite the bill carrying the full support of the White House (Restuccia, Schor, & Everett, 2018). While violent and sexual offenders were statutorily prohibited from accruing and applying "earned time" credits explicitly, the authors agreed to further revise the FIRST STEP Act to broaden the list of excluded inmates. This revision brought about new sponsorships in the Senate, including from Texas's conservative junior Senator Ted Cruz.

During this time, conservative groups were advocating for the bill's passage. Right-leaning think tanks like the Heritage Foundation and the TPPF to advocacy groups like the American Conservative Union and Freedomworks were active in the print and digital media in support of the legislation. Right on Crime, the conservative criminal justice reform campaign housed at the TPPF, started recording endorsements of the bill from similar organizations. Coupled with the endorsements received by Chairman Grassley's staff, it was patently clear that there was a groundswell of support on the right and from some on the left (Committee on the Judiciary, 2018). Other liberal and progressive groups, such as the American Civil Liberties Union, declined to endorse the bill, while groups like Van Jones's "Cut50" was one of the legislation's most vocal proponents. Law enforcement, notably the Fraternal Order of Police, the National District Attorney's Association, and the International Association of Chiefs of Police endorsed the bill as well.

On December 12, 2018, a final version of the bill (inclusive of the broad statutory exemptions) was agreed upon (Office of Senator Patrick Leahy, 2018). However, there simply was not enough time left in Congress to reintroduce or amend the legislation. To avoid this roadblock, authors and the leadership took S. 756 – the Save Our Seas Act, a bill which cleared the Senate unanimously in August of 2017 and returned from the House in late July of 2018 – and fully amended it to the agreed-upon language. The FIRST STEP acronym was retired, and the new legislation was simply referred to as the First Step Act. On December 18, 2018, the Senate passed the First Step Act. The House concurred with the sweeping amendment of the bill 358–36 one day later.

Provisions of the First Step Act

The First Step Act is largely separable into two main areas: prison reform and sentencing reform. The prison reform component comes largely from Cornyn and Collins' legislation and is focused on post-conviction custody and an inmate's transition back into the community through an interim mode of supervision. The sentencing component – taken from Grassley and Durbin's SRCA – adjusted the application and calculation of mandatory minimum sentence enhancements for certain narcotics offenses.

Prison reform elements

Titles I-III contained the prison reform elements of the legislation. Most notably, the legislation included the creation criteria for a risk and needs assessment in Section 101 that is to be used across all BOP facilities. The product of this tool would be used not only identify which inmates were most suitable for which programming but also to assign an overall dynamic risk score. Post-adjudicatory risk assessments, such as the model established by the First Step Act, have been in system-wide use by state corrections departments for over a decade (Cohen, 2017). The BOP tool is mandated to not only classify the risk of re-offense but to identify the inmate's risks and needs in order to place him in more appropriate rehabilitative programing. The assessment must also be administered periodically in order to gauge the successful mitigation of risk.

Inmates classified as low- and moderate-risk inmates would be eligible to earn and apply "earned time" credits by participating in and completing recidivism-reducing programs and training, up to 10 days for every 30 of quality participation. These credits can be used by suitable inmates to transition to home confinement or a halfway house. Section 102 clarifies that the original Congressional intent of "good time" credits to be the full 54 days – 15% of the original sentence – affecting as many as 4,000 inmates when the law took effect (Lopez, 2019).

Title III prohibits the shackling of women inmates while pregnant or postpartum, while Section 511 of Title V mandates that the BOP provide female inmates with feminine hygiene products. This provision was uniquely championed by advocates who often find themselves on polar ends of any given political issue: the progressive Left and the religious Right. While progressives see shackling and lack of access to feminine hygiene products as an inherent indignity, conservative see the practice as dangerous to the health and safety of the mother and the innocent child (Ferszt, 2010).

The bill also contained various "best practices" in corrections. It increased data collection and reporting. Section 506 mandates that officers be given special de-escalation training for dealing with the general population and mentally ill or cognitively-delayed prisoners. It prohibited juvenile solitary confinement outside of exigent circumstances and mandated the expansion of the medication-assisted treatment pilot program in the BOP. The bill also reauthorized the Second Chance Act of 2007.

Sentencing reform elements

Title IV contained the sentencing reform components of the SRCA. The 21 U.S.C. 841 mandatory minimum scheme for habitual offenders was lowered from 20 years to 15 years on the second offense, and from life to 25 years on the third offense in Section 401. It is important to note that under Section 401, only the "floors" of the enhancement – the immutable minimum sentence given for each offense – are reduced. The sentencing judge is still permitted to add up to 35 years for the first offense, and subsequent offenses have no upper boundary.

The title also broadens the "safety valve," and opportunity for departure from mandatory minimum sentences if an offender meets certain mitigating factors, such as little criminal history, no use of violence or weapons, or was not a high-ranking participant in a criminal enterprise. This provision mirrors legislation that has been passed in several states that have adopted determinate sentencing schemes. In the First Step Act, the mechanism for departure under 18 U.S.C. 3553 to apply to defendants with criminal histories up to four points of single-point offenses (such as low-level drug dealing), so long as the defendant does not have a previous serious or violent offense.

The application of 924(c) was prospectively corrected, making subsequent applications of the statute only valid if the sentence for previous predicate offense was completed. In other words, the same charge can no longer enhance off of one charge containing three or more counts of 924(c)-eligible criminal behavior; each enhancement would need to run its course before the next level enhancement would apply. This fix brings the law more in line with the intent of habitual offender laws. Once an individual has been sentenced and punished for a criminal act, only then would subsequent offenses trigger an enhancement above what was statutorily prescribed for the act itself. Were this clarification in place, Angelos would not have received the 55-year sentence for selling a small amount of marijuana three separate times.

Finally, the 18:1 disparity reduction from the Fair Sentencing was applied retroactively to sentences issues before the law's passage in 2010, affecting roughly 2,600 inmates (Lopez, 2019). However, Section 404 is not self-executing. The inmate or one of several enumerated federal stakeholders must petition the court for resentencing under the now-retroactive guidelines. Should the petition fail, no further petitions on the retroactive application can be entertained.

Justice, not jailbreak: next steps

Despite the breadth of the First Step Act reform, it offers very little to those currently incarcerated. All provisions – save for "good time" credit calculation fix and the explicit retroactive application of the Fair Sentencing Act of 2010 – were prospective. These two provisions are estimated to alter the sentences of no more than 4,600 federal inmates – a paltry percentage of the overall population. There is also a significant likelihood that certain inmates could be counted in both groups. Further, the accrual of "earned time" credits for lower-risk inmates only started once the bill had taken effect, and the credits cannot be applied until the risk assessment instrument is created and validated.

When components of Grassley and Durbin's SRCA were added to the First Step Act, "tough-on-crime" Republicans raised concerns that dangerous inmates might be moved to community confinement earlier than anticipated. While the prison reform-only bill that passed the House in May excluded 48 categories of federal offenses the prohibited inmates from applying "earned time" credits to earlier access to home confinement, the exemption list was expanded to 68 total offense categories in the Senate. Further attempts to broaden the expanded list to include nearly every federal crime were roundly defeated during the post-cloture amendment process. Inmates who have committed one of the 68 offense types would still be able to take and complete the expanded programming, but would not be able to use any credits earned. The effort to expand this list was peculiar, as (1) it removed the incentive from what the layperson would consider more "serious" offenders from participating in recidivism-reducing programming, and (2) it left untouched the risk-agnostic accrual and use of "good time" credit.

Finally, the compulsory analysis of BOP programming has revealed weaknesses in the legislation's approach. The foundational premise of the "earned time" risk-informed credit system is that inmates can earn a faster segue into community confinement by completing evidence-based recidivism reducing programs – although few are currently in practice in federal facilities that address dynamic criminogenic risk factors that, if treated, have been shown to lower the likelihood of recidivism (U.S. Department of Justice, 2019). If inmates are unable to avail themselves of programing that meets the standards set forth in Title I, the legislature's goals of segueing worthy inmates back into community settings sooner could be jeopardized.

To create the mandated risk assessment, Attorney General William Barr convened an Independent Review Committee (IRC), hosted at the Hudson Institute. While the Hudson Institute is to serve as a "project manager" for the IRC, the Committee's defined purpose is to assist the Attorney General in the completion of his academically intensive duties enumerated in the revisions to 18 U.S.C. 3631–3633 (p. 9). These duties include the development and validation of the risk assessment instrument.

However, perhaps the most praiseworthy feature of the First Step Act lay not within its provisions, but rather in the passage itself. While the federal government has on occasion displayed willingness to nibble around the edges of criminal justice reform, earlier presidents and congresses of each party have been unable to forward a comprehensive reform. The First Step Act was the first broad, albeit limited, criminal justice reform since the "tough-on-crime" era. It had fully succeeded where similar efforts have failed to gain traction. Prodding a sclerotic institution like Congress into action is no easy task, and First Step Act may be a case study in how bipartisan coalitional politics can be reliably expected to do so.

The future of federal criminal justice reform is unclear. As a subject matter, it has featured prominently in the runup to the 2020 Democratic primary elections, though with policy proposals so sweeping, devoid of nuance, and ignorant of what can be done at the federal level to affect state prison populations, it's difficult to see this as more than primary politics. The schism illustrated in the first House vote – that between the Democrats who would settle for an incremental reform and those who would vote "nay" for what was not in the bill – has not disappeared and will likely widen in the purity crucible of the primaries.

The Republicans too are far from united. Prison reform was ascendant policy proposal in the early days of the First Step Act simply because it was the least objectionable in a Republican-controlled Congress. While there are many in the party who wish to see further sentencing reforms, parts of the conservative wing of the Senate – the 12 Republicans who voted against the bill – are loudly opposed, and their opposition agitates the party's primary base. Far-Right conservative senators like Mike Lee can and do frequently expound on the benefits of criminal justice reform, but it only takes an allegation of a "jailbreak" to enervate the base and shut down discussion. Republican leadership was and remains sensitive of this dynamic, and was hesitant to advance the First Step Act until President Trump himself called for its passage explicitly.

This reality is reflected in subsequent proposals for criminal justice reform in Congress. Proposals such as the "Fair Chance Act" have to do with the role criminal histories play within the hiring process of the federal government or its contractors. The "REAL Act" would restore Pell Grant assistance in federal prisons, allowing inmates to take advantage of education and training opportunities while incarcerated. While laudable, these proposals are focused in both scope and ambition. The Administration has reiterated its willingness to support a "Second Step Act," though those discussions are just beginning anew in the autumn of 2019.

The signing

Sponsors, supporters, and advocates gathered in the Oval Office on December 21, 2018, as President Trump signed the bill into law. Several spoke to the momentous occasion, with Senator Cruz saying, "Right now, there are far too many young men – particularly, tragically, young black men – who find themselves decades in prison for a nonviolent crime. This bill corrects this and it's a great step in the direction of justice." Van Jones added, "And when you're trying to help people on the bottom, sir, I will work with or against any Democrat, with or against any Republican, because there is nothing more important than freedom" (White House, 2018b). Applause erupted as President Trump signed the First Step Act into law.

In a quintessentially "Washington" turn of events, the federal government shut down the following day.

Notes

1. Under *Furman v. Georgia* (1972), a *de facto* moratorium was issued against carrying out state and federal capital punishments. This moratorium was lifted in 1976 under *Gregg v. Georgia*, reinstated federally by the Comprehensive Crime Control Act of 1984, and expanded in scope under the Violent Crime Control and Law Enforcement Act of 1994. Three prisoners have been executed under federal jurisdiction in the post-*Gregg* era.
2. The fact pattern of a "serious drug offense" relevant to 21 U.S.C. 841 mandatory minimum sentence enhancements includes any offense under 21 U.S.C. or any state law carrying a 10-year minimum sentence. For example, the triggering threshold for a 10-year federal mandatory minimum sentence is 50 grams of pure methamphetamine and 80 grams of crack cocaine.

Disclosure statement

No potential conflict of interest was reported by the author.

ORCID

Derek M. Cohen http://orcid.org/0000-0001-9797-0406

References

Anderson, S. (2018, March 29). *In the case of fair sentencing act retroactivity, ussc report lends resounding endorsement* [web blog]. Retrieved from https://www.freedomworks.org/content/case-fair-sentencing-act-retroactivity-ussc-report-lends-resounding-endorsement

Cohen, D. M. (2017). *Right on Crime: Conservative reform in the era of mass imprisonment* (Doctoral dissertation). Columbus, OH: OhioLINK. (ucin1491305385860754).

Cohen, D. M. (2019, July 24). Tucker Carlson and John Kennedy get the First Step Act all wrong. *Washington Examiner*. Retrieved from https://www.washingtonexaminer.com/opinion/tucker-carlson-and-john-kennedy-get-the-first-step-act-all-wrong

Committee on the Judiciary. (2018, December 13). *Supporters of the First Step Act (S. 3649)* [Press release]. Retrieved from https://www.judiciary.senate.gov/imo/media/doc/Sentencing,%2012-13-18,%20%20First%20Step%20Act%20Supporters.pdf

Conlin, J. (2013). *The American past: A survey of American history, volume II: Since 1965.* Independence, KY: Cengage.

Deason, D., & Tolman, B. (2018, December 17). There's nothing 'courageous' about opposing the First Step Act, it's part of the GOP platform. *The Hill*. Retrieved from https://thehill.com/opinion/criminal-justice/421619-theres-nothing-courageous-about-opposing-the-first-step-act-its-part

Doyle, C. (2015). *Federal mandatory minimum sentencing: The 18 u.s.c. 924(c) tack-on in cases involving drugs or violence*. Washington, DC: Congressional Research Service.

Federal cocaine sentencing laws: Reforming the 100-to-1 crack/powder disparity: Statement of A.J. Kramer. 110th Cong. (2008). *(Testimony of A.J. Kramer, federal defender for the District of Columbia)*. Washington, DC: Federal Public and Community Defenders.

Ferszt, G. G. (2010). Giving birth in shackles. *American Journal of Nursing*, *110*(2), 11. doi:10.1097/01.NAJ.0000368027.79459.7f

Gallup. (n.d.). *Crime*. Retrieved from http://www.gallup.com/poll/1603/crime.aspx

Horowitz, D. (2018, May 10). House committee passes dangerous jailbreak bill. *Conservative Review*. Retrieved from https://www.conservativereview.com/news/house-committee-passes-dangerous-jailbreak-bill/

Horwitz, S. (2016, February 9). Former federal judge to President Obama: Free the man I sentenced to 55 years in prison. *Washington Post*. Retrieved from https://www.washingtonpost.com/news/post-nation/wp/2016/02/09/former-federal-judge-to-president-obama-free-the-man-i-sentenced-to-55-years-in-prison/?utm_term=.625a73fb324e

Hulse, C. (2016, September 16). Why the senate couldn't pass a crime bill both parties backed. *New York Times*. Retrieved from https://www.nytimes.com/2016/09/17/us/politics/senate-dysfunction-blocks-bipartisan-criminal-justice-overhaul.html

Johnson, C. (2017, January 20). In inaugural address, Trump decries 'carnage' and promises 'America first'. *National Public Radio*. Retrieved from https://www.npr.org/2017/01/20/510746700/donald-trump-sworn-in-as-the-45th-president-of-the-united-states

Kight, S. (2018, August 23). McConnell commits to moving forward on criminal justice bill after midterms. *Axios*. Retrieved from https://www.axios.com/mitch-mcconnell-commits-criminal-justice-reform-whip-count-69b62e17-3ef8-46b9-a95d-4073478d9924.html

Kimbrough v. United States, 552 U.S. 85 (2007).

Leadership Conference. (2018, April 25). *Vote "no" on H.R. 3356, the Prison Reform and Redemption Act, or any similar manager's amendment* [open letter]. Retreived from http://civilrightsdocs.info/pdf/policy/letters/2018/Sign-On-Letter-Oppose-HR-3356-4.25.18.pdf

Lopez, G. (2019, February 5). The First Step Act, explained. *Vox*. Retrieved from https://www.vox.com/future-perfect/2018/12/18/18140973/state-of-the-union-trump-first-step-act-criminal-justice-reform

Office of Senator Chuck Grassley. (2018, February 15). *Amid growing support, judiciary committee advances sentencing reform and corrections act* [Press release]. Retrieved from https://www.grassley.senate.gov/news/news-releases/amid-growing-support-judiciary-committee-advances-sentencing-reform-and

Office of Senator Patrick Leahy. (2018, December 12). *Senate & House lawmakers release updated First Step Act* [Press release]. Retrieved from https://www.whitehouse.gov/presidential-actions/federal-interagency-council-crime-prevention-improving-reentry/

Restuccia, A., Schor, E., & Everett, B. (2018, November 14). Trump endorses criminal justice bill that divides McConnell's GOP. *Politico*. Retrieved from https://www.politico.com/story/2018/11/14/prison-sentencing-congress-trump-mcconnell-990660

Schuppe, J. (2016, November 10). With Trump in White House, criminal justice reformers will look elsewhere. *NBC News*. Retrieved from https://www.nbcnews.com/storyline/2016-election-day/trump-white-house-criminal-justice-reformers-will-look-elsewhere-n681536

Seelye, K. Q. (1994, August 22). The crime bill: Overview; house approves crime bill after days of bargaining, giving victory to Clinton. *New York Times*. Retrieved from https://www.nytimes.com/1994/08/22/us/crime-bill-overview-house-approves-crime-bill-after-days-bargaining-giving.html

Svitek, P. (2018, February 16). Texas Public Policy Foundation head Brooke Rollins to join White House. *Texas Tribune*. Retrieved from https://www.texastribune.org/2018/02/16/tppf-head-brooke-rollins-join-white-house/

Trende, S. (2010, September 9). Misunderstanding the southern realignment. *RealClearPolitics*. Retrieved from https://www.realclearpolitics.com/articles/2010/09/09/misunderstanding_the_southern_realignment_107084.html

U.S. Department of Justice. Office of the Attorney General. (2019, July). *The First Step Act of 2018: Risk and needs assessment system*. Retrieved from https://www.nij.gov/documents/the-first-step-act-of-2018-risk-and-needs-assessment-system.pdf

United States Courts. (n.d.). *U.S. District Courts: Criminal defendants disposed of, by type of disposition and offense, during the 12-month period ending December 31, 2018*. Retrieved from https://www.uscourts.gov/statistics-reports/statistical-tables-federal-judiciary-december-2018

Ward, M. (2017, September 15). Texas prison-reentry model a focus of White House reform meeting. *Houston Chronicle*. Retrieved from https://www.houstonchronicle.com/news/politics/texas/article/Texas-prison-reentry-model-a-focus-of-White-House-12202178.php

West, A. (2018, May 4). A new hypocrisy for the left on criminal justice. *National Review*. Retrieved from https://www.nationalreview.com/2018/05/prison-release-reform-bill-progressive-groups-oppose/

White House. (2017, March 27). *President Donald J. Trump announces the White House Office of American Innovation (OAI)* [Press release]. Retrieved from https://www.whitehouse.gov/briefings-statements/president-donald-j-trump-announces-white-house-office-american-innovation-oai/

White House. (2018a, March 7). *Federal interagency council on crime prevention and improving reentry* [Press release]. Retrieved from https://www.whitehouse.gov/presidential-actions/federal-interagency-council-crime-prevention-improving-reentry/

White House. (2018b, December 21). *Remarks by President Trump at signing ceremony for S. 756, the "FIRST STEP Act of 2018" and H.R. 6964, the "Juvenile Justice Reform Act of 2018"* [Press release]. Retrieved from https://www.whitehouse.gov/briefings-statements/remarks-president-trump-signing-ceremony-s-756-first-step-act-2018-h-r-6964-juvenile-justice-reform-act-2018/

Index

Note: **Bold** page numbers refer to tables; *italic* page numbers refer to figures and page numbers followed by "n" denote endnotes.